La Verdad

A Witness to the Salvadoran Martyrs

Lucía Cerna
Mary Jo Ignoffo

Maryknoll, New York 10545

Founded in 1970, Orbis Books endeavors to publish works that enlighten the mind, nourish the spirit, and challenge the conscience. The publishing arm of the Maryknoll Fathers and Brothers, Orbis seeks to explore the global dimensions of the Christian faith and mission, to invite dialogue with diverse cultures and religious traditions, and to serve the cause of reconciliation and peace. The books published reflect the views of their authors and do not represent the official position of the Maryknoll Society. To learn more about Maryknoll and Orbis Books, please visit our website at www.maryknollsociety.org.

Published by Orbis Books, Maryknoll, New York 10545-0302 in cooperation with Santa Clara University.

Manufactured in the United States of America.

Manuscript editing and typesetting by Joan Weber Laflamme.

Library of Congress Cataloging-in-Publication Data

Cerna, Lucía.
La verdad : a witness to the Salvadoran martyrs / by Lucía Cerna and Mary Jo Ignoffo.
pages cm
Includes bibliographical references and index.
ISBN 978-1-62698-073-0 (pbk.)
1. Christian martyrs—El Salvador—History—20th century. 2. El Salvador—Church history. 3. Catholic Church—Political activity—El Salvador. I. Title.
BR1608.E25C47 2014
272'.9097284—dc23

2013040008

La Verdad

Jesus said, "Truly I tell you, there is no one who has left house or brothers or sisters or mother or father or children or fields, for my sake and for the sake of the good news, who will not receive a hundredfold now in this age—houses, brothers and sisters, mothers and children, and fields, with persecutions—and in the age to come eternal life."

—Mark 10:29–30

Para

Padre Daniel

Daniel V. Germann, SJ

1929–2007

Contents

Foreword by Michael E. Engh, SJ ix

Preface by José M. Tojeira, SJ xi

"My Blood Went Cold" xv

Introduction xvii

1. The Innocents 1
   1946–1960

2. The Devil's Gate 19
   1960–1975

3. Our Daily Bread 39
   1980–1985

4. The Open Window 65
   November 12–15, 1989

5. Cold, Like Ice 83
   November 16–23, 1989

6. Sacrificed 101
   November 23–December 3, 1989

7. Rescue 121
   December 1989–1990

8. Exile 137
   1990–2012

Epilogue: "Telling the Truth"
by Jon Sobrino, SJ 163

Acknowledgments 169

Bibliographic Essay 171

Index 179

Foreword

For the last twenty-five years, eight simple white crosses have stood in the grass immediately in front of the Mission Church at Santa Clara University. They were placed there by my predecessor as president, Paul Leo Locatelli, SJ. They remind us, he said, of who we are and who we aspire to be, not just as individual Christians, but as a Jesuit, Catholic university.

In the weeks following the terrible day of November 16, 1989, Jon Sobrino, SJ, lived in the Santa Clara University Jesuit Community. If Jon had not been traveling at the time, his name would have been on a ninth cross. We mourned with him as he slowly recovered from the shock, as he put it, of having his family dragged from their beds and murdered.

The story of these six Jesuits and their two coworkers has been told many times. But even in the days when Jon stayed in our community, another person of great faith had also arrived from San Salvador. Hers was a story of terrible trauma too, but of a very different kind.

Lucía Cerna's eyewitness account has never been told in its fullness.

As we commemorate the twenty-fifth anniversary of the martyrdom of our brothers and sisters at the UCA, we honor them by listening to the voice of this woman of great courage.

For those of us who continue to be inspired by the witness of Ignacio Ellacuría, SJ, and others who placed the service of faith and the promotion of justice at the center of a university's mission, we need to pay attention to Lucía's words.

A true education is conveyed not only in classrooms, but also by people who, quite simply and with their very lives, inspire us to do what the prophet Micah urged: "Act justly, love tenderly, and walk humbly with your God."

So let us listen to Lucía, telling the truth, *la verdad*. She has much—very much—to teach us!

MICHAEL E. ENGH, SJ
President
Santa Clara University

Preface

Before the killings I had known Lucía Cerna only by sight. She was the cleaning woman for the part of the UCA where the president's and vice president's offices were located. I had seen her on the few occasions when I visited there.

The first time I met with her personally was on November 16, 1989, at 6:40 a.m., in the house where I lived. Obdulio, the husband of Elba Ramos and father of Celina Ramos, had also come to tell us about the murders of the six Jesuits and his wife and daughter. He didn't know who had killed them, but Lucía was emphatic: "It was the soldiers, Father. I saw them."

A major guerrilla offensive had begun on November 11, and fighting in San Salvador was intense. Lucía and her husband and daughter had to flee their neighborhood when it was bombed and machine-gunned by the army. We offered them a room in a house of ours on the edge of the campus. From it, one could see the entrance to the yard in front of the Jesuit residence. After the priests were killed and the heavy shooting and explosions stopped, Lucía and her husband went to the window to look outside. They saw the soldiers leaving through the gate.

Trying to cover up what it had done, the army was claiming that guerrilla leaders had been meeting with the Jesuits at their residence, and that when the army came onto the campus to arrest them, the guerrillas fled, killing the Jesuits in the process.

Later, I spoke with Lucía in greater detail. She insisted that she and her husband had seen the soldiers. In her judicial testimony she explained that she saw them clearly because of the full moon and the flares the soldiers set off as they were leaving (there was no electric light in the area that night). The Cernas' testimony was especially important at a moment when the Salvadoran army and government were accusing the FMLN of the killings, when the media were being controlled, and when the military's discourse was focusing on threats and repression. Friends, lawyers, and people who knew the country well were all telling me that if the Cernas were going to speak, they should leave the country. They were willing to run the risk of testifying. The U.S. embassy said it would facilitate getting the family into the United States, and the Spanish embassy, after initially refusing to accept them as refugees, changed its mind and took them in while a judge was receiving their statements.

That is when this brave woman's torment began. The judge and the prosecutors arrived at the Spanish embassy, determined to destroy her testimony. They tried to confuse her and make her say that she couldn't be sure whether the people she had seen were soldiers or guerrillas. But she insisted: "They were soldiers, just like the ones I see on the street." They couldn't budge her. A Jesuit, Fermín Saínz, was with her during the interrogation. The prosecutors kept pressuring her, trying to make her look like a liar. Saínz finally couldn't take it anymore. Rebuking the prosecutors, he told them that instead of learning what they could from Lucía, they were trying to destroy her. As curfew approached, the judge left, saying he'd return the following day to finish taking her testimony. Lucía, her husband, and her daughter spent the night at the embassy. The Spanish ambassador, Francisco Cádiz Deleito, awakened her at midnight to tell her, "Pray, Lucía. They're going to come and kill us all." It fell to this courageous woman to calm down the nervous ambassador.

To accuse the army of killing the Jesuits, as the Cernas had done, seemed to us like signing their own death sentence, so after the interrogation ended, they went straight to the airport. The ambassadors of Spain and the United States accompanied them to provide security. The French ambassador offered his armored car, since the Spanish embassy didn't have one. Because the interrogation had lasted so long, Lucía and her family missed their flight. Because it would have been dangerous for them to have stayed in El Salvador for another night, France's minister for humanitarian affairs, Bernard Kouchner, who was in El Salvador, arranged for a French army transport plane, located in Belize, to come to El Salvador and take them to the United States. In the film of Lucía walking across the tarmac to the plane, Kouchner can be seen protecting her with his body, in case a sharpshooter tried to kill her.

The tension continued in Miami. Richard Chidester, the legal officer at the U.S. embassy in El Salvador, had offered to travel with the family, supposedly to help facilitate its entrance into the United States. But when they reached Miami, he turned the Cernas over to FBI agents, who in turn took the family to a hotel. The FBI agents said they were afraid that someone might try to kill them, and that they wanted to evaluate how much danger the family was in. But at the hotel Lucía and Jorge were interrogated for a week. There the pressure on them, and the attempts to discredit them continued. The head of the government commission dealing with the killings, Lt. Col. Manuel Antonio Rivas Mejía, was flown to Miami. He threatened to return them to El Salvador, telling them, "You know what will happen to you there."

They wanted Lucía and Jorge to say that they hadn't seen anything, and that a Jesuit, Miguel Francisco Estrada, had told them what they should say to the judge. Under threat of being forcibly returned to a sure death in El Salvador, Lucía and Jorge, in a moment of weakness, decided to say they hadn't seen anything, and that the version they had given had been invented by María Julia Hernández—director of Tutela Legal, the human rights office of the San Salvador Archdiocese—who had been present during the interrogation at the Spanish embassy. After giving this new version, Lucía and Jorge submitted to lie-detector tests—and failed them. The FBI leaked information to the media about the Cernas' retracting their testimony. They later returned to their original story.

The archbishop of San Salvador, Arturo Rivera y Damas, denounced the FBI in a homily, saying it had kidnapped the family and submitted Lucía and Jorge to psychological torture. Responding to the archbishop's charges, President George H. W. Bush said that in the United States, people aren't tortured. And so it was that, with difficulties but also with hope, Lucía and her family began their new life.

The Cernas became a symbol of courage and honor for those of us who witnessed their bravery in those terrible days. Lucía's convictions about justice and her affection for the victims led her to expose herself to what became a complex pilgrimage in which she would encounter a corrupt judicial system, mediocre diplomacy, lying army officials who were ready to kill, and FBI agents who mistreated her and were accomplices of a Salvadoran army officer later accused by the Truth Commission of covering up murders. She is an exemplary woman who became a victim herself because she tried to help in the search for truth when others—those with guns, arrogant government officials, and those who were financing an unjust war—were trying to cover it up. Her testimony—and her husband's—was a crucial part of the pressure that was needed to reach the first stage of the truth. Nearly forty days passed between her original testimony and the government's finally admitting that the army had killed the Jesuits and their coworkers. During that period, with the government insistently accusing the FMLN of the killings, the Cernas' testimony helped us to insist that the army was, in fact, responsible. Their brave and tough example was an incentive to all of us who were struggling for the truth at that moment. We realized we were at a disadvantage; we were up against a government that was able to send delegations to Washington, Madrid, and Rome. It also accused us of lying when we accused the army and claimed that the official investigation, supposedly scientific and impartial, implicated the guerrillas in the crime. Lucía and Jorge's example helped us see that establishing the truth was more important than protecting our own lives. We knew that in running the risks involved, we were contributing—just as Lucía and Jorge were—to saving lives in El Salvador. In the end, the army was forced to acknowledge that it was the guilty party. This left it totally discredited and, by weakening the position of the colonels who wanted to continue the war, helped to accelerate the peace process. Lucía and Jorge, brave peacebuilders, deserve all our gratitude.

José M. Tojeira, SJ
Rector Emeritus, UCA
Former Jesuit Provincial for Central America

"My Blood Went Cold"

I woke in the night, hearing a tremendous uproar inside the Fathers' home. I heard shooting, shooting at lamps, and walls, and windows. I heard doors kicked, and things being thrown and broken in the living room. I thought the war must be inside the campus. How could that be? I wondered. We saw soldiers earlier, so how could guerrillas get inside? The soldiers must be drunk, I thought. They were shouting bad words. I went to see what happened.

I got up to stop them. I wanted to say, "Why do you do this to the priests' home?" Jorge said no. Until that moment I did not think that they might kill me too. I would be dead now if Jorge did not say, "Don't go!" My God, I realized, they would kill us too. Shooting and shooting, I needed to stay and not move. There was only one wooden door between us and them. All they had to do was kick the door down and they could come to shoot us. We had no protection, but they believed nobody was there. That was our safety.

Padre Nacho was yelling—really, really yelling—on the path behind the house where we were. The shooting did not stop. It was serious. My blood went cold, like ice. I wished to go to stop the situation. I felt I had no hands, no arms, no power. I could do nothing to help Nachito, and he was yelling. My blood turned to ice, from the top of my head all the way down to my toes, and back up again. Then Padre Nacho yelled they are all *carroña* [scum] and "this is an injustice!" Now I wonder if he was yelling *carroña* and injustice because he knew I was in that room and he knows me. He knew I would hear, and I would tell. I would not let anything stop me from telling. After his words there was only quiet, very deep quiet. Then a huge bomb exploded and the garage and cars were destroyed. The house where we were shook with the bomb. Jorge put his hand on Geraldina, patting her back so she would not cry. He wanted to keep her silent. If they knew only a door separated us from the campus, they would have killed us too. In the quiet we went to look out the window again. There were soldiers there, with camouflage uniforms, and visors on their caps. I was afraid. How are the Fathers? I think I knew.

LUCÍA CERNA
Excerpt from Chapter 5

Introduction

Mary Jo Ignoffo

When Ignacio Martín-Baró, SJ—Padre Nacho—snapped a photograph of Lucía Cerna as she cleaned his office at the UCA (University of Central America José Simeón Cañas) in the spring of 1988, he captured an image of her at her happiest. She loved her job as a housekeeper at the UCA because she felt respected and trusted, for her a rare and new experience. At that moment in 1988, as civil war shattered El Salvador, she knew a little peace. Against all odds she owned a home, her husband had established a small business, and the two had a healthy baby daughter. Lucía recalls, "I wish I could explain how *happy* we were!"

The happy photo of Lucía sounds a disturbing alarm though. A small sign propped against Nacho's many books reads *Tortura Nunca Mas* (no more torture). Civil war raged barely outside the campus walls, and in fact, bombs had been detonated at university buildings on at least fourteen occasions between 1977 and 1986. Lucía's employers, the Spanish Jesuit priests who worked as university administrators, persistently lobbied for better living and working conditions for the majority of Salvadorans.

El Salvador, among the smallest Central American nations, has simmered in class struggle throughout most of its history. The fundamental conflict from the late nineteenth through the twentieth century lay in the fact that a relative few own most of the land, planted for coffee and sugar exports. For generations, almost-starving Salvadorans worked the land to fill the pockets of the growers. Full-out war erupted on the occasions when the poor protested and took up arms, most notably in *La Matanza* (the slaughter), an insurrection in 1932 to which the government responded by slaughtering an estimated thirty thousand people, and during the civil war the 1980s, when the civilian death toll at the hands of the military rose higher than seventy thousand.

The president of the UCA during the latter conflict, Ignacio Ellacuría, SJ, placed himself squarely in the middle of the country's conflict by speaking to both the political right—the government—and the left—guerrillas seeking an overthrow of that government. He was labeled a communist because he called for the military to halt atrocities in the countryside and was highly critical of the billions of U.S. dollars supporting the brutal military regime. Between 1977 and his death in 1989, Ignacio Ellacuría suffered death threats, had been expelled from the country, was forced into hiding, and heard bounties for his head announced over Salvadoran radio. He was specifically targeted for elimination.

Ellacuría and others at the UCA followed the mission of the university: to act as an intellectual conscience for the nation. He often reiterated the need to speak for the oppressed. "Our university's work is oriented," he said, "on behalf of a people who, oppressed by structural injustices, struggle for their self-determination—people often without liberty or human rights."[1] The commitment to speak out in favor of the majority of the people placed some of the Jesuits at the UCA in a corrosive political environment that ended up costing their lives.

Negotiations for peace in El Salvador's nearly ten-year war looked promising in early 1989, but chances for peace deteriorated as the year progressed. Right-wing candidate Alfredo Cristiani was elected president, and leftists were accused of the assassinations of Attorney General Roberto Garcia Alvarado and Minister of the Presidency José Antonio Rodríguez-Porth. The rightist government party, ARENA (Nationalist Republican Alliance) had little motivation to negotiate for peace. It held power and had almost limitless U.S. financial backing. The FMLN (Farabundo Martí National Liberation Front) retaliated by launching an attack unlike any other. In November 1989 guerrilla forces hit the capital city of San Salvador. The ferocity and success of the guerrilla attack stunned the government and military.

On the night of November 15, 1989, Colonel René Emilio Ponce, the chief of the Armed Forces–Joint Staff, gave an order to Colonel Guillermo Alfredo Benavides to "kill Father Ignacio Ellacuría and to leave no witnesses."[2] Benavides was told to use the Atlacatl Battalion,

[1] Ignacio Ellacuría, commencement address, Santa Clara University, 1982, Archives and Special Collections, Santa Clara University, Santa Clara, California.

[2] United Nations Commission on the Truth for El Salvador, *From Madness to Hope: The Twelve-Year War in El Salvador*, report of the Commission on the

an elite American-trained Salvadoran army unit, to carry out the order. Benavides and the soldiers entered the UCA campus in the early morning hours of November 16, 1989. The military men ordered five priests out of their beds to a courtyard at gunpoint, forcing them to lie face down on the ground, where they were executed at point-blank range with an M-16, and an AK-47 confiscated from the guerrilla forces. Another priest, a Salvadoran who had terminal cancer, made his way to the doorway, where he was also shot. When the soldiers came upon a cook and her teenaged daughter cowering in another room, they killed the two while they lay in a tight embrace. After the gunfire the soldiers lingered, smoked cigarettes, and appropriated a few cans of the Jesuits' beer. As they leisurely exited the campus, soldiers scrawled insignias of the leftist FMLN forces on some walls, pointing a finger of responsibility at the guerrillas.

The truth of that night might have died with the victims, or most certainly would have been delayed, if a witness had not come forward. Unbeknownst to the soldiers, a room in a building that had formerly been the Jesuit residence was also occupied. Lucía Cerna and her husband, Jorge Cerna, and their four-year-old daughter had been given a room in the empty house for the night by Padre Nacho because the Cernas' home had been without water and power for four days during an extended firefight between government forces and guerrillas that began on November 11. From darkened windows the couple watched uniformed soldiers prowl the campus. They could see that the strong military presence precluded any guerrillas from entering the grounds. They heard Padre Nacho yelling his indignant last words. Jorge and Lucía feared the worst for the priests, because after Nacho shouted, "there was only quiet, very deep quiet." The couple could not confirm their fears until dawn, when first light revealed the grisly scene. One by one, Lucía made out the figures prostrate on the lawn.

Leaving her little daughter with her husband, Lucía ran to the Jesuit Provincial House, not far from the campus. She burst in on Father José María Tojeira, the Jesuit provincial, as he was shaving. "They killed the Fathers! The soldiers killed the Fathers!" she blurted. Still in a bathrobe, he ran from the house to the campus. Lucía ran along, as did other priests, an older one falling slightly behind. When Salvadoran President Alfredo Cristiani announced over the radio that morning that guerrilla forces had killed the priests, Lucía knew he was mistaken. If she came forward, she thought, and stated that she saw soldiers and not guerrillas, it would help solve the crime. Since

---

Truth for El Salvador, S/25500 (1993), part IV, B.

her neighborhood had been swarming with guerrillas in the previous days, she was clear on their appearance. They dressed in shorts, not the long-pants camouflage uniforms of the army. One would not mistake the two.

Within days, Lucía and her husband, Jorge, gave sworn testimony to Judge Ricardo Zamora at the Spanish embassy. Both clearly stated that they had seen Salvadoran soldiers on the campus, heard Padre Nacho yelling, and described the shooting and destruction of the Jesuits' house. Lucía believed the government wished to know the truth. It never occurred to her that her testimony put her life in danger.

When a few of the Jesuits and a representative of the Catholic diocese explained to the couple that they needed to leave the country or risk being killed, the Cernas were truly surprised. Lucía presumed that the authorities, from President Cristiani to President George H. W. Bush, wanted to hear the truth about the killing of the priests and the women. Clinging to this line of thinking, the Cernas reasoned that even if they had to flee temporarily, the crime would be promptly solved and they could return to El Salvador.

The couple was given a choice to go to Spain, France, or the United States. They opted for Miami because Father Ellacuría had spoken well of it to Lucía. He had told her that it was not far from El Salvador, and that there were many Spanish-speaking people there. Upon their arrival in Miami, however, the tumultuous nightmare they found themselves in only grew worse. The U.S. Department of State and the FBI detained the family in a hotel, disconnecting the telephone, television, and any contact with the outside world. The family subsisted on American fast food delivered to them by FBI agents for the better part of a week. After three days of twelve-hour interrogations in which Lucía was accused of being a communist, a guerrilla, and a prostitute by the FBI agents and a Salvadoran colonel, she recanted her testimony. "Put me back in my home," she said. "Send us home." The couple felt their lives were more seriously threatened in Miami than in El Salvador.

The family was released to the president of the Association of Jesuit Colleges and Universities, Paul Tipton, SJ. He arranged for their immediate future, and flew them to Mobile, Alabama, to stay at Spring Hill College. Ultimately, Lucía testified to human rights lawyers for the United Nations, to the Jesuits of North America, to an investigating committee of the United States Congress, on tape for *60 Minutes*, and in countless other smaller settings. Her testimony is well documented if not widely known. The events of that night—what she refers to as "that history"—changed her life in ways that are still unfolding twenty-five years later. "My life changed in one moment, immediately! That is a fast big change. But I think also if we were not there, it would it still be a mystery, a secret about who killed."

The Cerna family ended up in Santa Clara, California. They had help with resettlement from Daniel Germann, SJ, a Jesuit associated with Santa Clara University. At that time he was living and working in East San Jose as a liaison between the working poor and university students. Dan found a place for the Cernas to live and solicited assorted household items. He shuttled them to immigration hearings and encouraged them to take English classes. He fielded employment options. He also demonstrated everyday American tasks—driving, pumping gas, changing a tire, grocery shopping, going to the dentist, and countless others—to help them acclimate to the United States.

Through Dan, my family and the Cerna family got to know each other. My husband and I had each been taught by Germann during our undergraduate years, and he presided at our wedding in 1985. He invited us to meet the Cernas early in 1990, and we were able to lend some help. After the first days and months we became friends with the Cernas. They asked my husband and me to be their daughter's godparents at her baptism. Lucía and Jorge held our babies when they came along, and when I had surgery or Lucía had surgery, one visited the other. We watched our collective three children grow up. Both families remained close to Dan through his final years dominated by Parkinson's disease.

As the twentieth anniversary of the Jesuit murders approached in 2009, I called Lucía to ask if she and her family would come to dinner "some night in November." In my mind it would be our own sort of memorial. "We would like to come on the sixteenth," was her immediate reply. And so our families shared a meal on that anniversary date, commemorating the murder of her friends, remembering the people of El Salvador who still struggle with poverty and exploitation, and grateful for our friendship through Dan, whose eightieth birthday would have been that week. November 16 is also the anniversary of my brother's death, and my sister even more recently had died in November. At that meal, in the month of all saints and all souls, we spent a few hours around the table, sharing stories in mostly English and some Spanish, laughing and crying. Our high school-aged children and the Cernas' college-aged daughter listened and asked questions and laughed too.

After that night I began to understand that relatively few people had heard Lucía and Jorge's perspective on the murders and what happened those years ago. Her official testimony is in written reports, but how does she feel about it now? What were the relationships she had with the murder victims, and how did the couple cope with leaving everything and everybody behind in El Salvador? I also wondered what had her childhood been like, and what brought her to that night? How do she and her husband feel about their native country? What was their experience as Spanish-speaking immigrants in America in the 1990s?

About a year after that meal I approached Lucía with an idea to interview her and to record the interviews. Aside from official documents in 1989 and 1990, no one had recorded Lucía's personal story. I believed it would make an important primary historical source and should be placed in an archives. At first she thought I wanted to hear what she witnessed. "I already told that to Father James," she said referring to James S. Torrens, SJ, who had published an article in *America* magazine about her testimony in 1990. When I explained that I was interested in her life story, what happened before the murders and what has happened since, she was surprised and somewhat emotional. Her daughter, who was in the room, explained, "No one has ever asked just about her before. They usually ask what she saw on that night."

She agreed. "My history is sad," she said. "I have not spoken of it. But now is the circumstance to tell my biography." Over the next two years she and I met, sometimes alone, sometimes with her husband or daughter or my daughter. We recorded over fifty hours of conversational interviews during 2011 and 2012. The first few were emotionally difficult for Lucía, and I asked her if perhaps this was not such a good idea. The initial difficulty faded, and our conversations became more free flowing, sometimes sprinkled with humor, and not in any particular chronological order. I was not an objective interviewer. I am sympathetic to Lucía's life experience.

Through the interviews, I also became better acquainted with Jorge Cerna. I had not realized that he too had seen the soldiers on the campus that awful night. Why, I wondered, was Lucía identified in some official documents as the sole witness when Jorge had seen the soldiers too. Initially, that first week, Jorge was reluctant to say what he had seen for fear of reprisals. Yet he made a statement under oath at the Spanish embassy before fleeing El Salvador, and he made the same statement to the FBI in Miami. But since Lucía had worked at the property, could identify the voice of Ignacio Martín-Baró, knew the victims and had an emotional attachment to them, she was the stronger witness. In Miami, Jorge was ridiculed for "allowing" his wife to give witness. He chuckles at reporting this, as if he had the ability to control her determination to speak out. In some ways Lucía was reported more often as the witness simply because of the emotion she brought to the testimony.

Like Lucía, Jorge has navigated the traumatic upheaval of fleeing El Salvador to protect his family. As Lucía notes: "If he had been away from me that night, he would not understand. But he was with us. . . . He understands why I am different now." They have been together to cope with the psychological fallout of the Jesuit murders.

Salvadoran and U.S. officials presumed that, like many poor people in El Salvador, the Cernas *wanted* to come the United States in 1989. Nothing could be further from the truth. At that time they were well established and, by El Salvador's standards, successful. They had achieved a middle-class lifestyle, and prospects for their daughter's education were far better than their own had been. Besides his homegrown bakery business with customers throughout the district, Jorge left behind a large family, with both parents living. His mother repeatedly asked them to return to El Salvador. When Lucía's mother died, they could not go to mourn her because they were still awaiting immigration documents. Neither Jorge nor Lucía ever harbored any desire to come to America.

After a half-dozen interviews, I told Lucía that I thought her story would make an important book. Her life illuminates so many issues that still face our world: poverty, childhood hunger, limited opportunities for education or healthcare, abusive militaries, corruption in government, and loss—what she repeatedly called "deep, deep loss." For Lucía, all these are wrapped up in faith. In spite of accusations against her ranging from lying to communist affiliation to prostitution, after leaving so much behind, and in the face of real hatred, she is able to say, "I think of God, always, because he is the basis for life. . . . I had nobody with me—no parent, no father. And to not have God in my heart? I believe totally."

This book is the result of our recorded conversations. Each chapter has two parts, one by Lucía and one by me. Lucía's parts are her *spoken* English words, taken directly from transcriptions of our interviews. Her choice of words is sometimes sharp and literal, common attributes of someone learning English as a second language. Her English words distill the stark reality of her family's story. The only changes I have made are for clarity. For each chapter I have written an essay as an accompaniment to her recollections to offer historical or social context. The essays also identify many of the Jesuits with whom Lucía worked or those she came to know in the United States.

Much of what I have written she would have had no way of knowing. For example, while she was well aware of El Salvador's civil war, she had no idea of the U.S. financial support of the Salvadoran military. "I do not understand politics, and I don't have time to watch TV." When that subject comes up, she says, "I don't know about that. I only say what I know." Lucía's strict adherence to reporting only what she knows firsthand, without extrapolating or deducing possible causes or effects, underscores her credibility.

It is surprising to me how well Lucía and I have been able to communicate. In a literal sense we do not speak the same language. Notwithstanding the occasional translation from her daughter, or one of us thumbing through a dictionary, we have managed to understand each other with a depth that catches me off guard. A verse from the Acts of the Apostles has come to my mind again and again: "And how is it that we hear, each of us, in our own native language?" (Acts 2:8). I do not have an answer other than to presume that the Spirit of God generates the love and respect that we have experienced during the interviews.

The Company, to use the common nickname for the Society of Jesus that Lucía and many in Latin America use, plays a leading role in her narrative. Her loyalty is not ideological or theological or philosophical. It is based on how she was treated by the Jesuits at the UCA. The late Dean Brackley, SJ, an American Jesuit who worked for years in El Salvador and with whom Lucía spoke on a few occasions, writes, "Love 'honors' others; it accords them *respect*, perhaps our deepest human need."[3] Lucía believes the priests at the UCA lived and taught self-respect and mutual respect. "The priests appreciated my work. . . . They offered respect. Never before did I have that." To this day the respect that Lucía was paid at the UCA sustains her. Lucía's life plays out as a paradigm for Brackley's assertion that respect is "perhaps our deepest human need."

Saint Ignatius, the founder of the Society of Jesus, drew a following about him because of a radical personal transformation while recovering from a severe leg injury. His process of listening for the will of God, of distinguishing the good Spirit of God through spiritual exercises, echoes down through the centuries from Jesuits scattered during a great suppression and those martyred in the years since to

---

[3] Dean Brackley, *The Call to Discernment in Troubled Times: New Perspectives on the Transformative Wisdom of Ignatius of Loyola* (New York: Crossroad, 2004), 213.

the Society of Jesus today. This historical continuum since Ignatius includes a modern-day litany of those who died at the UCA: Ignacio Martín-Baró, Ignacio Ellacuría, Segundo Montes, Amando López, Joaquín López y López, and Juan Ramón Moreno. Other men who escorted Lucía through the aftermath of the assassinations and offered help and friendship include the late Fermín Saínz, Paul Tipton, Dean Brackley, and Dan Germann; former Jesuits Joseph Berra and Richard Howard; and contemporary California Jesuit, James Torrens. All, in the tradition of Ignatius, attempted to find God in all things in order better to give glory to God in this time and place.

A memorial to the tens of thousands who died in El Salvador's civil war stands adjacent to a sculpted mural in Parque Cuscatlán in San Salvador, not far from where Lucía grew up. Twenty-five thousand names of women, men, and children etched into the black granite represent only about one-third of those who died. Monumento a la Memoria y la Verdad—a monument to the memory and the truth—reminds Salvadorans of their friends and neighbors, sons and daughters, who died during those horrific war years. In a similar way Lucía's memorial to the UCA martyrs and others she has lost since is here in this chronicle. Here is her testament to the truth.

Lucía frequently uses the English word *curious* to describe something unusual or interesting, or something she does not quite understand. Recently, I experienced something quite curious. I recalled a poem I had written in 1978, long before I met Lucía, published in my college's literary magazine, and I located it in an old file. For some unaccountable reason, I composed part of that poem in Spanish, as if foreshadowing my friendship with the Cernas. Reading the poem felt suddenly eerie when I realized how strangely apt it is for Lucía Cerna's choices in 1989 and for her life now. Entitled "Abandoned Things," two of the verses read:

> Mis paquetes y bolsas
> que son llenos
> de los posibilidades y potenciales
> de mi vida
> yo abandono
> para la una perferencia
> que es la mas importante
> para mi viaje.

So as I live my life,
I leave packages and bags
abandoned
unused
and I'll never know what lies
within them—
what could have been or what might have happened.[4]

Lucía Cerna cannot turn back the clock, cannot save the UCA martyrs from assassination, and can never know what may have been if she had not spoken of what she saw and stayed in El Salvador. When she publicly spoke the truth, she gave up everything, "home, brothers and sisters, mother and father, property." Her journey has brought her family to the United States, to a life full of "deep, deep loss" but also full of grace and full of God.

The path of Lucía's life led her to the night she saw and heard soldiers attack the UCA and murder eight people. Her choice to speak the truth came out of the depth of her convictions and the whole of her life experience. Her choice to speak the truth has also had lifelong implications for herself and her family. Lucía says: "We were there that night, and those several hours changed our life forever. I never thought about changing my life. I only told the truth. I was a housekeeper. I never wrote about anything political. I only told the truth, and they did not like it. For that I had to leave my home and family and country. For that."

[4] Mary Jo Hull, "Abandoned Things," *The Owl*, Santa Clara University (Spring 1978).

1

The Innocents

1946–1960

Lucía Cerna

I know sadness with victory. I know hunger. The worst part of my life was when I was a child. A child. I ask myself, because my mind is open now, how did I grow up? I sincerely do not know. My history is sad, but I don't forget. I have not spoken of it. But now is the circumstance to tell my biography.

I grew up in Antiguo Cuscatlán. Everybody in that town knew me as Luz. I answered to Luz because no one told me until I went to be married that my name was really Lucía. Now the place where I grew up is the botanical garden, but then everything belonged to Walter T. Deininger, a millionaire. This man was owner of so much, just incredible, including San Benito, sugarcane fields, and orange groves called *Pirineos*. He had a dairy with so, so many cows! And then the *cafetales*, where the coffee beans grow. From Antiguo Cuscatlán to the farm and the *cafetales*, he had a lot. Many years later one side became part of the UCA. But when I was a child, that was all orange trees, more than I could count.

This man Walter Deininger, whom we called Don Baltita, owned all the houses for the people working on his land. He was very small. He was German and very white, but he spoke fluent Spanish. He was really a millionaire, this man. My mother's family worked there. That is why I lived in Antiguo Cuscatlán. My grandfather dug deep holes to catch the rainwater so that the crops would not flood. Sometimes it rained too much, and flooding is very bad for crops. For digging, my grandfather was paid about seven *colónes* for two weeks, less than three dollars. Another aunt and uncle worked in the processing plant making brown sugar. If my cousin went to the plant with a soup can or a coffee can, he brought it back full of sugar. Sometimes he stopped to give us a little sugar.

When one aunt was young, she worked cleaning the Deininger house. I was maybe in fifth grade when she was working there. His home was a big Victorian house, beautiful, beautiful, totally beautiful! Such a big garden! The botanical garden is still very beautiful. He had only a wife, and she went every afternoon with two dogs to walk around their other farm on the north, a sugarcane farm, and back to the *Laguna*. They were quiet people.

This man also had a dairy, with a lot of cows and horses. When a cow died, he sent somebody to butcher it and give the meat to everybody in the town. With him, nothing was forbidden. Several times I went with a bowl to bring the stomach and make soup at home. Other people got a whole leg to take home. It was very good because that was the only time we had meat.

For every Christmas this man bought many toys for the children! He had a very nice car, but he did not drive. He had a driver. He was very rich, but he did not have guards around him like the other rich people. That rich man was very good to the people, and I think he liked Salvadorans. Many years after I had gone, he went to visit somebody and died of a heart attack. He left an order in his will that those living in the houses on his estate could buy them, but very cheap. So my aunt could pay little by little and then own her house. She only had to pay about thirty dollars. She owns her house now. It was wonderful for those people. They could never buy a house without that will. That man was a very good man.

I lived in the house of my grandfather. He was no good.

My mother was a servant in another home, far away, and so my younger brother and I lived with our grandparents. It is common in El Salvador for children to go with grandparents and the young mother goes to work as a domestic servant. It's awful. I don't like it. My mother came on her day off once or twice a month. I do not know who my father was. When I asked my mother, "Who is my father?" she never told me. A child should not grow up without a father. I felt shame not knowing a father.

When my mother came on her day off, my younger brother Óscar and I walked with our grandfather a long way to the bus stop. Returning to our home with our mother, we tried to hold her hand, but she was busy talking to her father. When we got home, the children were sent to the patio, and the adults talked. The next morning my mother would leave again for the bus.

I do not feel good when I remember *how* my mother suffered. I wanted to give more when I grew up, and my mother was my priority. I thought her heart was suffering, but she never explained to me. I felt that my mother loved my brother Óscar more than me, and I asked her why. She said because I looked like my father—but she would never say who my father was, even though I asked. I think some Hispanic families do not usually have good communication. It is very bad to grow and not know your father.

I think the people of that town would say my family was the most poor of all. I will tell you why.

I picked up garbage nobody wanted, but I needed it. We had hunger. We never forgot, never, because how is it possible to raise a child with no mother and no father and live like this, like animals?

We were always together, Óscar and me. When we passed the orange grove, I did not take an orange from the tree. "We are poor," I told my brother, "but the tree is not mine, and I do not take." If the orange was on the ground, I took, cut out the bad part with a knife, and gave half to Óscar, half to me. If I found a banana, half to me, half to Óscar. When the guards saw me pick oranges off the ground, ones the birds knocked down, they let me, even though it was forbidden. They knew my family. They only said, "*hola, cipota*"—"hello, child." They knew me because the guard station was almost in front of my home. My aunt washed and ironed the uniforms of the guards for pay.

Our house was one room with a patio for cooking. My grandmother slept on *un tapesco*, no mattress. Only rich people had mattresses. My brother Fernando was twelve years older than me. He had another father. He was with us sometimes. Óscar and I slept on the brick floor and shared one blanket. We did not have another one, so I did not wash it every day. I only washed it if it looked dirty, or on Sunday. Very early in the morning I went to the river to wash that blanket, but it had to dry the same day to be ready for the night. It was a lot of work to squeeze the water out of that blanket.

I tried to take care of my brother like a mother, advising him not to be away too long, or to help, or to do homework. I wanted to help him. In our home nobody was allowed to speak at the table. Nobody. Only eat quietly. Never talk to my grandpa; he never asked what I did in school or how Óscar was. Never. No one ever paid attention to us. Kids were supposed to work and be quiet.

Early in the morning, when it was still dark, the church bells from Santos Niños Inocentes woke me. We had no clock, no radio, no electricity, only an oil lamp with a soaked rag. The bells were our clock, Bing! Bing! Bing! That meant it was time to work. First, take out the chicken and the rooster that lived in our house and sweep out their droppings. Then start a little fire with sticks in the stove so it is warm when we bring the water. We did not have water coming into the house. Before breakfast we went to the river for water. Holding hands, Óscar and I went for water. I brought the water in the full jug on my head to wash and to cook.

It is curious. The river coming from the mountains was warm in winter or summer. So when I poured water on my head for a shower, it was not cold, just nice. I never wondered if the river was clean or not. There was no purified water. We drank from the river. We washed clothes in the river. The river was the river. We needed water. There it was.

There was no time in the morning to bring wood. There was no one to get wood, not my grandmother, not my grandfather, not my older brother, just me. So with Óscar I would go, but the night before. It was scary because it was in the camp, about a kilometer from the house, and there were animals and snakes. I tried to be an example for Óscar and I said, "*No tengo miedo*," I am not afraid. I explained to him that he must help because we needed the wood for cooking. And he understood always. We collected the sticks, tied them together with a belt, put the bundle on my head, and back home we went.

I was very skinny, but I climbed the trees with *un gancho*, a tool to pull the fruit. When I was high up and pulling the fruit, my brother Óscar stayed below to pick up the green fruit. We let it ripen at home, and then, with avocadoes for example, we were happy. I made breakfast with beans, only beans, and a little lard. Everything was measured. I learned to measure everything, because we had so little. With coffee we never had milk. The most difficult was grinding the corn on the *piedra de moler*, making powder, and after that making tortillas. I did not have a lot of strength. I planted *quisquiles*, a vegetable, on the patio, and a coffee plant. The *quisquiles* grew and they hang like grapes. I grew up very fast because my grandmother had arthritis that contracted her hands. I took care of the cooking from a very young age.

I did not learn at home. I learned by watching other women. I looked to a neighbor to see what she was doing, and I copied her—

carrying water, making tortillas, washing clothes with soap in the river. I did it all, even when I was just six years old. To wash clothes in the river, we scrubbed with a stone and some soap. One day I lost the soap in the river. I was so upset about the lost soap. I had to wash those clothes! My grandfather wanted those pants! When I lost the soap, I left the clothes at the river and ran to my chicken. I took one egg from that chicken and went to the store of Nina María. I paid one egg for a new soap and went back to the river to finish the clothes. My grandfather's pants were difficult to wash and to squeeze dry. I put one leg under my foot and twisted, twisted until water squeezed out. Then I put them on a hanger. Good clean pants. After that I was more careful with the soap.

My grandma started to lose her mind.

Many times she took off her clothes and went out in the street. My grandpa did not care, but I was ashamed to see her naked. She left the house and was going around naked. I thought how can I resolve this? I decided to tie her leg to the table so that she did not wander away when I was at school. Óscar helped me to tie it tight. I came from school and she was still tied to the table. It was very hard, very hard. She had bowel movements on the floor, and there was only me to clean up. With paper I took and threw away and washed with water and a broom and soap. I always had that broom, washing, washing. We did not have disinfectant, only water. One neighbor told me to try chlorine to clean the floor, but that was a terrible mistake! It had a terrible smell and was very bad. My grandpa did not care. He was no help. He just went with other women.

I cooked vegetable *chipilín* soup; here they call it spinach, but there it is *chipilín*. Several times I made that soup and gave it to my grandma. Instead of eating the soup, she poured it over her head, like a shower. Then I had to clean her and find something else for us to eat. My grandma pulled and pulled her hair until it came out. She was hurting herself. She would not permit a comb, so with my fingers I combed and tied up her hair in a bun so she would not pull it anymore. I had no family to help me. My mother was working far away. My grandma's other daughters came and looked and said, "oooooo," or "poor Luz," and went away. They offered no help. They did not come back because their mother was crazy.

Three times my grandma went to the psychiatric hospital, and three times she came back. Every time she was sick and they took her to the psychiatric hospital, she came back with the same problem. I never knew a diagnosis, but now that I work in healthcare, I read a lot about dementia. She had dementia and maybe schizophrenia. I was a kid then, and I did not understand.

The worst day was when my grandpa came home from work and he was drunk. He came in the door shouting at me, "I'm hungry! I'm hungry!" He had his pay that day, and before he came home he got drunk. He had *un corbo*, one big machete the men use to work. He shouted at me and waved that machete in my face yelling, "I'm hungry! I'm hungry!" I was scared. I thought, Oh, my God! Now I would say to him, Why do you do this? But then, I was just scared. I hid my brother on the patio. "Stay here!" I said to Óscar, and left him hiding in a cupboard. I ran to the *guardia* (guard station), just one block away. They heard his scandal in the street but did nothing until I told them he had the knife. The guards came and took my grandpa to jail. He spent Saturday and Sunday in the jail and came out Monday to go to work. We were in peace at home for two days.

We were supposed to be a family, but we were not a family. It was kids alone. It was hungry kids alone taking care of one drunk and one with dementia. We had no support, but I looked to the neighbor and repeated what I saw. I did for my family. That family did not teach and did not love. From my childhood my grandfather was no good. It would have been good to have one grandpa giving care, helping, especially with my grandma. She slept on the floor, with only me cleaning her, and my grandpa took another woman. Kids know everything, especially me because I was curious and listened. He had another woman. And when my grandmother went to the psychiatric hospital, he went with other women.

It is very curious. My older brother, Fernando, lived with us and worked learning carpentry in the shop of the Deininger estate. I washed and cooked for him too, and took care of my grandmother, but never one coin did he give me. Never. But here is the story about him. When he finished learning carpentry and could work on his own, he became interested in the woman living next door. But she had a husband and two children. I was only a child, but I could see. People think because you are a child that you do not know. But I know. My brother took that woman and they went to the city to live and work, leaving the husband and two kids. And soon that woman had a new baby.

They sent for me to care for her while she had the baby. I was twelve, and I went to care for her, rubbing oil on the belly, and putting on a warm brace. I cared for her for a couple of weeks. After the baby came, I went back to my grandmother's house again. Later, that woman had three more children. But later, much later, my brother discovered that the first baby was not his. It was the woman's husband's baby, the man she left behind. And so my brother was angry and divorced her. He married again, but had no more children. But now that I am an adult, I wonder why he never offered any support to me. Even one coin. But he never did.

I started school at seven years old. In El Salvador we study from January and finish the year in November, with no vacation. I wanted to get to school early, to talk to my friends and to laugh and be happy. "*¡Hola!*" I would say, pretending everything in my life was just fine. I went at 7:45 a.m., so I had to do all my housework very fast. I had to run to get the water, to make tortillas, and to cook. Then at noon I went home to eat again tortillas, beans, the same, three times, always the same. I had to be responsible as a child.

I went to the school in the morning and afternoon, the whole day in the school, but the time was divided. One class was manual arts, and I learned to embroider. I had a classmate, and her mother had a store. When she finished with the sugar, she gave me the sack for free. I think she knew I was poor. I washed it, and I learned to make a pillowcase from that sack. When I sold the pillowcase, I reminded her to give me the next sack. I used the money to buy thread for the next one. Then I made a table cloth. Before it was finished, I was offering it for sale in the town. I did not have time to do that job stitching during the day; only in the night after the dishes were washed, I did that job. Then I bought more thread to continue working. By second grade I was making things and selling, selling, to buy my book for one year. Paying with my art, I never stopped stitching and selling, stitching and selling.

With that money I could buy a pencil. Other children with good families throw away the small pencils. I picked up any small piece of a pencil because I appreciated having a pencil that I did not have to buy. I made my own *papel de paque*, six pages of newsprint sewn together with my needle and thread. When I learned my ABCs, I remember I started like that. The teacher showed me how to write each letter in that book I made. I enjoyed participating in dramas in school, dancing or acting. Once I dressed like an old lady and put dust in my hair and borrowed a skirt. I walked bent over with a cane, and everyone thought I was old! It was fun.

The teacher loved me a lot, giving clothes from other children to me and my younger brother. One day she gave Óscar white pants for church on Sunday. He was so proud to wear those pants! He asked me to take care of the special pants. He called them *pantalones de leche*, or milk pants. He was proud wearing clean, white pants. The first-grade teacher gave me several dresses, and I took them to my aunt who was a seamstress. She cut the dresses for me, and after, I had my clothes! I had to make my own underwear from other clothes. They were not good, but for me, okay.

One day I went to the school for September 15, Independence Day. That day is also my birthday. The whole school was together in line listening to the director and teacher explaining a lot of things about independence. I was in the line and suddenly my nose was bleeding, a lot, and I felt dizziness, and boom!—to the ground, my body dropped. Somebody brought one brick, a hot brick, with a very strong smell, and the brick stopped the bleeding. They told me to sit down for a while. I had anemia but never saw a doctor. There was no doctor for my family, only an herbalist. Several times I suffered that problem with a bleeding nose and dizziness, but I never knew what happened to me. The teachers stayed with me until the dizziness passed and I was awake again, but no parents or grandparents, no, only teachers. I think the teachers loved me.

I never stayed in a grade for more than one year.

I loved school and wanted to learn everything. From the start until sixth grade I was confident in school. The teacher asked me to help clean the school, and I was happy to help. Here in the United States they say hall, but there it is called a corridor. I mopped it bright and shiny. In that school they taught me to clean and I thought, okay, if I clean the school like this, I should also clean the home like this. So I learned. I have good memories of how they were with me, very good teachers. They never said, "Luz is very poor," but they gave me some clothes for myself and for my brother. I was always very grateful, and I showed it. My mother could not buy anything. She was really, really poor. I don't know how it was she thought to have children. Anyway, I got everything I could for my brother.

Every Tuesday nuns came with the priests, Jesuit priests, for catechism. No one ever told me to go. My grandmother never said to go. I wanted to go, and I took my brother with me. The priest called the children with a puppet. It was very funny, and he would make the puppet speak. I liked to go because I was happy there and they had prizes! For example, they asked questions and I answered immediately. For correct answers they gave candy or a cookie. When I won, I shared with my brother or brought something little to my grandmother.

When I was alone, I talked to God. The priest in Antiguo Cuscatlán knew my situation because I told him in confession. I was suffering. He couldn't say to me "don't worry" or give advice. He only said that things could change very soon. But that suffering went on for years and years! Until I grew! But I think of God, always, because he is the basis for life, to believe in something. I had nobody with me—no parent, no father. And not to have God in my heart? I believe totally. I believe. Always I went to the church, to the mass, once a week when the priest came, and during the week I talked to the nuns.

In my country Dia de la Cruz is a big celebration. The teachers and nuns and priests prepare for a big event. My teacher directed me to learn a poem to recite on the stage at the *guardia*. I worked very hard and learned that poem. Even today I remember it, "*¿Quien tuviera dos alas para el vuelo*?" Who has two wings to fly? And I waved my arms like wings and said that whole long poem with great drama and movement. They clapped and clapped for me. And I won first place! Happy, happy! The prize was one big basket of fruit—a pineapple, mangos, oranges, and also *cinco colónes* [about two dollars] for me! This was a very happy day, and for that I always remember that poem:

> And then, a sound is heard through the hills and lush
> groves,
> As if a storm rolled through the slopes:
> Animals arrive with a strange fervor
> To drink the tears that the mountain sheds.[1]

My grandmother died in our home. By that time my brother Fernando was a carpenter, and when she passed away, he prepared everything for the funeral. They put a lot of flowers on my grandma's body. Many, many people came to the house to see my mother and

---

[1] Alfredo Espino, "Ascension," in *Jicaras Tristes* (San Salvador: National Council for Culture and the Art of El Salvador, 1996), 13, trans. Jesús Ramos (2012).

aunts. I was on the patio helping to make tamales and thinking: "Why do they come now? Why are my mother and aunts here now? Why is everybody so nice and happy now?"

When my grandmother passed away and my grandfather was with another woman, I did not have support anymore. Where would I go? I was fourteen. I went to work in San Salvador as a servant in a house. That is when I left Antiguo Cuscatlán. I wished for more school, but I had to go to work.

One of my friends at school was Milagro Navas. I knew her from first grade. We played together as children. We talked and laughed and jumped rope. I had to stop school after sixth grade, but she continued to study in a private school in Santa Tecla, closer to the city. Her family was not wealthy but had a medium-style life. Now she is the *alcaldesa*, mayor of Antiguo Cuscatlán. She has had that job for many years, and she is good and works a lot for the city. When I go to the *alcaldia*, courthouse, she calls out, "Hey, Lucía!"

Many years later my grandpa was very old. He retired, and my mother cared for him with money from retirement in that house in Antiguo Cuscatlán. Sometimes I helped. For example, he liked tobacco, so I took tobacco, or a shirt, or a pair of pants—anything to help. But they did not love me. I tried to respect and recognize that she was my mother and he was my grandpa. So I did these things out of respect. But we did not have an attachment or a bond. No, they did not teach me how to love. But finally, finally, he told me, "Luz," *porque* he called me Luz, "you are a hero." He told me, "I am proud of you."

When I left Antiguo Cuscatlán to be a servant, the orange trees were still there. About the time I visited my mother and grandfather, the Deininger estate and the orange trees disappeared. They started to build the UCA. The Jesuit priests made a big campus where the orange trees were. It is curious. After many years I went back there to work at the UCA.

Mary Jo Ignoffo

The desolation of Lucía's childhood brought us to silence. We sat together, quietly, letting her story have the air in the room. Her memories of hunger and of searching for food and for love tumbled out through anguished tears, not in a self-pitying way, but as if they had not been spoken, perhaps ever. I had no consoling words. How is it that I have known this woman for more than twenty years and had not heard these things? I never asked. The certainty that she speaks for most of the people in the world took my breath away.

Plain, raw hunger lurked every day of Lucía's childhood. She was not alone. Hunger has haunted El Salvador's children since the Spanish Conquest. From the sixteenth-century armed invasion, to the debt peonage of the following two hundred years, through a late-twentieth-century civil war, countless Salvadoran children have lived in a state of chronic malnutrition and hunger. Although there has been some recent improvement, as of 2010, according to World Bank statistics, published online, 21 percent of El Salvador's children under age five are stunted, that is, suffer low height for their age. Thirty-eight percent of children aged six to twenty-four months are anemic. El Salvador ranks 106 out of 182 countries on the Human Development Index. In other words, most countries are better off, but far too many are worse. We have work to do.

For me, Lucía's personal account offers a microscopic look at global hunger statistics. Even though I am aware of general percentages of world hunger, her explicit descriptions of the consequences of poverty brought the reality home as no statistical graph can. Paltry allotments of food; lack of sanitation; drinking, bathing, and laundering in the same river—these images speak louder than numbers. According to the United Nations, 870 million people worldwide suffer from chronic undernourishment. I fear my naivete may be typical for an American.

The emotional conversation moved to the firmer ground of everyday life. She patiently explained to me common things in El Salvador. The *guardia,* for example, is not a police station, as I had guessed, but a guard shack for security in the plantation's housing district. She demonstrated grinding corn for tortillas and squeezing river water out of a pair of pants. She showed me a pillowcase she had embroidered. There are no disposable diapers in El Salvador, she noted. Instead, cloth from old clothes is carefully washed to be made soft for the babies and torn down to size. She had no underwear, so she fashioned some from castoffs. We talked about the differences in vegetables available there—*chipilín* and *quisquiles*—and our comparative spinach and chayote.

"What was your chicken's name?" I asked Lucía. She looked at me blankly. Perhaps she did not understand the question. As a child I also had a pet chicken, which is odder than one might think since I grew up in central Los Angeles.

"It had no name," she said. "It was *la gallina.*"

Of course. Her chicken was an insurance policy, a bank, and a grocery store all at once. My chicken was an exotic pet. Hers was a means to survival.

El Salvador was a colony of Spain for its first three hundred years. Early in the nineteenth century Spain began to lose its grip on the Americas, and independence from Spain was won by Mexico and the provinces of Central America on September 15, 1821. El Salvador united with other Central American provinces as the Federal Republic of Central America. In 1824, El Salvador published its own constitution, the first independent constitution adopted in Central America. Yet it remained linked with its neighbors until its National Assembly formally proclaimed its separation from the Central American Federation in 1841. Nevertheless, El Salvador celebrates its independence on September 15, commemorating its separation from Spain rather than from its neighbors.

Lucía was born on Independence Day in 1946. At the time, hopes ran high for social reforms and democratic ideals. The brutal dictator Maximiliano Hernández Martínez had just been overthrown by a military-led revolution. A new constitution drawn up and adopted in 1950 extended the right to vote to women.

During the 1950s large estates like the one where Lucía lived provided their workers and families two meals each day, always the same—beans, *maize* (corn) to make tortillas, and coffee.[2] Pure coffee was too valuable to provide to workers, so it was cut by two-thirds with cornmeal. Foraged tropical fruits sometimes supplemented meager diets. Not surprising, Lucía was anemic, malnourished, and underdeveloped.

The nominal ration and roof overhead were offered in exchange for the work of her maternal grandfather. He worked on a team of ditch-diggers assigned to avert sometimes torrential rains from the crops on the coffee and sugar plantations of Walter T. Deininger. Every other necessity—water, clothing, herbal medicine—came by hard work or the charity of others. Lucía graphically details daily routines, the stark reality of a child struggling to survive, and life in a home without love. Lucía and her younger brother, Óscar, scavenged for food and wood, cowered in fear of a drunken, violent grandfather, and kept watch

[2] Alistair White, *El Salvador* (New York: Praeger Publishers, 1973), 118.

over a mentally ill grandmother, all the while expecting the return of a mother too distracted to love.

"What was your mother's name?" I asked.

"Dolores."

Mother of Sorrows. Lucía's mother, an extremely poor and apparently profoundly unhappy woman, can be depicted as images of Nuestra Señora de Dolorosa have for centuries, with a tear-streaked face. Dolores gave birth to her daughter, Lucía, on the feast day of Our Lady of Sorrows on September 15.

El Salvador of the 1940s and 1950s was held in the economic and political grip of an unofficial coalition between a brutish military and a tightly knit oligarchy, sometimes called the Fourteen Families. The military held control of the population on behalf of the elite society that dominated the cultivation, production, harvest, and export of coffee, cotton, and sugar cane. By the mid-twentieth century, the Fourteen Families had branched out to include almost two hundred members, descended from founding families or from successful later arrivals. If economic influence were not enough, the oligarchy also supplied the government with leaders who firmly and quickly suppressed any challenge to the status quo. The coffee elites, backed by the military, successfully resisted demands for change from the poor.

Many elites scorned the poor as though they were a contagion. One wealthy woman of El Salvador's oligarchy was quoted as saying: "Look at how they live! They live like pigs; they have children with different men; their houses are made of cardboard." Her description of *la chusma*—the rabble—included "the toothless, the crippled, the degenerate, the lazy, the drunken, the mad, less than animals!"[3] Lucía was born to the *chusma*, to a poor, single mother whose family was employed by one of the country's large landowners.

The family lived in a feudal-style housing district belonging to Walter Deininger, just outside present-day San Salvador, edging Antiguo Cuscatlán. The ancient "place of gems and jewels" had been the capital for the indigenous Pipil, a branch of the Aztecs of central Mexico. According to legend, when the Spanish invaded in the 1520s, the Pipil resistance was led by a ruthless warrior named Atlacatl. It is doubtful if such a character ever lived, but the superhuman exploits associated with him are so entrenched that he is still reported as an important historical figure in El Salvador's national story. He represents strength

---

[3] Robert Armstrong and Janet Shenk, *El Salvador: The Face of Revolution* (Boston: South End Press, 1982), 12.

in the face of insurmountable opposition. The Salvadoran poet Alfredo Espino writes about Atlacatl:

> That indigenous Atlacatl, with a body figure
> Of robust biceps and an upright chest,
> And who in a legend of heroes and gods, would
> Have been one of a bronze statue of Hercules.[4]

During El Salvador's civil war of the 1980s, an elite military regiment trained to combat communism by the U.S. Army called themselves the Atlacatl Battalion. The modern soldiers effectively co-opted the legend and the ruthless attributes surrounding their ancient hero in a cultural justification for their own aggressive brutality.

Don Baltita, as Lucía recalls Deininger, was by all accounts a decent man who contributed to schools, churches, and hospitals. As she described the *patrón*, I wondered if she might be exaggerating his benevolence or overlooking his place as one of the country's big landowners. Who was this Deininger?

Walter T. Deininger was born in Guatemala to German parents, educated in Hamburg, and, beginning in 1912 at the age of twenty-one, managed the family enterprises in El Salvador—vast sugarcane fields, coffee plantations, a dairy, and a collection of exotic plants and trees from around the world.[5] His father had been one of the immigrants to consolidate colonial lands farmed by rural people. The consolidation by a relative few resulted in a landless population, large-scale agribusiness in coffee and sugar, and an inability for the country to feed itself.

As a member of one of the earliest immigrant families, Deininger was part of the oligarchy, a bona fide member of the elite, an association that during World War II saved his life and his fortune. Lucía would never have guessed and had no way of knowing that her Don Baltita spent World War II in an American detention camp for German prisoners of war. Violating its own Good Neighbor Policy,

---

[4] Alfredo Espino, "Atlacatl," in *Jicaras Tristes*, 97, trans. Jesús Ramos (2013).

[5] Information about Walter T. Deininger comes from public records, such as passenger ship lists and immigration papers, and from Internet links for tourism in El Salvador and the country's national parks. Ship manifests give his place of birth, age, and marital status. Deininger traveled to Europe several times in the course of his life. He is buried at Cementerio do los Ilustres in San Salvador.

which claimed not to interfere in Latin American affairs, the United States demanded that Latin governments identify and detain enemy nationals. State Department officials presumed that people of German ancestry in Central America were necessarily pro-Hitler, escalating fears of sabotage and espionage at America's back door. The United States also wished to stockpile prisoners as potential bargaining chips in trade for American prisoners of war in German camps.[6] Deininger was one of those chips.

Despite the fact that Walter Deininger had not been born in Germany and that he had made his Salvadoran citizenship official by terminating dual citizenship with Germany in 1939, the Martínez government, under great pressure, handed him over to the Americans. Deininger went to Texas by way of Mexico in 1943 and was incarcerated at the Kenedy Alien Detention Camp for the duration of the war.[7] His German-born wife was not sent to detention because official U.S. State Department policy stated that women were not a threat.[8] Señora Deininger remained at the estate on the edge of Antiguo Cuscatlán, awaited her husband's safe return, and attempted to cast a protective shield over Walter's family legacy.

Some of Deininger's fellow prisoners were repatriated to Germany, some Jews among them, and others were exchanged for American POWs. Deininger's allies in the Salvadoran government, his prominent place among the elite, along with his wife's presence in Antiguo Cuscatlán, proved invaluable in allowing his return home with property intact.

If Deininger was hostile to the U.S. policy and his government's complicity in it, he did not take it out on El Salvador. He remained the *patrón* that Lucía describes from the end of the war until his death in 1968. He bequeathed large portions of his land to be set aside as parks. The Jardín Botánico La Laguna is a showcase for Deininger's imported plants and trees. The seven-acre garden in Antiguo Cuscatlán draws locals to calm ponds and hiking trails, but its herbarium has brought international attention. Since it opened to the public in

---

[6] Max Paul Friedman, *Nazis and Good Neighbors: The United States Campaign Against the Germans of Latin America in World War II* (Cambridge: Cambridge University Press, 2003), 113.

[7] National Archives and Records Administration (NARA), Washington DC; *Alphabetical Manifests of Non-Mexican Aliens Granted Temporary Admission at Laredo, Texas, December 1, 1929–April 8, 1955*; Record Group: 85, *Records of the Immigration and Naturalization Service*; Microfilm Serial: *M1771*; Microfilm Roll: *1*.

[8] Friedman, *Nazis and Good Neighbors*, 152.

1978, it has developed a library and plant database for the rare species collected there.

Parque Nacional Walter T. Deininger is in the department of La Libertad, near the sea. A ten-mile hiking trail skirts the park, and there are several spots to take in panoramic views of the ocean below. The botanical garden and national park are only two highlights of his many generous gifts. But Deininger's most important contribution, and one that Lucía notes with gratitude and respect, may be the least known. His last will and testament offered employees the opportunity to purchase their homes for an exceedingly low sum, well within the means of many. For workers to have a chance to own a house was unheard of in El Salvador in the 1960s. Lucía's aunt paid "little by little" and owns her home today. Deininger's bequest had a discernible impact on the lives of some of El Salvador's poor.

Lucía's fond recollection of Deininger, however, is tested by the reality of her childhood, and the image of this kindly man is tarnished by childhood hunger and disease. Lucía and her brother were not permitted to pluck an orange from the vast groves, so they resorted to collecting rotten oranges off the ground. They had meat only when a dairy cow dropped dead and could be butchered and divided among the workers. Collecting cow innards to make soup was perceived as a great gift. Deininger's beautiful Victorian manor house, whose housekeeping staff included Lucía's aunt and which Lucía visited only through the back door, stood as magical as any castle. It is in sharp contrast to the one-room shanty that Lucía shared with three or four family members.

Most of Lucía's childhood memories are unpleasant, so she had no difficulty in quickly identifying the happiest. Dia de la Cruz, one of El Salvador's most beloved holidays, borrows from ancient indigenous rites marking the beginning of the rainy season and incorporates the traditional Christian adoration of the Savior's cross. A presentation of song and dance was prepared by schoolchildren and held at the local *guardia* or security station. Lucía had been instructed to learn and recite "Ascension," a poem by Salvadoran poet Alfredo Espino. "Who has two wings to fly?" Espino wrote and Lucía recited.

> From here, I see the sea,
> so blue, so sleepy;
> if it were not a sea,
> it would gladly be another sky![9]

---

[9] Espino, "Ascension," in *Jicaras Tristes*, 25.

Arms waving and words flowing, Lucía gave a dramatic rendering to Espino's bird in flight over El Salvador's stunning natural landscape.

A young intellectual of the 1920s, Espino's collection of ninety-six poems in *Jicaras Tristes* (sad vessels) is popular in El Salvador but is not considered particularly significant by literary critics. Perhaps it maintains its popularity for its beautiful imagery, an escape from the reality of daily life in El Salvador. For Espino, beauty was visible only at a distance, always out of reach, and disturbed by human conflict. Up close, the scene loses its appeal.

> Night approaches.
> The sea can no longer be seen.
> And how repugnant, how sad
> To have to begin the descent.[10]

After an ongoing dispute with his parents over choosing a suitable marriage partner, Espino committed suicide. Lucía never knew that. For her, the poem recalls personal affirmation, a very unusual occurrence for her in her youth. The prize awarded her—approximately two dollars and a fruit basket—was more money and more food than she had ever had at one time.

"What was the name of your church?" I asked.

Without hesitation she reported, "Santos Niños Inocentes."

Church of the Holy Innocents! How sadly apt! The bells that ring morning, noon, and night are from a church dedicated to the biblical holy innocents—infants slaughtered by the fearful politics of an insecure and misguided King Herod. Each insufficient meal of Lucía's childhood was heralded by bells tolling from that church of the innocents. Surely the children of El Salvador, Lucía and Óscar among them, are modern *inocentes*, children sacrificed to keep the wealthy and powerful in business.

From earliest childhood Lucía wished for education. School had been a crucial respite from a grim home life. At school she found respect and success. She was one of the fewer than 20 percent of Salvadoran children in the 1950s to finish primary school. It is not surprising that she would not be among the 4 percent who finished secondary school.[11] Having finished sixth grade was an accomplishment that placed Lucía

---

[10] Ibid.

[11] White, *El Salvador*, 231.

in a special minority. Her brothers were lucky enough to become tradesmen. Lucía had to forgo more education to become a servant.

Lucía expresses very little ambiguity. She speaks with surety. That was not love. There was love. Here was despair. That is hope. That was respect. Where is the justice? Lucía opened my eyes, shining a light on suffering, exposing hunger, rendering a world that is foreign to me in all aspects. "Everybody in that town knew me as Luz," she said. We can visualize a little street urchin, selling stitched sugar sacks. Today, she is for us a reflection of little Luz, a light of hope and resilience, illuminating the life of the poor in the country named for the Savior of the world.

The UCA grew up on the land that had been the orange groves of the Deininger estate. The Jesuit order had received a formal request on November 17, 1964, from the Catholic bishops of Central America, with papal approval, to establish a university in San Salvador. Twenty-five years less one day later, one of those Jesuits to whom the request was made, Joaquín López y López, was murdered with his colleagues on the campus he helped found. Something went terribly wrong.

2

The Devil's Gate

1960–1975

Lucía Cerna

After my grandmother died, I went to work as a servant in San Salvador. Óscar went to a vocational school and learned to be a brick-mason. My mother and I went to visit him maybe once a month, and he seemed happy. I brought shoes or pants, or whatever I could, to help him. My mother worked for people who were not nice, and I encouraged her to find another job, but she did not. She worked hard for nothing.

I went to work as a servant in the home of Niña Martita. She was very good and was confident with me because, although I was poor, I never took. That is very important. I do not take. The teachers taught me that. I did not learn that at home. I did not get a good example in my grandparents' home, but in the school, yes. This house had enough to eat, so it was very good for me. They appreciated my work. Still, I wanted to be more than a servant.

While I was working at that house I met my first husband. I married when I was maybe eighteen, but I don't remember exactly when. We went to the *alcaldia* to be married, and I discovered my proper name is Lucía. I always answered to Luz, so when the officer said no, you are Lucía, I was surprised. I asked my mother. She just shrugged and said, oh well, we called you a short name, Luz. Starting then, though, people called me Lucía.

My mother and my aunt did not marry. But I preferred to be married, so I married. I saw in my family what happens to children when the parents are not married. I thought to myself, if I am not married, I will not have children. It is important for safety and responsibility. I did not have anybody to advise me, no one to say this man may not be good. He was ten years older, and I thought he was a good man. Now I know, when you start bad, you finish bad.

My husband worked for one of the Fourteen Families that owned everything in El Salvador. He worked for Ernesto Regalado Dueñas, the grandson of General Tomás Regalado of the Tomás Regalado dynasty. That family was very rich and powerful. Don Ernesto's home in the *colonias* had an amazing view of the whole of San Salvador. From that house you could see the whole city! And inside the house was spectacular. My husband worked as a gardener and a landscaper. He knew a lot about flowers. He built beautiful fountains for that rich millionaire family, and he took care of the big swimming pool and golf course.

Here is the story about how that Regalado family became so rich.

The family started many years ago with the first woman, Concepción Regalado. The people called her Concha. The woman was very poor, and suddenly the family had a lot of money, and her son also had a big family with many millions of dollars. How did she get that money? The older people say that this woman, Concha, made a pact with the devil to make the family grow and grow with all the money and so many properties.

Doña Concha Regalado was married to the president. He told her he had a problem. There are too many people in the jail and we cannot provide clothes, blankets, and food for all the prisoners, he told her. Concha told him to take all the criminals out of jail to work for the city. She used her money to buy a ball and chain for each prisoner. So the prisoners did the work of the city, but they could not run away because of the ball and chain. This was her idea, and this is what the president did.

Many years later, after Doña Concha died, people said you can hear the sound of the balls and chains at night on the streets of San Salvador. The workers at the Regalado home also said that the night she died, they heard yelling in the Regalado land offices. The oldest people say even more. They say she is the fire from the volcano at Izalco, called *el Puerto del Diablo*—the devil's gate. Many people say that since she made a pact with the devil, la Conchita appears in the fires of Izalco.

The Regalados were very rich, similar to Walter Deininger. Both properties also had infirmaries. I don't know if they still exist or not. I remember Concha's son, Don Tomás, named after his father. He also had a lot of money, in Guadalupe, close to Antiguo Cuscatlán. He built a mansion with big gardens and a golf course and everything was totally beautiful. Concha's grandsons, including Don Ernesto, grew up in that home. That man Tomás had a heart attack in his bathroom and somebody found him dead. My husband told me, because he was often at that house, that the wife became a drunk when she was all alone in that mansion, always drunk. The white, beautiful castle was very near to the UCA, with only a bridge to separate it. Now it is a beautiful museum.

Don Ernesto's home had a lot of big dogs. My husband showed me the German Shepherd and Doberman. The family had a cook just for the dogs. She made *sopa de res*, meat soup, for those dogs. Big bowls with meat! I saw that, under his supervision. It was not a little bowl, no. It was a big bowl for each! Too much! My husband had the job to brush the teeth of the dogs. They had huge, gold teeth. Their teeth were made of gold! He also showed the collars that the dogs wore on their necks. The collars were made of teeth. I was so afraid of those dogs! They had many puppies too, but I was terrified of the big dogs with the gold teeth. For his work my husband was paid the normal wage. Nothing extra, no food, no help, nothing. That was the lifestyle of rich people during those years, and I saw it. I do not understand how they have a lot of money and do not work hard.

Don Ernesto was kidnapped by the guerrillas.

That started the bad situation in El Salvador. Guerrillas took him and killed him. My husband was planting flowers one morning, near the gate. He saw Don Ernesto leave for work and turn out of the driveway where there were a few construction workers on the street. They held up signs to slow the cars, and when Don Ernesto slowed, the kidnappers took him. My husband ran to tell Helen de Regalado, his wife, and together, with my husband driving, they chased the kidnappers. My husband carried a pistol with him. They never found them, even though they drove to the mountains looking. Days after, when his body was found, Helen became a widow and went to Europe, leaving that home empty. They had two little children, and she took them away. She was afraid for her children. I was upset when that happened. When people have the money, they leave El Salvador. Many people go to the United States because they have heard how life is in the United States. But she decided Europe would be better.

That history is very true. Concha Regalado somehow found money when she was poor. After she became rich, she treated the people in jail with injustice. Maybe it was a pact with the devil. Anyway, the Regalados had a big defect, and later the truth came out. Don Ernesto was kidnapped and murdered, and his wife and children had to leave El Salvador.

My husband changed jobs after Ernesto Regalado died because there was no more work on that property. He also changed his life and started doing bad things.

My son was born in 1970. My daughter was born in 1971, the same year that Don Ernesto was kidnapped. We lived outside San Salvador, close to Santa Tecla. We had a nice family. I visited my mother and brother when I could. I thought I was happy. My children were learning and growing. I did not work outside the home. I became friendly with my husband's sisters. But then my husband took up with another woman. She lived just across the street. One day I saw the woman was pregnant. I asked my husband about her, and we argued. I was upset. He had another woman with another child the same age as my son.

My husband was looking for money. He worked all that time for the Regalados and started doing similar things about making a pact with the devil. He learned about *El Libro de San Cypriano*, an evil book that explains how you can make money, how you can go inside a bank and take money and nobody will see. He loved reading that book! One day I touched it, and I felt cold, cold, cold. It was very scary. He did not like to listen to things about God. I told him when I came from church, and he'd say "I don't believe anything that the priest says. This is the truth!" he yelled, holding *El Libro de San Cypriano*. He set up a little altar, and put a figure there with wine, water, and food. I asked, "What is that?" and "Why are you doing that?"

"Forget it," he told me. But I would find him there in the hammock at midnight smoking *puros*, long Cuban cigars. If I put on the light, he got very angry.

"What are you doing?" I asked. "Are you a *brujo*?" He was acting like a witch. Soon he appeared with a car. "Where did you get the car?" I asked.

"Forget it!" he said to me.

I thought he was fine. He had his own home, children, and a job. But he changed, first the mind and then the face. Maybe he was depressed; I don't know. But when his face changed to hate, I felt scared. Nothing but scared. He started to give me reason not to love him because I was so afraid. Was it not enough to have a family and be happy? But his face changed, and he became a different man. I did not want to be with him again. I started to hate, too. No love.

One day I did not like the altar there anymore, and he kept putting wine and tortillas there, and praying. I picked it all up and threw it away in the garbage. When he came back he was so angry, so angry. He kept hitting me and yelling. The man changed character. After that I could barely sleep. I thought he would hurt me or my children. One night he came home drunk, but now he had a gun. He chased me through the house shooting. He wanted to kill me. I cried for my children. I begged him not to hurt the children. He kept shooting, and I ran to a neighbor and then to his sister's house.

When I went back after a day, he said he would kill me if I ever came back. I had no help, no one to give me advice. To be poor is one thing, but to kill me too? It could not be possible. I wanted my children, but he refused. We went to a court reconciliation and I told him if you let me stay in one room of your property, we can both care for the children. They should have a mother and a father. He said live with me in our house as a wife or leave with nothing. He and the attorney were laughing and laughing.

"Well, Señora," the attorney said to me, "he says he loves you. Live with him or lose your children!"

It was a terrible, terrible situation. I don't remember where I went. It was a very bad moment for me. I was disoriented, and nobody I knew understood what happened to me. He took my children. He did not pay attention. He told me and the lawyer told me: "Don't take these children again. You have permission to see them one day a month." He gave me the last Sunday of each month. When I went on the last Sunday of every month, the children were not there. He hid the children from me. I bought things for my children, sometimes a pair of shoes, or a toy, or a blouse. When I went to see my children, they were not at home. So I left the gifts for my children. As I walked away, my ex-husband set fire to the gifts I brought, and he laughed and laughed. The children thought I left, and he poisoned their minds with hate. They never got one gift I left. I went to tell the lawyer, and he did not pay attention because my husband paid him money. The official records say that I abandoned my children. Those years later, when I came to the United States and was interrogated about the massacre at the UCA, they accused me of abandoning my children. I had a choice to be dead or to be gone. Bad choice.

He must have learned from that evil book, because he got his money.

Maybe he had his own pact with the devil. He bought property. After I left, because I did leave, he appeared with two more cars and two commercial trucks. He married twice again, but he was never happy. He killed the happiness. Finally, many years later, when the children were grown up, somebody assaulted him. Two men came to his home and offered good money if he delivered something. He accepted. When he drove for the delivery, the men pointed a gun at him and made him pull off the road into a plantation. He had a helper with him, a ten-year-old boy, and the boy ran for help. But the men beat my ex-husband so badly that he was unconscious in the hospital for three months. He lost an eye and an ear and had such a bad infection that he had a terrible smell. When he got out the hospital and was home alone at his sister's house, he hanged himself. That is what his money got for him.

My children grew up with hate. What can I do? Pray to God. I take time to think about it, but always I pray to God. When someone poisons the brain with hate, it is very difficult to change the mind. Both these children are adults now and have come to the United States. I sponsored them. But they still have in their minds the lies their father told them. They speak to me, but it has been difficult.

I got a job working as a servant in a house.

I worked in a house that had a dairy, cleaning and cooking and attending the family. I became friends with a coworker there. Her name was Cecilia. She had the job to wash the big one-liter bottles for the milk. She brought the milk to the electric pasteurizer. We built a very strong friendship. When she invited me to the farm of her parents, I saw, Ooooohh, a lot of fruits—bananas of every kind, mangos, oranges, pineapples. I never knew anyone who had so many fruit trees! The family had a big house, very big, with the farm. And the whole family—seven children—grew up in that big home. I was happy to get to know that family.

When they were children they went to school in the city every morning. They walked over a mile at 6:30 a.m. At 11:30 a.m., when class in the city finished, they walked back home to eat. After eating, they walked back again to start at 1:30 p.m. That family did a lot of walking! But everybody felt free. The parents had a big farm. The children picked avocados, and as they ripened, their mother sold them from the patio. There were chickens, turkeys, all with little chicks, walking around the patio. Their father planted a lot of sugarcane, and then the sons helped to cut the cane to send it to make sugar. Even though it is cut in December, it is not necessary to plant it again. It grows again in the second and third year. The fourth year it must be planted again. The father also planted sesame seeds near the sea. When it is ready, it is put in the sun to dry. The sesame seeds are put in bags and sold to a seed plant. Other crops were pineapples and sometimes corn. At that time, they never used fertilizer or insecticide. Later, after an infestation, it was necessary to use insecticide. Then there was a shortage of the chemical, and only the farms of the rich had a supply. Poor or middle-class people could not get insecticide and lost their crops.

The oldest brother was very tall, like the father, and handsome. He was a character, and sometimes he got into trouble. Once, he took the horse named Gorrión (sparrow) to the city. He drank some beer, and then he gave beer to the horse. He made a big commotion when he and the horse went inside the bar together. The police were called, and that behavior worried and upset the parents.

The mother was a midwife. She did that job her whole life. She went to classes at the hospital and earned a certificate. Midwives are common in El Salvador. She advised women about everything that is good for the woman and for the baby. When someone did not have support, she took the woman into her own home to care for her and the new baby.

It was through Cecilia that I met her brother Jorge. He was the youngest son of the family and the favorite of the mother. She wished him to continue in school, but he was influenced by others and did not go. So she insisted that he learn a trade. So Jorge became a baker. When he was young, maybe about eighteen, he worked in a big bakery in San Salvador called Victoria. He went back to the farm for holidays or celebrations.

When I started to know Jorge at the farm, we walked in the orchard, talking and getting to know each other. Once he reached up to get an orange. "Which one do you want? You can pick any one." This was a big surprise for me. I never could choose an orange from a tree before. After picking the orange, we enjoyed it together. Another time when I went to visit them, his father sent us to cut coconuts, but a lot! They had so many! Meantime their mother was cooking at the house, making tortillas, and we were all inside talking. It was a beautiful life.

All this was so new. For me, this was all a big surprise and very good because I found a good family. My family was destroyed. My family never was together, never! The look of Cecilia and Jorge's family was so different for me. Everything in my life was improving. Then after, when I was to be married to Jorge, Cecilia was very, very happy. And his parents, too, they were very, very happy.

Mary Jo Ignoffo

On her own to make a living, fourteen-year-old Lucía left Antiguo Cuscatlán and found work as a domestic servant in a San Salvador home. She told me this as if it were the most natural thing in the world for a fourteen-year-old to do. "I had no support," she explained. "No choice." The middle-class mistress was kind, and there was food. Lucía's body had a chance for nourishment and to recover from delayed physical development. Comparing working conditions with her mother, whom she visited about once a month, she felt better off. She counseled her mother to find a different household with better working conditions, but to no avail. Lucía wished for a close bond with her mother, but in relaying episodes or conversations, it seems that the daughter was the more stable, more inclined to give advice, and had her feet on sturdier ground.

Within a few years Lucía met and married a man ten years her senior. Many poor women in El Salvador, Lucía's mother and aunts among them, do not marry. With little social or economic benefit to marriage, women routinely have children and fend for themselves. A marriage does not ensure food or stability. In fact, a marriage can exacerbate poverty, with another mouth to feed or spousal abuse to endure.[1] Lucía felt different. "I preferred to marry," she told me. "From my childhood I said I would not have a child if I was not married." Her own experience of never knowing a father is quite painful to her and led to this conviction. She and her husband registered their union at the court house.

For a while Lucía was content. She had a son and a daughter, born at the start of the 1970s. From her point of view she had what she needed and wanted—a family with enough to eat, a home, a husband with a job. She was almost living a middle-class lifestyle. Her husband worked at an estate high on a hill overlooking busy San Salvador. It belonged to Don Ernesto Regalado, the heir-apparent of the allied Regalado, Dueñas, and Mathies families. By the 1970s this family

[1] For a description of marriage practices in the 1960s, see Alistair White, *El Salvador* (New York: Praeger Publishers, 1973), 245.

dynasty was the country's largest producer of coffee and sugar. Profits allowed them "to move into finance, real estate, commerce, tourism,"[2] dominating the country's economy with banks, including Banco de Comercio, utility companies, and automobile dealerships. In Lucía's recollections, the names of husbands and wives, little children, and even the dogs, came easily.

The disparity of wealth in El Salvador is heartbreakingly obvious as Lucía describes the possessions and property of the Regalados. The extent of palatial homes, offices, and businesses, seemed to her incalculable. She found it puzzling that she never saw them work. "I do not understand how they have a lot of money and do not work hard."

Accompanying her husband to Don Ernesto's home when he worked there gave Lucía a unique vantage point to observe an utterly alien lifestyle. Among her husband's tasks at the Regalado home—landscape work, cleaning the swimming pool, maintaining the golf course—the most startling of his routines, to my ears at least, was brushing the teeth of the huge Doberman and German Shepherd guard dogs. Evidently the dogs' teeth had been resurfaced with gold, and any teeth that had been removed were fashioned into fierce-looking collars. The gold teeth needed special care and attention, including brushing after meals. As if the dental work were not enough, the animals ate more meat in one meal than Lucía had eaten in her entire childhood.

The enormous guard dogs were not simply an odd status symbol. The wealthy could not presume that their place in society was enough to keep them safe from assault. When Lucía notes that Don Baltita Deininger traveled with only a driver and no bodyguards, she points out that he was unique in his class. Few other oligarchs garnered good will or could expect personal safety in public. Estates implemented intricate security measures as the elite became targets from tens of thousands of the hungry and jobless. The oligarchy's grip on the wealth of the nation depended on the guns of private security guards and military soldiers. And as often as not, security guards and soldiers were one and the same.

Don Ernesto's grandfather and the original Regalado patriarch, General Tomás Regalado, had taken over the government of El Salvador by coup d'état just before the turn of the twentieth century. His presidency assured the political power of the coffee growers. El Salvador's coffee families remained in control of the government from the time of the general's battlefield death in Guatemala in 1906 until

---

[2] Jeffery M. Paige, *Coffee and Power: Revolution and the Rise of Democracy in Central America* (Cambridge, MA: Harvard University Press, 1997), 18, 23.

the Great Depression.[3] In 1931, a reformist president was elected, but some military officers staged a coup, ousting the reformer and installing their own president, Maximiliano Hernández Martínez. When starving peasants revolted in 1932 under the leadership of communist Agustín Farabundo Martí, the Martínez government annihilated any and all protestors along with anyone who had the bad luck to be nearby. An estimated thirty thousand, many of whom were indigenous Pipil, were killed by government soldiers in what the Salvadoran people call *La Matanza*—the slaughter. Martí was shot for inciting the uprising and became a martyr for the poor. All reports of *La Matanza* were ordered expunged from libraries and official documents. Despite the purged documents, the people did not forget.

From that time on the elites could not maintain complete control on their own. They needed the military, no matter how distasteful its tactics. The oligarchy forged an uncomfortable alliance with a brutal military. In return, military officers received generous compensation and were allowed to act with impunity as they lined their pockets. Oligarchs looked the other way when the peasantry was victimized. The expedient alliance between the elite and the military persisted for the remainder of the twentieth century.

Historians point to *La Matanza* as the defining moment in Salvador's history and assert that "the paranoid anti-communism, fear of social reform, remoteness from the poor, dehumanization of the political opposition, and willingness to tolerate the most severe repressive measures in defense of the agro-export order were the ideological heritage of 1932."[4] *La Matanza* provided a horrific blueprint for the civil war of the 1980s, a precedent for the wholesale massacre of those who would demand change from the status quo. Gross economic imbalance fixed the path to violent confrontation.

The kidnap and murder of Don Ernesto Regalado in 1971 marks an unofficial beginning to that war. The February morning began normally enough, and Lucía's husband was digging up an area to plant flowers down a slope from the main house close to the road. Don Ernesto left the house, as was his habit, drove down the driveway and turned onto the road below. In plain sight road workers flagged Ernesto to slow down. As he did, a number of the men jumped into the car and sped off. That Lucía's husband witnessed the kidnapping and followed in pursuit is a demonstration of his loyalty to the Regalados. It also provided Lucía a front-row seat to her country's history.

---

[3] Ibid., 14, 22.
[4] Ibid., 126.

The mutilated body of Ernesto Regalado Dueñas turned up on a public road days later. The audacity of the kidnapping and the violence of the murder enraged El Salvador's oligarchy. The crime had the hallmarks of an organized hit; no one could claim it was a random act by a rogue malcontent. An active insurgent movement announced itself as a viable and formidable force in El Salvador when it targeted the heir-apparent to the powerful Regalado dynasty. Historians point to this event as an indicator that guerrilla groups had already organized to confront an unresponsive government and an oppressive military. Civil war went undeclared for another decade, but Ernesto's death put all parties on notice.

The widow Regalado-Dueñas fled El Salvador with her young children. Workers on the estate were let go, including Lucía's husband. A bad end came to the Regalados, local folklore claimed, because Concha, the original matriarch, had made a pact with the devil. The public's attempt to make sense of the kidnap and murder led it to braid together history and legend. In this way Concha's cruel personality is attached to the unpredictable fury of El Salvador's volcano Izalco, its eruptions spewing flame, ash, and rock, indiscriminately wiping out villages and farms at unpredictable but deadly intervals. Salvadorans called the hellish approach to Izalco's vaporous steaming mud *el Puerto del Diablo* (the devil's gate) and considered Concha's unscrupulous behavior toward political prisoners as evidence of her demonic pact.

Concha Regalado's pact took an alarming and personal turn as Lucía's husband embarked on a serious exploration and subsequent obsession with the occult. It started, Lucía maintains, when he worked for the Regalados, and she dates his malevolence to that time. Over the next couple of years Lucía became aware of an escalating hostility. She discovered that he had fathered a child, exactly the same age as her son, with a neighbor directly across the street. Still, she chose to carry on, working through life's challenges. She was puzzled to think this was not enough for her husband. He wanted money.

He studied *El Libro de San Cypriano*, a book of black magic and the occult dating from nineteenth-century Spain and Portugal. Although often attributed to the Roman Catholic bishop Cyprian, it has no association with that canonized saint, who lived centuries before. The book contains precise instructions for gaining riches through incantation and alignment with the devil. The makeshift altar that appeared in Lucía's home became a monument for her husband's obsession. His daily offerings of drink or food or some trinket offended her sensibilities. When Lucía asked if he practiced witchcraft, he answered with his fist.

In a fit of disgust Lucía dismantled the altar, and it very nearly cost her life. "He filled them with hate," she laments about her children. He denied her visitation rights. When she was questioned by the FBI in Miami after the murder of the Jesuits, she was reminded yet again. The Salvadoran Colonel Rivas shouted at her that court records in El Salvador show that she had abandoned her children and that she was not a fit mother. Child abandonment was only one of the crimes she was accused of in Miami. Barely able to speak about these events of almost forty years ago, Lucía's wounds from this separation are still raw.

Don Ernesto had been raised in a "beautiful castle" near where the UCA would be built. Lucía's husband often made deliveries to this house where Ernesto's parents lived. The father, Tomás Regalado González, died in 1969. He had been one of the original benefactors for the establishment of the UCA.[5]

Initially, the UCA was welcomed by the oligarchy, including the Regalados, because the University of El Salvador, the country's only school of higher education, was perceived as leftist. El Salvador's elite presumed a Catholic school would affirm its inherited position in society. Surely a Catholic school would be more amenable to the political agenda of the rich than its secular counterpart at the University of El Salvador. A new Catholic institution seemed just the solution to educate the future leaders of the country, including wealthy families like the Regalados.

When the university opened in 1966, it had just over three hundred students instructed by fourteen professors. Within a few years the school purchased about thirty-five acres, and in February 1969, moved to the new and current campus. During the 1970s, new facilities, classrooms, library, a cafeteria, and computer center were added. By the end of 1989, when the priests and two women were killed, the university had sixty-five hundred students with 240 faculty members and an annual budget of US$3.24 million.

The new University of Central America José Simeón Cañas (UCA) veered from initial expectations almost immediately. Naming the

---

[5] Charles J. Beirne, SJ, *Jesuit Education and Social Change in El Salvador* (New York: Garland Publications, 1996), 19.

school for José Simeón Cañas signaled at least a nod to a human rights consciousness. Cañas had been a Salvadoran priest who, when Central America gained its independence from Spain in 1823, convinced the new government to abolish slavery, the first country in the Americas to do so. By the time the UCA was named for Cañas, his advocacy for enslaved men and women was ancient history. It is unlikely that many in 1960s El Salvador expected Cañas's advocacy for the oppressed would filter down through the years. But it did.

The rector and president at the time of the UCA's founding in 1966, Florentino Idoate, SJ, said at the school's inauguration that its mission was to "collaborate in human progress and advancement, in all the gigantic tasks to bring about the transformation of the world according to the plan of God, to make it more and more balanced, more comfortable, more human and more just."[6] The inauguration must have been a moment of pride and great hope.

Perhaps some dignitaries and officials gathered for the inauguration took Idoate's words as standard-issue clerical rhetoric. For me, his words went to the heart of the matter. Of anything I read in preparing for this work with Lucía, Idoate's vision caught my faith and hope, both at once. His succinct declaration says we humans can collaborate with God to move the world toward love and fulfillment. God beckons us toward balance, comfort—for all, that is—and justice. To my mind, Idoate captured the essence of our human journey together toward that new creation to which we are called.

In even more explicit language, the first issue of UCA's magazine *Estudios Centroamericanos* (ECA), at the end of 1969, stated that the purpose of the institution was to be "an intellectual conscience for the nation."[7] The school would not rely on textbook theories and philosophies, but its professors looked to the "national reality," the day-to-day life of Salvadorans, to teach economics, sociology, psychology, theology, and ethics.

UCA's administrators ran headlong into the ruling oligarchy's presumption that it reaped earthly benefits—riches, education, power—because it was the will of God. In this spiritual Darwinism, the thinking went, the poor should accept their lot as part of God's will. They could anticipate better accommodations in the world to come. Catholic teaching, colored with notions of predestination, fit nicely with the life of the rich. It affirmed the status quo as God's will.

---

[6] Ibid., 78.
[7] Ibid., 99.

The archbishop in San Salvador at the time of the school's founding, Luis Chávez, had a long tenure and an established friendship with the oligarchy. He welcomed the UCA because it brought a stronger Catholic presence to education. It was not very long before he was pressured to censor scholarship at the UCA. The school nurtured the emerging field of liberation theology, a theological approach that calls for liberating humans from oppression and injustice. It frames a Christology that places Jesus in human history, reacting to the social and political structures of his time and place. In this analysis the Gospels show that Jesus demonstrated a "preferential option for the poor," consistently standing with the poor, the oppressed, the diseased, the outcast—*la chusma*, if you will. Previously, Catholic theology most often emphasized the divine nature of Jesus, minimizing his human suffering and rendering his humanity almost invisible.

The UCA emerged as a school of unprecedented independence—partly because of the preference of Jesuits involved in the school's founding, and partly by chance. It was born free from control by the oligarchy. Although it received some government funding, it was not completely dependent upon it (which turned out to be fortuitous when the government suspended all funding during the civil war of the 1980s). More surprising, though, is that the school had no official ties to Catholic ecclesial authority. Archbishop Chávez could comment or recommend, but he had no real authority. The official religious affiliation of the UCA was not more explicit than its "Christian inspiration." Since it was run by the Jesuits, the school was commonly viewed as Catholic. In reality, it was neither a public institution nor an officially Catholic one. When a member of the ruling class exerted political or financial pressure on either a government official or the bishop to rein in the UCA, it had little effect. Neither had any influence to force UCA to comply with any agenda. The Christian-inspired institution, governed by a board of directors that for most of its history has been all Jesuit, was only answerable to the superior general of the Jesuit order in Rome.

From its earliest days the UCA fostered independent scholarship unique to the marginalized developing world. Its publications and the research of its faculty issued far-reaching commitments to justice. Without independence from church and state, the university most certainly would have been shut down—either by officials in the Vatican, on the one hand, who showed consternation at liberation theology in general and Ellacuría's book *Teologia politica* in particular,[8]

---

[8] Ignacio Ellacuría, *Teologia politica* (San Salvador: Ediciones del Secretariado Social Interdiocesano, 1973), translated into English as *Freedom Made Flesh: The Mission of Christ and His Church* (Maryknoll, NY: Orbis Books, 1976).

or by the government, on the other hand, because the writings and teaching of Martín-Baró and Montes demanded a more equitable society.

The tack toward social justice at the UCA was not merely an invention of the Jesuits. The Second Vatican Council, which opened in 1962 at the behest of Pope John XXIII, issued documents urging just solutions to social issues. The cardinals who selected Angelo Giuseppe Roncalli at age seventy-six as pope in 1958 did not expect anything more than the status quo. The aging pontiff displayed surprising vitality by calling the Second Vatican Council to finish what the first had to abandon in 1870 because of the Franco-Prussian War. John XXIII signaled a church reevaluating its mission and actions in the world.

A month before the council opened, the pontiff called the church to a fresh start. "The prophetic words of Jesus, pronounced in view of the final consummation of the world, inspire the good and generous dispositions of men—especially at certain periods in history—to a fresh start toward the highest peaks: 'Lift up your heads, because your redemption is at hand' (cfr. Luke 21:28–33)." The pope also made a specific plea for social justice. "Where the underdeveloped countries are concerned," he said, "the Church presents herself as she is. She wishes to be the Church of all, and especially the Church of the poor."[9]

The same can be seen in the council's opening statement:

> Coming together in unity from every nation under the sun, we carry in our hearts the hardships, the bodily and mental distress, the sorrows, longings, and hopes for all the peoples entrusted to us. We urgently turn our thoughts to all the anxieties by which modern man is afflicted. Hence, let our concern swiftly focus first of all on those who are especially lowly, poor, and weak.[10]

Pope John XXIII died before the Vatican Council closed, but his successor, Paul VI, promulgated *Gaudium et spes (The Church in the Modern World)* on December 7, 1965. The very first line calls for Christians to stand in solidarity with those in need. "The joys and the hopes, the griefs and the anxieties of the men of this age, especially those who are poor or in any way afflicted, these are the joys and hopes, the griefs and anxieties of the followers of Christ" (no. 1). In other words, we are all in this together.

---

[9] Pope John XXIII, radio address, September 11, 1962, translation available on the conciliaria.com website.

[10] "Message to Humanity," October 20, 1962, in Walter M. Abbott, ed., *The Documents of Vatican II* (Piscataway, NJ: The American Press, 1966), 5.

Three years later, in 1968, building on Vatican II, the Roman Catholic Conference of Latin American Bishops convened a regional conference in Medellín, Colombia. In the resulting document the bishops asserted that the real-life situation of most Latin Americans could not be taken as the will of God. They made it clear that "social injustices existent in Latin America . . . keep the majority of our peoples in dismal poverty" (no. I-1). Hunger and poverty are preventable, and the bishops asserted, human suffering through poverty requires action—in this world, not the next. Jesus, during his life, the bishops pointed out, treated the poor and disenfranchised—*la chusma*—preferentially. Furthermore, the bishops quoted *The Development of Peoples,* an encyclical of Pope Paul VI: "When so many communities are hungry, when so many homes suffer misery, when so many men live submerged in ignorance . . . any arms race becomes an intolerable scandal" (no. I-13).[11] Feeding the hungry takes precedence over national security.

Both Vatican II and Medellín inspired some theologians to study the Gospels through the lens of the developing world. Latin American bishops concluded that a serious and faithful reading of God's word must include addressing the grinding poverty and starvation of the majorities of the Latin American populations. The bishops identified poverty as a wake-up call from God, not a divine order.

Latin American bishops did not universally agree on statements coming out of Medellín. Yet the documents that emerged from those meetings mapped out the social problems of the times and theology to actively address the problems. "It is certainly not enough to reflect, to be more discerning, and to áspeak. Action is required."[12] These are words to live by, even today—or perhaps, especially today.

When Archbishop Chávez approached retirement, El Salvador's oligarchy favored Óscar Arnulfo Romero to replace him. Romero was a studious and soft-spoken conservative who had a history of ministering to the elite. Romero's appointment disappointed most at the UCA, who expected that he would look the other way when confronted with the violence eating its way through the Salvadoran countryside. Archbishop Óscar Romero had a friend, however, who pushed him to see the face of Jesus in the poor of El Salvador.

---

[11] Second General Conference of Latin American Bishops, *The Church in the Present-Day Transformation of Latin America in the Light of the Council* (Washington DC: USCC Division for Latin America, 1968), 58; the quotation is from *The Development of Peoples*, no. 53.

[12] In Alfred T. Hennelly, ed., *Liberation Theology: A Documentary History* (Maryknoll, NY: Orbis Books, 1990), 89.

Rutilio Grande, SJ, was a native of El Salvador and had been on the path to priesthood since his youth. He studied for a time in Spain and in Belgium; he helped train Central American seminarians; and he taught at Colegio Externado San José, the Jesuit high school in San Salvador. In 1972 he picked up the work of a parish priest in Aguilares, a town about twenty miles outside of San Salvador. Grande was considered an activist because he spoke out on behalf of the poor. He was also accused of being a communist. He is quoted as having declared that Jesus himself would be considered a communist in El Salvador: "If Jesus of Nazareth returned, coming down from Chalatenango to San Salvador, I dare say he would not arrive, with his preaching and actions, even to Apopa; they would arrest him for being a subversive and would crucify him again."[13]

Grande stood as friend and master of ceremonies for Óscar Romero's installation as bishop in 1975. Two years later, on March 12, 1977, while driving from Aguilares to El Paisnal to preside at mass, Rutilio Grande and two passengers were sprayed with bullets from high-powered rifles. The government claimed the priest was killed by a bandit carrying a pistol. Grande was hit eighteen times, a feat no pistol could accomplish. Romero pleaded with the government to carry out a full investigation; it declined to do so.

For the one-year anniversary of Grande's death, Jesuits at the UCA wrote and published a brief account of his life.[14] The authors noted that, for them, Grande's life typified the mission of the Jesuit order as articulated in the 32nd General Congregation of the Society of Jesus: "the service of faith and the promotion of justice." An unfortunately prescient and chilling passage asks: "Who killed Rutilio Grande? Rutilio Grande was the victim of injustice and the institutionalized violence that predominates in El Salvador."[15] Although it is impossible to determine which of the Jesuit authors penned that particular line, the very real threat of violence and death had to be confronted on a daily basis. Ignacio Martín-Baró said not long before he died, "There is an environment of the possibility of being killed at any moment of the day, and the possibility of being involved in a violent clash at any moment, and you have to count on that."[16] Ultimately it exacted its cost once again on November 16, 1989.

---

[13] Quoted in Joseph E. Mulligan, SJ, "Remembering a Salvadoran Martyr," available on the thewitness.org website.

[14] UCA, *Rutilio Grande Mártir de la evangelización rural en El Salvador* (San Salvador: Universidad Centroamericana José Simeón Cañas, 1978).

[15] Ibid., 117.

[16] Ignacio Martín-Baró, *60 Minutes*, April 22, 1990.

It is widely accepted that Grande's death marked a turning point for Archbishop Óscar Romero. The loss of his friend inspired forceful leadership in the face of death threats and ultimately his own assassination in 1980. In the three years between 1977 and 1980, Romero's tenure as archbishop was characterized by increasingly emphatic calls for justice for the poor. On December 10, 1978, he said:

> Who will put a prophet's eloquence into my words
> to shake from their inertia
> all those who kneel before the riches of the earth—
> who would like gold, money, lands, power, political
> life to be their everlasting gods?"[17]

At the same time that the Catholics of El Salvador, both rich and poor, reacted to the deaths of men like Grande and Romero, Lucía was struggling to survive. In the days and months after losing her children and home, she cannot even recall where she lived, except to be certain that she had no help from her family. Eventually, she found work as a servant in a home that also had a dairy. At that home Lucía met a lifelong friend, Cecilia.

Cecilia brought her new friend, Lucía, to the family home about forty miles from San Salvador, in San Pedro Nonualco. Nestled in the foothills on the outer edge of Volcán San Vicente, it is about an hour's bus ride from San Salvador. When Lucía told me about visits to the home, she is still amazed at how much fruit their farm produced—avocados, pineapples, mangoes, bananas, oranges, enough to eat a piece whenever one desired. The family was never wealthy, but neither was it short of food.

How is it that this family did not suffer from poverty as terrible as Lucía's? Looking into the community of San Pedro Nonualco, I discovered that early in the nineteenth century the area had been a cluster of communal farms. Later, as coffee growers consumed most of El Salvador's communal lands, San Pedro Nonualco was somehow overlooked. This fortuitous yet unintended circumstance allowed small-scale cultivators to survive. Even as late as 1970, almost 70 percent of the land in San Pedro Nonualco was in the hands of locals.[18] Cecilia's family's orchards and fields were partly due to this situation.

---

[17] Óscar Romero, *The Violence of Love*, foreword by Henri Nouwen, comp. and trans. James R. Brockman (Maryknoll, NY: Orbis Books, 2004 [1988]), 105.

[18] David Browning, *El Salvador: Landscape and Society* (Oxford: Clarendon Press, 1971), 213.

Another significant aspect to the family's ability to succeed and farm is precisely that it was a family—marriage and children who could help work the land put them on the path to success. Furthermore, the mother valued education. She sent the children to school. She herself had been certified as a midwife, a process that many who practiced midwifery did not have access to in the 1950s. In a country with a severe lack of medical care, the midwife is a crucial part of the community. She routinely took pregnant women into her home to care for them through delivery of their babies.

Here Lucía met Jorge, the youngest son of seven children and the acknowledged favorite, born to a careful and moderately successful farmer and a midwife. Lucía observed the family and was drawn to the bonds so absent in her own experience. The bounty of the orchards and fields, and the simplicity of the family's farm life appeal to her even today. Today, if she could be assured of her family's safety from El Salvador's roaming *maras* (gangs), she would be quite happy to retire there. She would go back in a heartbeat.

3

Our Daily Bread

1980–1985

Lucía Cerna

For many years my aunt was a nanny for two daughters of a very wealthy woman. She was a tall, beautiful, and very rich lady from one of the Fourteen Families. When her daughters were grown, she recommended my aunt to work with the priests. The woman knew Father Fermín Saínz. That is how my aunt came to work for the priests, and therefore how I came to work for the priests. Father Saínz knew me through my aunt.

He hired me to work at Loyola Center, a new retreat building up the hill in Antiguo Cuscatlán, close to the UCA. It is a beautiful place. It had three big pavilions, and each one had fifteen bedrooms for the people who came for a retreat. There was a large auditorium, and it had a very big kitchen, with people there to attend to the guests. When I started working there all those years ago, Father Saínz had only two gardeners and one woman to clean the whole building. There were no machines; it was all manual work. He asked me to come to work, and I did, but part time, without benefits, only my pay every two weeks.

Father Saínz had a friendship with that very wealthy woman, and together they built the retreat center. Her money paid for that, and so she was the cofounder. I met her several times when she went to visit Father Saínz. She was a very elegant lady, and I was happy to greet her.

"Welcome! Come, Father Saínz is in his office."

"Thank you, Lucía, I know my way to the office. Thank you."

I saw that she had a wonderful education, and I was amazed with how she spoke—so sweet and patient, a very nice lady. Oh, I was so proud. She knew me. She knew my name! In El Salvador we do not have money to feel proud about, but when a poor person knows a rich one you feel good knowing such an important person.

When I was working in the retreat building I often went to visit my aunt in the Jesuit residence at the UCA where she was a housekeeper. She asked Father Gondra to give me the opportunity to work. He was director of maintenance and he lived in that residence. He put me on call to clean offices at the UCA when someone called in sick. He provided a uniform, a very neat and clean uniform, and shoes. If somebody was sick, I could work. Again, I did not have benefits or *Seguro Social*, which allows money to be withdrawn from pay to go to medical insurance or to have the ability to get a loan for a house. At that time, in 1980, I did not have enough work to receive benefits. I worked in the morning for four hours when Father Gondra called me, and after I walked up the hill to work in the afternoon at Loyola Center. He began to call more often.

My aunt worked there for a long time, maybe seventeen years, until she got arthritis and could not work anymore. She has very good memories from working for the Jesuits, knowing them from when they were younger priests until they grew old in El Salvador. She is still living and has these memories. She was the housekeeper in their home, and when she was on vacation, for example, they asked me to come from the UCA offices to take her place. I cleaned rooms, washed and ironed clothes, answered the telephone, and helped the cook to pass the food at the meals. There was a lot of laughing and joking at those meals, they were not quiet. No, they were very funny with each other and with us.

Between them the priests had different opinions. Even with different opinions they stood together in bad situations. They talked during meals when I was there, but some, for example, Father López y López, did not like to talk politics or philosophy at the table. No politics. And philosophy? I don't know. He was different from the others. He liked to help people but didn't like talking. I know they were friends, laughing and talking. Everybody knew he was sick, and that he came from a rich family to join the Company. He ate fast to leave the table and go to his room so he did not hear about politics and philosophy. He was very simple.

Padre Ramón [Moreno] never talked politics either. He avoided being interviewed. He was so quiet, very quiet. He was the librarian for the province. That the soldiers killed Moreno means that they did not know whom they were killing. That was injustice.

The house had a chapel and a retired old priest was the chaplain. The Fathers had mass there at 6 o'clock in the morning. It was only for the Fathers, not outsiders. I think each father was assigned one mass a week. There was a big church on the campus, but that was for special occasions.

It is curious that this is the house where my husband and daughter and I stayed the night of the massacre. Never when I cleaned it did I think I would stay there one day. For this reason I told the investigator in Miami that I would know that house even if I were blind. He demanded to know how I knew about that house where we stayed on the night of November 15. I know every hall, every room, every corner, and every window because I cleaned it.

After my aunt returned from two weeks off, I went back to the offices in the rectory at UCA. The Fathers at the UCA did not accept other women there, so when I was busy at the house taking my aunt's place, they took on *un mensajero*, a messenger, who also cleaned the halls and the bathroom. Only I had the keys to all the offices.

I lived with Jorge in a rented a room in Colonia Luz.

When our daughter was born, we moved to an apartment in Antiguo Cuscatlán. It was larger, and we did not have to share a bathroom. Jorge was working for the big bakery in San Salvador, and I had my job at the UCA and Loyola Center. We saved our money. I kept the *colónes* in a matchbox. Finally, one day we had three hundred *colónes* in the small box. I saw a notice in the newspaper that three hundred could be a down payment on a new small house in Soyapango. I went to see the engineer for those houses and his wife, who was also his secretary, and she instructed me to bring a paper from my employer that said I had a job.

When Jorge and I wished to qualify to buy a house, I went to see Father Ellacuría because I still had only four hours of work at the UCA.

"Padre Ellacu" [pronounced ya-cu], I said, because that was his name for short, "is it possible to have more work?"

He said, "Lucía, I have watched you, and after four hours you do not go home. You stay here and finish. You deserve to have more time here. You will have six hours of work here."

I was so happy! "Really?" I told him. Then he said that the provincial needed someone to clean his office.

"Let me talk to Father Tojeira and maybe you can also work there."

That is how I came to be working at the UCA in the morning and in the provincial's office in the afternoon. Together the jobs made ten hours, and I was really, really happy. It is hard for me to explain how happy I was at that time. This was all because of Father Ellacu. I worked very hard at my job because I was grateful. I wrote a letter to tell the Fathers how thankful I was.

The UCA provided the paper to say I had a job, and my application for the house from Fondo Social para la Vivienda was approved. In this way, money is taken from each paycheck, but not too much, to pay a mortgage loan for twenty years. Because Father Ellacu arranged for more work for me, Jorge was not on the application. If we applied together, money would be taken from both of us. This way, the money was only taken from my paycheck.

We had our own new house in Soyapango. Our daughter was about one year old when we moved there. It was not a big house, but it had a living room, a kitchen, and two bedrooms with a bathroom. And a very nice patio. Jorge made many improvements, working on his days off. We did not have a camera at that time, but Jorge found one in the river and fixed it to take a few pictures. Those are the only pictures we have from that time. When we left El Salvador we had to leave our house abandoned. Jorge's sister went to Soyapango and got our few pictures to save for us.

Now I can say how it was to work at the rectory offices at the UCA.

Padre Ellacu was quiet—quiet and peaceful. He was the president and the rector of the UCA. He enjoyed seeing children and babies. I never saw anything disturb him, and he was thankful for my cleaning his office. He expressed his appreciation to me. Once when he was away and I was cleaning his office, I saw a book on the shelf about Don Ernesto Regalado. I took it down to read because I remembered that history. My ex-husband's name appeared in that book about the kidnapping, and I knew the book was true.

The padres were interviewed many times, often for television. Usually the interviews were held in the garden. The first time I saw Padre Ellacu and Padre Nacho speaking English in an interview, I was amazed! I had no idea they could speak another language, and so fluently! I was so amazed to discover that they could speak English. I felt like clapping for them. After, when they were finished, I said to Padre Nacho, "*¡Que bueno!*" How wonderful that you speak English so well!

"Ay, Lucía. You are happy for anything! The smallest thing makes you happy."

I never thought big things. I remember when the Fathers asked me if I wanted to take an English class in the university. "Me? Why should I take classes in English?"

"You will need it when somebody comes here and speaks English, or if you go to Europe or the United States."

I said no, no, and Padre Nacho said, "Well *mujer* [woman], you are stubborn, but it is open to you if you wish."

Father Ellacu said the same and then he added, "Any day you decide to go, it is open. You do not need to tell me. Just go."

Father Ellacu and Father Nacho were in politics, but they were mediators. They tried to stop the killing, on one side or the other, to bring peace to El Salvador. They went to many meetings and conferences, always mediating for peace. Father Ellacu was so different, he was calm, but Father Nachito, he was active always. Some people thought Padre Nacho was a little fussy. He was not fussy with me, just happy. Every morning, even when it rained, even with an umbrella, he came to his office at 5:30 a.m. to work. I arrived at six o'clock. I made fresh coffee, checked and cleaned the cups, and took care of the pantry. When I was finished, I knocked at his office door. "Good morning, Father Nachito, good morning!" I told him every morning, "Coffee is ready."

"Okay, Lucía, thank you." He always said thank you, and he was happy with me.

"Why do you come to work so early?" I asked.

"Why stay in bed? When married we like to be in bed. When not married, only sleeping with a pillow, it is better to be up and to work," he joked.

"You could be married."

"No, Lucía. I study and that is my life. If a woman married me, she would suffer. I have no time to attend a wife."

When he was working in his office, he did not want me to dust his books—and he had a lot of books, like a library! He only wanted me to dust the desk and lamp and table and be done. Then he would say, "Lucía, please, if somebody comes or asks for me, do not disturb me unless my door is open." When he was grading student papers, the students were worried and came to see him. I always made sure no one knocked on the door to see him unless his door was open. Students would say, "Is Father angry?" when they came to talk or ask something. "Is Father there?"

"Yes, he is. The door is open, so don't be afraid. *Toca la puerta*." Knock on the door.

Some people thought he was fussy. If you did not do something correctly, he could get annoyed. He wanted the bathroom very clean, with fresh towels. Only he was like that. The other priests did not seem to notice if something was clean or not. With me, Padre Nacho was excellent. I knew him very well, and if he seemed annoyed, I went to the garden and cut a rose and brought it to him in a vase.

"Father, I am here. It's Lucía. Knock, knock."

He would smile and say, "Oh, that is beautiful! Thank you." And after he was in a happy mood.

Once when I was pregnant with my daughter, he saw me up on a ladder cleaning the windows. "*¡Ay, Lucía! Cuidado!* [be careful]" "Don't fall from that ladder. Leave the windows." But I was happy then, really, really happy. I was not thinking that working on the ladder was a problem for a pregnant lady. No, I enjoyed my job. Later, after my daughter was born, I rested at home for three months. On the day I went back to work I got my broom and Father Nachito said, "Lucía what are you doing here?"

"I am here to work," I told him.

"No, go back home. Take another week to rest. That is a gift from us. Today I will call Mrs. Bustamante in payroll and she will pay you for this week." I was so grateful, and I brought my baby for him to see.

Father Nachito helped many people. When he saw the need of the people in the parish at Jayaque, for example, he gave guitar classes to students to raise money to buy toys at Christmas for the poor children. When he held an event in the auditorium at the UCA, admission was to give one new toy. He collected lots and lots of toys for the poor children in the parish. He could sing and play the guitar very well, and lots of people enjoyed hearing him.

He taught me many things that improved my life. Always tell the truth, he told me. One day he called me to his office and said, "Lucía, when that person called you, I heard you say '*Mande*' [What do you want me to do?]. Please, never say *mande*' You do not need to take a command. You can say '*¿Qué es lo que quiere, Señor?*'—Can I help you, or What would you like?" He taught me different but very good things, very good things for my future. He taught me to respect myself and to ask others to respect me too. That was very important for me to learn.

One year Padre Nachito and Padre Ellacu asked a secretary to buy a cake. It was September 15, and those priests wanted the cake for my birthday, but it was a secret. The secretary put it in the conference room downstairs, and they were all there when they called me from my cleaning. Señora López called, "Lucía, please come."

The Fathers and secretaries were there, and they sang "Happy Birthday." There were candles to blow out on that cake! Oh, my God, I cried for happiness and for the surprise. Never before did I have a birthday cake.

This is how I organized my life.

I left home at 5 o'clock in the morning and took the microbus and another bus that left me in front of the UCA. This was Monday through Saturday. I arrived at work at six o'clock to start cleaning. I was happy, never angry, never lazy. When I arrived in the morning, I made sure my uniform was clean and my hair combed. Then I could greet everybody.

The guard in the UCA opened the rectory, and I was alone sometimes when Father Nachito was out of town in Spain. Even when I was alone in that building, I was never scared, never. It was a beautiful life for me, and I have good memories. I enjoyed giving my service. When the students came for admission at 6 o'clock, I was in administration, cleaning the floors bright.

My attention went to making the big *café* when they arrived in the morning at six o'clock. I was the first to put on the coffee. When it was ready, Father Nachito had some.

"Does it taste good, Father?"

"Yes, it's good, thank you."

"May I have permission to clean your office?"

"Yes, of course, Lucía," and he took his coffee out to drink while I quickly cleaned his office. The priests say, "Thank you, Lucía, *gracias*, Lucía." They never discriminated because I was poor or a servant. Such respect I did not have before.

Father Nachito and Father Ellacu did not like noise. They were fussy about that. For example, when a guest or the secretary walked in the hall, and high heels went clack, clack, clack, they did not like it. "What is that?" one would shout. Soon the secretaries tiptoed past their offices. One time a guest made the noise—clack, clack, clack—and Father Nacho opened the door and shouted, "Stop that noise!" No, they did not like that noise. Now I think it is funny, but I never laughed then. I was totally serious. My shoes were flat and did not make noise. I knew the system in that building was quiet. Father Ellacu, as president, had his office on the third floor with his secretary. The vice-president, Padre Nacho, was on the second with his secretary.

Father Segundo had his office on the second floor, but he moved to another building.

I remember my worst day. One room was always locked, and I was forbidden to go there. Only Father Nachito had the key. In that room was a big machine that made a lot of noise, chuck, chuck, chuck. This is where the priests got information and news. I think now that machine was a telex. It was forbidden for me to go there. I do not know who cleaned there. I did not. I never went inside.

One day I was cleaning in the next room, and I must have hit the plug. Suddenly that big noise stopped. I knew I had done something terrible. Immediately, immediately, I went to knock on Father Nacho's office door to tell him of my mistake. "I am sorry, Father. I unplugged something, and the machine stopped."

"Really? Lucía, how did you do that?" He went to see. After he saw and plugged it in again, he said, "Don't worry. I put it back again. Be at peace."

It was a big relief for me because I was really, really worried because that machine stopped.

The priests had computers in their offices, but I did not touch them, only cleaned the screens with a special spray. I was instructed not to move the books, only lift the books, dust, and put them in the same place. In the same place! I should not change anything around, just clean and go. Only Saturdays or when they were traveling did I take down the books to dust. Father Nacho told me, "Don't let anyone in while I am gone," so I made certain to keep his office private.

There were some rules, but I followed them. No one was allowed who did not work in the rectory. One woman came selling Avon, but I did not let her in. Instead, I went out to see her because it was forbidden to invite her in. Whenever the priests had a conference or there was someone talking privately and they did not close the door, I moved away. I knew it was not for me, and I left the area so they could speak freely. I think I saved my job because they came to know that I gave privacy. I could always find something else to do—wash toilets or clean windows in another room. Always I was busy, but not nearby, because I knew it was not my business. I saw how they were, and that was my education.

At noon I had my lunch and then walked off the campus a short distance to the Jesuit province offices. I worked there from one until four o'clock. Here is where Father Chema's [Tojeira] office was. I was not very close to him, because Father Chema did not work in the rectory on the campus, and he traveled a lot. When he came back after travel, he said, "Nice to see you," and then he closed the door and went to work. With the Fathers in the rectory it was different. Other Jesuits stopped in to pick up mail or to attend a meeting. I knew Father Richard Howard from the province offices, and I saw Father Joseph Berra there too. Father Howard lived in Santa Tecla, and Father Berra lived at the philosophy house. I said hello, and they were friendly when they came. It was a very big surprise for me when I saw these two in the United States when I first came.

After work on Saturdays, when I worked just until ten o'clock, the secretaries to the priests hired me to clean their shower rooms at their homes. They had servants, but no one to clean the shower rooms. One week I went to a secretary's home, and the next week to the other. They paid me cash, usually 35 *colónes* for cleaning and sometimes for ironing too. With the cash I stopped at the street market before taking the bus to go home. I always had my basket with me. I wanted to stock our refrigerator for the week. I would pay one *colón* for a tomato, one *colón* for green beans, one *colón* for bananas, one *colón* for eggs. There was a man who sold fish, from the ocean at Libertad. He was smart. He had a speaker on his car, announcing that he had fish for sale. With my fruit and vegetables, I bought one fish. My family would enjoy that fish.

Jorge is a baker.

He worked in a big bakery in San Salvador called Victoria. After we had our daughter, his cousin came to care for the baby while we were at work. When she told us that she was to be married, we talked about what we should do. For me, it would be very difficult to find another job. And I loved my job working for the priests. They gave me respect. I qualified to buy a house because of them. I did not want to leave my job. But Jorge had his skill, so it would be easier for him to find another job. He did not quit immediately but began to plan. He started to build an oven on our patio to bake his bread in our home in Soyapango.

On all his days off he worked on our house, with paint or concrete, from early in the morning. The neighbors asked, "How did you do so much in such a short time?" He always took time for our house. When his plans were in place, he took vacation from Victoria Bakery and started to build a wood-fired stove with bricks. I never thought he could do it, but he did. I don't know how, because I kept working. But when I came home every day, it was more and more complete. It had bricks, bricks, and bricks, until as high as my waist. Then he built it higher still, and I was amazed. Amazed with his ideas and with his ability to build it, even with a curved top. When he fired the stove to try it, I was afraid it would burn our house. But everything was fine. He did a very good job.

He did all of this to start his own business so he could care for our daughter and I could keep my job. He quit his job at the big bakery. He prepared everything for a full bakery—racks for bread, pans, all the supplies of flour, brown sugar, and semolina. Our daughter was under his care while he was working on the patio at home. When he went to buy supplies, our girl sat on his shoulders, holding his hair in her little fists to hang on. She bounced along on his back many times. Jorge built a business with that oven. By this time our daughter was almost two years old.

On the first day that the bakery was open, he told all the neighbors and many people, "Tomorrow I open my bakery, and I give the bread for free." At 5 o'clock in the afternoon many people came to see the new bakery on our patio. They saw the big oven.

"Oh, very good!" they said while they were looking. They became his good customers.

Every morning he woke at 3 o'clock to prepare everything. He had two boys to help, and he directed, "You make this one; you make this one." He baked 150 pounds of French bread in the morning. Then in the afternoon he baked sweet muffins and other breads. He also baked *semita* from semolina flour, a flat bread. You have that with marmalade. He did very well and was working, and our daughter was always happy at home. We had to teach her not to climb up to the oven. "It's hot! Get away from the oven." So she learned. At first I thought she would be afraid of the stove, but she was not. And Jorge let her roll some dough. We have one photo from that time, and she is white with flour!

One problem was that Jorge had to deliver his bread every morning from six until eight a.m. I left for work at 5 a.m. That left no one with our daughter. So we bought a TV for her to watch and told her not to open the door of the house. He gave her a bottle of milk and turned on the TV. And she knew if someone was at the door not to open it. She watched TV, pretending nobody was at home.

When he built the bakery on the patio, I could not hang the laundry to dry anymore. So he built a roof over part of the patio and stairs to take the clothes up for drying. At first I did not believe this would work, and I was afraid to climb the stairs. But he was right, and it did work, and the clothes dried very fast up there. Each night I left the diapers in water, and in the morning I got up at 4 o'clock to shake and squeeze the diapers and clothes, leaving them out to wait for the sun to dry. In El Salvador we do not have disposable diapers. We wash diapers every day. I always washed them with vinegar and soap, no bleach. But they were very white and clean from the vinegar. When they were dry in the day, Jorge took them inside and folded them. That was our system. It was not easy, and it was work, but we were happy. I wish I could explain how happy we were.

Little by little he grew the business. Soon, Jorge offered the bread to one store, then another. He always gave the store a bonus. For example, the store paid one dollar, but he put four more loaves for the store at no charge. That way the store was happy too. He bought the flour for twenty-five dollars a bag, and all the bread he baked brought in about fifty dollars a bag. So he made his earnings. Jorge gave credit to the people. Some paid for the bread every week, some every fifteen days, and others paid for a month. He bought a bicycle and paid somebody to deliver bread. For one month that worked very well. Every day the man delivered the bread. When he came back he got paid. But after one month he did not return with the bicycle. Oh well, that is normal in El Salvador. Later, another man asked for an opportunity to work.

"Okay," Jorge told him, "here is a basket. You can go to deliver the bread." Just like the other man, this one delivered the bread. He took the big basket on his head and delivered the bread and came back for his pay. That went on for about two weeks. Then he one day he did not come back. No more basket.

Once Jorge had a problem when a mouse ate the inside of some of the bread, but he did not notice. He sold the bread to a store, and they saw that the inside of the bread was gone. When the store owner complained, Jorge said, "Oh, I don't know what happened. I will provide you with other bread." After that he checked every time to make sure the bread was okay. And you know, it is curious. We never used a bank, never. The money was in a bowl. That was our bank. One bowl. When our daughter heard the ice-cream man, she went to put her hand into the bowl. She knew where the money was.

The bakery was famous in the neighborhood.

The bakery needed his attention every day, so he did not have the opportunity to visit his parents in San Pedro Nonualco very often. He was very close to his parents, I think, because he was the youngest son, and he was good to them. Sometimes they came to see us, and they were so happy to see his business, and what he had made. My mother-in-law was amazed with the bakery and with what Jorge did and how he worked and cooked lunch for our daughter at the same time. I saw him so busy! And I never knew he could make the stove of bricks. I don't know how he did it. Sometimes I took our daughter to visit the grandparents. If I did not work on a Saturday, we could take the bus and stay until Sunday.

People liked to come to get bread or sweet rolls. For Christmas the people came to roast chicken in the brick oven.

When they came to pick it up, they said, "Is my chicken ready?" and I heard Jorge say, "Five more minutes." We were very active, and we laughed so much with the neighbors. We knew everybody because of the bakery and had people coming all the time. That is why, when we came to the United States, life was so different. We did not know anyone. We could not speak English. It felt like we were in a cage. All the time in El Salvador we had so many people around, and here we were alone. We wanted to go back.

Everybody in the *colonia* knew us because of the bread. They would come at 4 o'clock, 5 o'clock, or 6 o'clock for hot bread. When I went to work with the priests, I was already with Jorge. And the priests appreciated my job, and I was happy. They offered respect. This is the reason I said okay when the FBI in Miami said, "We will send you back."

"Okay, I will go back. We are happy there. You do not believe us here. Put me back in my home."

We were living in peace in our little home with a bakery. When we left, Jorge's bakery had been open about three and a half years. It was a normal life, and until the war came to Soyapango, we lived in peace in our house.

Mary Jo Ignoffo

"Jorge had his art," Lucía very accurately described her husband's work. His mother's insistence that he learn a trade paid off. Jorge's bakery offers us a snapshot of a Salvadoran entrepreneur, one who not only provided for himself, but also allowed his various workers a level of employment they would not otherwise have had. He also personified community, delivering bread often on credit, roasting Christmas chickens, and attending to the day-in and day-out baking of the daily bread for hundreds of families. The output of Jorge's enterprise is remarkable, not only by El Salvador's standards, but for any hand-built business in any country. He went through 150 pounds of flour each day, not to mention sugar, leavening, or lard. For every dollar invested, he took in two. His careful calculations and hard work provided bread for an entire district and sometimes employed delivery men or young workers. Unlike setting up a small business in the United States, he filed for no permits or business licenses. The no-bank, all-cash enterprise enabled him, along with his wife's work, to reach the Salvadoran middle class, all the while personally providing daycare for his infant daughter. The little family found a way to endure even while its country boiled over in civil war.

The happiest period of Lucía's life, full of affection, security, and respect, began when she went to work for the Jesuits in 1980. Father Fermín Saínz hired her to clean rooms at Loyola Center, a retreat house in Antiguo Cuscatlán. High on a hill, the center was born of Saínz's spirituality and funding from a woman of the oligarchy. The Spanish-born Saínz had taught philosophy and psychology in Central American seminaries and later at the UCA. He lived down the hill in the Jesuit residence at the UCA, as did his colleague, Father José María Gondra, the UCA facilities manager.

Gondra also hired Lucía for housekeeping chores at the rectory (*rectory* in El Salvador means the offices of the rector, not a residence for priests). Gondra was known as a bit tight-fisted, sometimes a good asset in such a position, and initially he hired Lucía only as a replacement when a regular worker was sick. A job at the UCA opened new doors for Lucía. "They offered respect. Never before did I have that." The respect was disarming, and she was drawn to the manners, language, demeanor, and education of the Spanish Jesuits. In a sad irony, Fermín Saínz, the man who initially hired Lucía, was also the one who ushered her to the airport in a hasty escape from the country after the murders in 1989.

The Jesuit province for all of Central America is headquartered in San Salvador under the direction of a provincial, at that time José María Tojeira—Padre Chema. The curia, or offices of the province on Avenida Rio Lempa, is quite close to the provincial residence Casa Cinquenta, or 50 Mediterráneo. In addition to province offices, the UCA, and Loyola Center, the Jesuits had other households in El Salvador, including at Santa Tecla, a Jesuit high school called the Externado San José, a residence called el Despertar, and a house for Jesuits studying philosophy.

Although Saínz and Gondra were the first to hire Lucía, the Jesuits with whom she had the most contact were those whose offices were in the rectory, Padre Ellacu (Ignacio Ellacuría) and Padre Nacho (Ignacio Martín-Baró). "They were my family," Lucía recalls. "I considered them my parents, the parents I never had." Ellacuría's willingness to extend her hours and ask Provincial Tojeira to hire her allowed Lucía to qualify to purchase a home. More important, it provided the security for raising a child and for her husband to establish a small but profitable bakery business.

As Lucía cleaned offices, bathrooms, and bedrooms at the UCA, when she helped serve food at dinners, or when she mopped the floors of the provincial offices, she did not notice conflict between or among the Jesuits of the UCA. Her university was around the dining-room table, and although she was not seated and did not enjoy education or perspective, her schooling came from listening to the Jesuits. She noticed that some, like López y López, did not talk politics. She knew that he had strong associations with the oligarchy, and in fact came from a wealthy family. For her, that was irrelevant. He was humble. Others were more outspoken and engaged in lively discussion. "They were for the people," she says. Besides their work on campus, they also went to countryside parishes on weekends.

UCA's Jesuit community was not of a single mind, and tensions showed over the years. The underlying disagreement was not simply siding with rightists or with leftists. One group of Jesuits, the ones embracing liberation theology, believed that the church and the university were obligated to speak on behalf of the poor, who had been silenced by oppression. Another group of Jesuits, while they may have acknowledged the desperate state of the poor, did not feel that the church or the university should engage in these ultimately political and social agendas. Those issues were better left to officials in government. Father Joaquín López y López, one of the school's original founders, was in the latter camp.

The rift in the community was significant enough in 1974 to prompt the provincial to write with concern to Pedro Arrupe, SJ, the head of the Jesuit order in Rome. Arrupe wondered how a community could conduct business and survive such internal disagreement.[1] When

[1] Pedro Arrupe, SJ, to Miguel Francisco Estrada, SJ, 1974, in Charles J. Beirne, SJ, *Jesuit Education and Social Change in El Salvador* (New York: Garland Publications, 1996), 109.

bombs started exploding on the UCA campus, arguments seemed beside the point.

Any ideological divide within the Jesuit community at the UCA was lost on Lucía. Maintenance workers, janitors, gardeners, and household staff, Lucía included, were largely unaware of the broader implications of the Jesuits' day-to-day work. Occasionally, a worker watched one of the priests interviewed in the garden or caught a glimpse of one on television or in the newspaper. Lucía would have been hard-pressed to describe a communist. She knew rich from poor. It never occurred to Lucía that anyone would wish to harm these decent men, the ones from one camp or the other. She was unaware that Ellacuría had received a series of death threats.

The scholarship of some Jesuits and lay faculty at UCA drew attention to the campus from both supporters and detractors. The most persistent and consistent message from the institution to the country and the world was the fact that the majority of people in El Salvador had no say in their present or future economic, political, or social reality. The military and the oligarchy exploited the poor and acted with impunity against the majority, who had no options. These messages were not well received by the government, the military, and by the United States.

The leading voice from the UCA was its president, Ignacio Ellacuría. After completing the requisite theology and philosophy degrees necessary for ordination as a Jesuit priest, he continued to study theology under the Jesuit theologian Karl Rahner. He went on to pursue a doctorate in philosophy under the Basque-Spanish philosopher Xavier Zubiri. By the time Ellacuría studied with him, Zubiri's career included teaching stints at the University of Madrid, Institut Catholique in Paris, and at the University of Barcelona. By the 1960s his teaching was restricted to seminars and lectures around the world. Ellacuría's doctoral dissertation focused on Zubiri's three-volume *On Essence,* published in 1963. From the time that Ellacuría completed his dissertation in 1965 until 1983, when Zubiri died, the two collaborated in study, lectures, and publications. According to the *Encyclopedia of Philosophy*, "Zubiri would not publish something, or even present a lecture, without first showing the material to Ellacuría."[2]

Ignacio Ellacuría was often accused of being a Marxist. While his most strident accusers may have had only vaguest notion of Marx's philosophy, Ellacuría was steeped in philosophical thought. If he was

---

[2] David I. Gandolfo, "Ignacio Ellacuria," Internet Encyclopedia of Philosophy, www.iep.utm.edu/ellacuri/.

a Marxist, it seems to me, he would have said so. His mentor, Zubiri, was not a Marxist, and Ellacuría most often responded to accusations saying that he was something much more radical—a Christian. Ellacuría repeated over and over, in speech and in publications, that the majority of the people must have political, social, and economic self-determination. His colleague Jon Cortina, SJ, an engineering professor at the UCA, put it another way. "The radicalism that cost . . . their lives was not Marxism of any kind but simply radical hope."[3]

Ellacuría took seriously the carnage caused by civil war in El Salvador. He spoke to both sides of the conflict and on a number of occasions, spoke to representatives of the U.S. government or emissaries of the church. In the spring of 1983, Ellacuría and colleagues Jon Cortina, SJ, and Dr. Ricardo Stein were invited to the U.S. embassy to share their views on the state of affairs in El Salvador. Ambassador Deane Hinton wrote in a secret memo to the State Department—declassified in the 1990s—that Ellacuría "proceeded to read from well-prepared notes a careful, almost tautological analysis of the situation. According to Ellacuría's 'personal opinion,' the Reagan Administration policies have yielded some good results but have not solved the real problem in El Salvador." Ellacuría told the others that he believed the Reagan Administration policy had failed because it was based on two incorrect assumptions. Namely, "1. that a Marxist regime is so unacceptable that anything, including war and repression, would be preferable, and 2. that the negotiated presence of the FMLN in a power-sharing or representation scheme will inevitably usher a Marxist regime into power." Ellacuría suggested that "the US shift policies and attempt a 'pre-dialogue' with the FMLN through a personal, official and secret emissary from President Reagan."[4] The memo from Hinton does not relay his own opinion.

Things turned out as Ellacuría feared: the United States did not change its policy, and the guerrillas did not back down. The predictable result was an indefinite number of years of violence, death, and war. Author Teresa Whitfield notes that the "view held by Romero and shared by the Jesuits of the UCA all their lives, [was] that each and every political decision or action should be measured against the

---

[3] Jack Miles, "A Survivor's Story: El Salvador, Father Jon de Cortina Recounts the Still Unsolved Murders of His Jesuit Brethren on Mission in U.S.," *Los Angeles Times*, May 16, 1990.

[4] Deane Hinton, secret memo, 0 311382Z MAR 83, cited in Arthur Jones, "A Look at Declassifed State Department Documents," *National Catholic Reporter*, special supplement, "El Salvador Revisited" (September 23, 1994), available on the natcath.org website.

interests of the majority of the people and not the demands of ideology or political dogma."[5] These priests had a fundamental commitment to democracy, and pointed out policies of governments, militaries, and foreign aid that did not expressly benefit most of the people. The mounting crisis faced by the poor was much too urgent to tolerate lip service and lies for very long.

Liberation theology was born of poverty.

The concept of liberation in theology is rooted in the meaning of the word. From Latin *liberatio*, meaning "setting free" or "becoming free," one etymology calls the word a "noun of action." The term *liberation theology* was coined in 1968 by Gustavo Gutiérrez, a Peruvian priest who has since become a Dominican and teaches theology at the University of Notre Dame in the United States. The Catholic Latin American bishops who gathered in 1968 in Medellín plainly stated pastoral responses to entrenched poverty. They said, "The Church in Latin America should be manifested, in an increasingly clear manner, as truly poor, missionary, and paschal, separate from all temporal power and courageously committed to the liberation of each and every man."[6] While the Medellín conference did not codify liberation theology, it opened the door to a theology of the reality of people's lives.

Critics of liberation theology most often accuse it of being a Marxist philosophy. They would say that when theology seeks to transform society—land reform, for example—that it is advocating a redistribution of goods just as Marx suggested. These critics also accuse liberation theologians in general, and Catholic workers in particular, of inciting the masses to revolutionary actions against the state.

Within the church, liberation theology faces critics on at least two fronts. Some, while not accusing its practitioners of Marxism, suspect that it is out of balance. These would say that in searching out equitable relations in society, dimensions of faithful religious thought and practice have been put on the back burner. Ideally, faith and justice are partners in addressing poverty. Some advocates of liberation theology, this group of critics would say, have abdicated the faith piece of it and neglect devotion and traditional rituals.

---

[5] Teresa Whitfield, *Paying the Price: Ignacio Ellacuría and the Murdered Jesuits of El Salvador* (Philadelphia: Temple University Press, 1994), 216.

[6] Second General Conference of Latin American Bishops, *The Church in the Present-Day Transformation of Latin America in the Light of the Council* (Washington DC: USCC Division for Latin America, 1968), 97.

Another criticism came from the Vatican. Joseph Cardinal Ratzinger (later Pope Benedict XVI), writing on behalf of Pope John Paul II in 1984, initially acknowledged the gravity of the problem of social injustice:

> The scandal of the shocking inequality between the rich and poor—whether between rich and poor countries, or between social classes in a single nation—is no longer tolerated. On one hand, people have attained an unheard of abundance which is given to waste, while on the other hand so many live in such poverty, deprived of the basic necessities, that one is hardly able even to count the victims of malnutrition.[7]

Ratzinger's document goes on to criticize the practitioners of liberation theology and warns the faithful of "deviations" that could be damaging to Christian life because they use, "in an insufficiently critical manner, concepts of . . . Marxist thought." "Theologies of liberation," he writes, show "a disastrous confusion between the 'poor' of the Scripture and the 'proletariat' of Marx."[8] Borrowing any notions from Marx, according to the official church, is inherently flawed because Marx was an avowed atheist. Having articulated the problem, "the shocking inequality between rich and poor," the document offers no approaches for solving it.

A few years after Ratzinger's criticism, the Conference of German Bishops wrote in 1987 in its adult catechism that Jesus Christ *liberates* from sin. An essay entitled "The Renewed World" explains that "sin often embodies itself in oppressive structures, in alienating human, economic, and political situations, which for their part then are the occasion for selfish behavior, envy and conflict, discord and violence."[9] Interestingly, the Conference of German Bishops recalibrates the discussion, moving away from ideology and challenging us to analyze our institutions for ways that they can be oppressive.

The work at the UCA has been a catalyst to the development of the field of liberation theology, particularly publications by Ignacio

---

[7] Sacred Congregation for the Doctrine of the Faith, "Instruction on Certain Aspects of the 'Theology of Liberation,'" August 6, 1984, available on the vatican.va website.

[8] Ibid.

[9] German Bishops' Conference, *The Church's Confession of Faith: A Catholic Catechism for Adults*, trans. Stephen Wentworth Arndt, ed. Mark D. Jordan and Walter Cardinal Kasper (San Francisco: Communio Books Ignatius Press, 1987), 209.

Ellacuría and Jon Sobrino. Each authored pioneering books and articles, and in 1984 the two founded the theological journal *Revista Latino-americano de Teología* to encourage scholarly exploration of liberation theology in Latin America and around the world.

Ignacio Martín-Baró, SJ, adapted the premises of liberation theology to the study of psychology. His *liberation psychology* translated those symptoms and behaviors normally attributed to individuals to a larger national or cultural context. Before analyzing an individual's psychological debilities, he asserted, a collective recognition of traumas, inequities, injustices, and a restoration of a national historical memory is required. This is a tall order in a country where the government repeatedly denied the occurrence of large-scale massacres—from *La Matanza* in 1932 to *El Mozote* in 1981. El Salvador's denial of state-sponsored atrocities was echoed by strident denials of the U.S. Department of State throughout the 1980s.[10] Martín-Baró's efforts to restore historical memory in El Salvador made many in power wish to silence him.

Martín-Baró was a native of Spain and had lived in Colombia and Ecuador. He was a Fulbright Scholar, and he did his doctoral studies at the University of Chicago. His dissertation was approved exactly ten years before his death, on November 16, 1979. Invited as keynote speaker to psychology associations, and accepting short visiting posts at other universities, he used travel as a way to broadcast issues facing El Salvador.[11]

Martín-Baró traveled to Cuba but did not appear on Cuban television, fearing reprisals at home.[12] In an interview on *60 Minutes* that aired on April 22, 1990, five months after his death, he said, "The problems of this country are not the problems of communism or capitalism. The problems of this country are the problems of the distribution of wealth, the very basic needs. In this country when you ask for satisfaction of those basic needs you become a subversive." Being known as a subversive took a toll on Martín-Baró, and some who knew him reported that he was increasingly nervous.[13] One wonders if his agitation upon hearing the "clack, clack, clack" of high heels outside his office door and his apparent short temper with students were

---

[10] Whitfield, *Paying the Price*, 170.

[11] Nelson Portillo, "The Life of Ignacio Martín-Baró: A Narrative Account of a Personal Biographical Journey," *Peace and Conflict: Journal of Peace Psychology* 18/1 (2012): 81.

[12] Ibid., 82.

[13] Ibid.

symptoms of trying to cope with "the possibility of being involved in a violent clash at any moment."

In the foreword to Martín-Baró's *Writings for a Liberation Psychology*, published after his death, the editors wrote, "Like Bruno Bettelheim, who preserved his own mental health in the death camps of Nazi Germany by assigning himself the task of observing and analyzing the psychological effects of the extreme situation, Martín-Baró kept himself whole by converting every atrocity and every loss, but also every act of heroism and sacrifice, into an object lesson in the study of human behavior."[14] He had founded the IUDOP (University Institute of Public Opinion), which carried out public opinion polls, measuring public interest in economic and political issues. At the time of his death in 1989, Martín-Baró was the only psychologist in the entire county of El Salvador holding a PhD.

Sociologist Segundo Montes, SJ, in the first study of its kind in El Salvador, set about analyzing the financial impacts of Salvadoran migration to the United States. He discovered a circular pattern wherein as the civil war worsened, the fewer acres of Salvadoran land could be in production. Many rural residents were chased out by the war. Others fled El Salvador to avoid forced conscription or guerrilla recruitment. The United States, on the other hand, claimed Salvadorans migrated to the United States to escape poverty. Montes proved they were driven out by war.

Montes also discovered, partly through extensive polling of Salvadorans in the United States, that remittances sent from migrants back to their relatives in 1988 amounted to US$1.3 billion. His empirical data demonstrated that the Salvadoran economy was addicted to the over US$1 billion per year in remittances. This placed remittances among the three largest sources of foreign income in El Salvador, along with U.S. economic assistance (military aid) and earnings from coffee exports. Montes's startling conclusion: *the poor are crucial to El Salvador's economy*.[15] Pointing out this counter-intuitive reality put Montes in danger. His personal appearances before committees of the U.S. Congress in Washington DC made matters worse.

---

[14] "Foreword," in Ignacio Martín-Baró, *Writings for a Liberation Psychology*, ed. Adrianne Aron and Shawn Corne (Cambridge, MA: Harvard University Press, 1994), 3.

[15] Segundo Montes and Juan José García, *Salvadoran Migration to the United States: An Exploratory Study* (Washinton DC: Center for Immigration Policy and Refugee Assistance, Georgetown University, 1988), 36.

The Carter Administration had appointed Robert White as ambassador to El Salvador in 1980, a year full of violence and repression. A Fulbright Scholar and longtime diplomat, White had briefly served the Peace Corps as its director for Latin America in the late 1960s. Returning to the State Department, White had a penchant for annoying his superiors by focusing on human rights issues. He had his work cut out for him in El Salvador.

Early in his tenure he met with Archbishop Romero and, because he was Catholic, attended mass at the Cathedral. The archdiocese broadcast the Sunday masses over the radio so those in the countryside could also hear their bishop. White was in the congregation on the Sunday (March 16, 1980) when Romero read aloud the letter he had written to President Jimmy Carter requesting the elimination of foreign aid to the Salvadoran government. As the most visible representative of the U.S. president, White took in each desperate word Archbishop Romero spoke:

> As a Salvadoran and archbishop of the archdiocese of San Salvador, I have an obligation to see that faith and justice reign in my country, I ask you, if you truly want to defend human rights:
>
> - to forbid that military aid be given to the Salvadoran government;
> - to guarantee that your government will not intervene directly or indirectly, with military, economic, diplomatic, or other pressures, in determining the destiny of the Salvadoran people.
>
> In these moments, we are living through a grave economic and political crisis in our country, but it is certain that increasingly the people are awakening and organizing and have begun to prepare themselves to manage and be responsible for the future of El Salvador, as the only ones capable of overcoming the crisis.
>
> It would be unjust and deplorable for foreign powers to intervene and frustrate the Salvadoran people, to repress them and keep them from deciding autonomously the economic and political course that our nation should follow.[16]

---

[16] Archbishop Óscar Romero, letter to President Jimmy Carter, February 17, 1980, available on the progressive.org website.

Romero called for a new way to do business in El Salvador, a way where the people would "manage and be responsible for the future." In this scenario the corrupt military would be made just or abolished. The following Sunday his message, also broadcast over the radio, was specifically directed to soldiers. They were not obligated, he pleaded and instructed, to follow orders that went against God's law. Please do not kill civilians, even when ordered to do so. For military officers these were fighting words.

The archbishop was well aware that his pleas on behalf of the people made enemies in military and political circles. He knew his life was in jeopardy. He lived in simple quarters and insisted on driving himself around San Salvador in a beat-up Toyota. He was not an evasive target. Yet those who wished him dead also wished to make a statement, and so they killed him in dramatic fashion. The day after he spoke directly to his country's soldiers, Romero went to La Divina Providencia to preside at a mass in the chapel of a cancer hospital. He gave a short sermon and walked to the altar, where he was shot in the chest. The shooter chose to kill Romero at the altar, in the presence of believers, at the foot of a crucifix. It is as if the assassin and those who directed the assassination took down the bishop, the church, its believers, and Jesus himself, all at once.

Well over 100,000 people gathered in the plaza outside the Cathedral for the funeral of the slain bishop. Dozens of visiting bishops and clerics processed through the people mourning the loss of the humble shepherd. At some point gunfire erupted and bombs exploded, apparently coming from the National Palace, the government building. Yet the government blamed the disruptions on leftists. As many as forty people died, and hundreds were injured as the panicked crowd tried to escape the barrage.

The assassination of Romero briefly gave the Carter Administration pause, although Ambassador White and other U.S. officials believed the Salvadoran government when it claimed that the crime was being investigated. Evidence, however, was not gathered by the government or its police. Even a decade later, America's Watch (today's Human Rights Watch) stated: "Ten years after his death, the case is collecting dust," stifled by the ARENA-controlled Supreme Court.[17] The long arm of the military obviously had a stranglehold on the judicial system too. The United Nations later proved that Roberto D'Aubuisson,

---

[17] America's Watch, *El Salvador's Decade of Terror: Human Rights Since the Assassination of Archbishop Romero* (New Haven, CT: Yale University Press, 1991), 34.

founder of the ARENA party and candidate for president in 1984, commissioned death squads to carry out political assassinations, including that of Archbishop Óscar Romero. The alleged triggerman has been identified as a man who has lived in both California and in Flordia. D'Aubuisson died in 1992, but his portrait hangs today with great dignity in one of the main government buildings in San Salvador.

Sadly, the fate of Romero foreshadowed the massacre at the UCA. The archbishop's life and that of the university had followed a remarkably similar script. Initially, each was conservative and applauded by El Salvador's oligarchy. Over time, with evidence of cruelty against the *campesinos* mounting, each took a serious look at the Gospels to direct their respective futures. The soft-spoken and compliant Romero turned about when his friend Rutilio Grande was gunned down. Romero emerged one of the most outspoken advocates for the poor.

Ronald Reagan's election on November 4, 1980, did not bode well for Carter appointee and centrist Ambassador Robert White. El Salvador's oligarchy and military, however, held great celebrations over Reagan's election.[18] It appeared that, once and for all, a leftist insurrection could be suppressed. Strangely or predictably, depending on one's viewpoint, a series of new atrocities began just after the Reagan election. Some have attributed the unprecedented increase in death-squad activities as resulting from the right wing being emboldened by Reagan's anti-communist agenda.[19] The events of November 1980 through 1981 are among the most brutal of the civil war.

On November 26, 1980, Ignacio Ellacuría was tipped by an anonymous phone caller that he might "not survive" the week.[20] He sought help from the Spanish embassy and fled the country for about a year and a half.

On November 27, 1980, just hours after Ellacuría escaped, six representatives of the Revolutionary Democratic Front (FDR), a coalition of labor unions and social democratic groups, were taken at gunpoint from a meeting at the Externado San José, a Jesuit high school. Their tortured bodies were found the next day, dumped on a road leading out of the city.

---

[18] Margaret O'Brien Steinfels, "Death and Lies in El Salvador: The Ambassador's Tale," *Commonweal Magazine* 133/18 (October 26, 2001).

[19] Ibid.

[20] Beirne, *Jesuit Education and Social Change in El Salvador,* 165.

Five days later, on December 2, 1980, four American churchwomen—Jean Donovan, Ursuline sister Dorothy Kazel, and Maryknoll sisters Ita Ford and Maura Clarke—were commandeered by National Guardsmen as they drove from the airport in a van. They were raped and murdered. Ambassador Robert White had hosted two of the women the night before at the American embassy. When he learned that bodies had been found, he went to the site, near Santiago Nonualco, and requested forensics tests, but he was turned down by Salvadoran authorities. Ultimately, evidence indicated the guardsmen had acted upon orders, yet no superiors were convicted. Those who had the authority to issue the orders to those guardsmen, the head of the National Guard and the Minister of Defense, retired to Miami.

After the murders of the American women, the Carter Administration limited U.S. military aid. But U.S. funding of the Salvadoran military was accelerated with the newly elected President Reagan's anti-communist crusade. Secretary of State Alexander Haig, prone to dramatic misstatements, claimed the women had exchanged gunfire with the guardsmen. Evidence proved otherwise. Ambassador White was unceremoniously fired by Haig. A month after the women were killed, two leaders of land reform in El Salvador and two Americans with them were shot at the Sheraton Hotel in San Salvador. These murders set back the reform movement and introduced an era of unchecked brutality.

Many of these who were tortured, gunned down, and murdered actively worked for reform and for change in El Salvador. They knew the danger. Many received threats. Yet, the events that unfolded on December 11, 1981, took aim not at activists and workers but at simple *campesinos*. On that December day hundreds of Salvadoran villagers were massacred at El Mozote, a village in the department of Morazán.[21] The military believed the village was a base for guerrillas. Other nearby villages had been destroyed, and some survivors of those skirmishes fled to El Mozote. A lone woman managed to escape the roundup. Rufina Amaya hid herself, watching as men and women and children, including her husband and children, were separated by gender and age. Mothers and daughters were raped, and some butchered. Others listened in horror as their children called out last pleas before being shot. Group by group was summarily executed by the military in a cruelly twisted anti-guerrilla attack. Rufina's husband was beheaded, and four of her children were killed that day.

---

[21] For a full description, see Mark Danner, *The Massacre at El Mozote* (New York: Vintage Books, 1994).

Both the *New York Times* and the *Washington Post* identified the U.S. funded and trained Atlacatl Battalion as the perpetrators of the massacre, where one thousand people were killed. The Reagan Administration claimed the reports of the massacre were exaggerated. Amaya spent the rest of her life, until her death in 2007, reporting what she saw at El Mozote, pointing out the mass graves of the villagers. Eventually, official excavations confirmed Amaya's claims. Finally, in 2011, the Salvadoran government acknowledged crimes at El Mozote and issued an official apology.

Vice-President George H. W. Bush was the highest-ranking U.S. official to call El Salvador's government and military to task. In a clandestine visit in 1983, Bush was helicoptered to a remote presidential retreat, where he met with El Salvador's president, Álvaro Magaña, and the highest military leaders.[22] Flanked by the now infamous Colonel Oliver North, he threatened to cut off U.S. military aid if human rights abuses did not end. Witnesses say that when the topic of the murdered churchwomen came up, Bush pounded his fist on the table. That Bush confronted the Salvadorans is admirable. Unfortunately, his threats were hollow, because U.S. money kept flowing, even though human rights abuses did not end; the money financed tens of thousands of civilian deaths.

Between 1972 and 1990, besides Romero and the churchwomen, eighteen Catholic priests were murdered. Presumably officials in the Catholic Church would be alarmed by the calculated elimination of its bishops, priests, and nuns. Local bishops spoke out against the brutality. An editorial in the UCA's journal *ECA (Estudios Centroamericanos)* in 1975 asserted that "to see in priests subversion and communism is to look at reality through eyeglasses loaned by the dominant classes; it is political ineptitude, and even worse, it is culpable blindness."[23] Many of these church workers offered what Lucía experienced at the UCA: respect. Its transformative power allowed the poorest of the poor to come to value themselves and to expect their government to value them too.

When Pope John Paul II visited Central America in 1983, he publicly scolded Nicaraguan priest Ernesto Cardenal for joining the Socialist government of the Sandinistas in Nicaragua. The pope had taken a strong and public political stand in his native Poland in support of the Solidarity labor union. Was Cardenal's political stance so very different? It seems the pontiff could not see that in Central

---

[22] John Solomon, "A Wimp He Wasn't," *Newsweek* (March 20, 2011).

[23] Quoted in Beirne, *Jesuit Education and Social Change in El Salvador*, 106.

America anti-communists were killing poor people. The church withdrew Cardenal's faculties to work as a priest. Today, Ernesto Cardenal is a world-renowned poet.

During the 1980s I was only vaguely aware of life in El Salvador. That is to say that I was slightly more aware than most Americans—for two reasons. My aunt is a Maryknoll sister, Sister Lilla Hull. And second, I had friends who were Jesuits. When Archbishop Romero was assassinated, I remember thinking that most archbishops, in America at least, would not be at the vanguard of advocating for the poor. The complexities of who killed him were lost on me, but I understood him to be a martyr.

The rape and murders of the churchwomen was another story. I was horrified and indignant. I could imagine that they were colleagues of my aunt. I knew she was not a political person but one looking to help address world poverty. I understood that elements of security forces committed the crime. Only as time went by did I understand that few in El Salvador, and fewer still in the United States except the families of the victims, were interested in who raped, murdered, and buried the women. I suspected that if any men were brought to trial, they could very well be scapegoats for the guilty parties. The murders of those women still haunt.

4

The Open Window

November 12–15, 1989

Lucía Cerna

We have lived that war in our country. Everything is really true. For example, when Father Rutilio Grande was killed, they were on the road waiting for him when he went driving his jeep. Soldiers killed him and two others. This was before Romero got killed. The activists were very angry. It happened in Chalatenango, about two hours from the UCA. And Father Alas, they tortured him. Somebody saw, but nobody will say. It is too scary to say something in El Salvador. Monseñor Romero was shot even while he was saying mass. Somebody saw, but nobody would say. All those people there, somebody saw. If you say, you will be killed. Simple.

Only one of the Jesuits at the UCA was Salvadoran, and that was Father López y López. He did not teach, but he was the director of the center for job training for poor people who could not attend school. The people could learn a trade. Everybody knew he had prostate cancer, but he said, "Ay, I don't care." He always said good morning, and for breakfast he liked to drink a beer. Afterward he walked to his office in the training center. He was a very good man, very humble.

Sometimes I did the laundry, but he did not want his clothes washed too much. "Every three days I change my clothes," he told me. He was very humble, even though he was from a rich family in Santa Ana. They had big properties of coffee and fruit near a lake. On weekends he went to see his family, and he always brought back boxes of oranges for everybody. When I think now, I wonder, who could kill him? How could the soldiers kill him? For me, it was a deep loss, deep loss.

The print center at the UCA had its own building on the campus. Here it produced magazines and made flyers. When anyone requested a magazine, it was sent. They sent magazines everywhere. Father Rogelio Pedraz was the director, and there were many people working there, mostly men. Father Rodolfo Cardenal worked as editor. For a while he had an office on the second floor of the administration building, and so I saw him more often. A woman editor worked for Father Cardenal, checking in Spanish that there were no errors. I think Father Cardenal and Father Pedraz worked well together.

Father Cardenal was living inside the campus, but after the soldiers came to examine the rooms three days before the massacre, he decided to leave that house and live in Santa Tecla. He saved his life by going to live in Santa Tecla. The other priests did not believe that there was danger, but Father Cardenal moved to Santa Tecla the day after the soldiers came. He did not want to live in that house after that. There was another priest, Father Ibisate, whom we all called Ibis. He had lived on the campus but moved to Casa Cinquenta with the provincial. That is where he was that night. He has passed away since then.

Padre Segundo Montes was also with poor people, working for human rights. He calculated how much money Salvadorans in the United States sent back to my country. He was worried about Salvadoran immigrants. One Saturday he was looking for me at the UCA. He asked for me in several offices and found me dusting in one.

"Do you have relatives who went to the *Estados Unidos* [United States] illegally?" he asked me.

"No, I do not," I said.

Then he explained that he had an opportunity to help with immigration papers, and he wanted to know if my family needed help. Padre Segundo was a very good man. And he was tall and very, very handsome. He had blue-green eyes and beautiful manners.

Father Sobrino was away. He went to some countries like Vietnam and Thailand. His personality was easy and happy. I felt he was a good man and never offensive. He was a teacher, and his office was in another building, not in the rectory, so I did not attend him. I did not know him very well. Father Ellacu was the rector, and Father Nachito the vice-rector. Their offices were in the rectory, and each had a secretary. At one time or another there was someone else in the rectory, a *techano* or *licenciado*. I think they instructed mathematics.

Still in my mind I do not understand, or maybe I do not want to understand, why someone felt the need to kill them. I knew them. They did not have guns, or bombs, or weapons. Their defense was their brains For example, I remember one interview years ago when Roberto D'Aubuisson wanted to be president. He was interviewed with Father Ellacu on television, and I saw them.

D'Aubuisson pointed at Father Ellacu and said, "You are a communist!"

Father Ellacu answered by saying [something like], "I am not a communist. I am a Christian, and you, Señor D'Aubuisson, are a hypocrite. You say you are for the people of El Salvador, and you are not." [José Napoleón] Duarte won as president instead of D'Aubuisson. That interview made it so D'Aubuisson did not win. I think it made him hate Father Ellacu.

One day U.S. Ambassador [William] Walker came to the rectory to give a donation of books for the library at the UCA. It was maybe eight months before the massacre; I am not sure, maybe eight months or a year. Walker was one hyper man. I remember him when he arrived at the UCA rectory, and I opened the door. "*Buenos dias, Señor*"—good morning, sir. He was very unpleasant, and he did not say hello or speak to me. He spoke fluent Spanish, but he did not take notice of me. Maybe he did not like Latino people. Or maybe he did not speak to me because I was wearing my apron and was therefore a servant. I was happy that I did not have to travel abroad and be interviewed by this angry man.

I showed him and two other men to the conference room on the first floor of the rectory. Two guards stayed outside. The guards were Salvadoran military, and they had very elegant uniforms. They looked very good and important. Father Ellacuría, Father Nachito, and Father Segundo, too, received the donation from Walker in the big conference room with a glass door. They closed the door and talked and talked. There was a big round table, and that is where they sat. It was a small group. I did not see the books, only the paperwork they were doing to accept the gift.

The two guards disappeared. They went looking around. I left my trash basket and broom, and I followed them upstairs. They were looking in the bathrooms, opening cabinets and searching.

I asked, "Excuse me, Sir, what are you looking for?"

"Nothing, only looking. Sorry—*disculpe*."

"If you are done, go downstairs, please," I told them. There was nobody to put discipline there. It was not my property, but I was taking care. Nobody told me to take care. But I did. The offices were all locked. If the guards were looking for something, they did not know that I had the key to every office.

I went to tell Father Nachito's secretary. "Did you see those guards go upstairs?" She was busy typing and did not notice the men go upstairs.

"Where, where?" she asked me and went looking for them. Those secretaries write on the typewriter so much and very fast. But she did not notice people in the building. It is private, and usually when someone rings the doorbell, they answer through an intercom from the second floor. She did not know the men came in with the ambassador.

Later, I told both Padre Nacho and Padre Ellacu. I commented about the guards, and they said, "*Estan locos*"—they're crazy. They did not pay much attention to my comment. I did not understand. I had doubts. My simple thought was if these people were curious, why did they come here?

I told the secretary again, and she said "Ay, Lucía, don't pay attention."

I insisted, why did they come here? I asked again, "Father Nachito, excuse me, but do you think they came with good intentions?"

"I think they will give a good donation of books," he said.

That is good, I thought. "No, I am saying something else. Do you think they are good people?"

"Yeah, they are."

The priests' error was that they trust too much. When the ambassador came to donate books, I did not see a good sign. If you trust, you do not send someone to search. From that incident I could immediately identify Ambassador Walker at the airport on the day when we had to leave El Salvador. He did not speak to me on that day either. That Walker was a hypocrite too.

For us, the worst part of the war was when it came to Soyapango. A military helicopter flew over the district firing at guerrillas. It was loud, like a roaring lion. Our house was hit, making a hole in the roof. The FMLN opened sides of houses to crawl in and escape the firing. They did not ask permission, no, they just cut the hole. Guerrillas went in the psychiatric hospital and from inside shot at the helicopters. The guerrillas killed too. There is so much revenge. In the civil war the guerrillas killed and the army killed, they both killed.

Monday and Tuesday, November 13 and 14, when we slept at night, Jorge put a mattress over me and our daughter. This way the bullets would not hit us. He did not sleep but kept watch. We were living under that mattress! It was Jorge's idea to do this. Things got worse and our supply of food ran out. There was no water, and the river was not close. Soyapango was the town worst hit by the war. In our home we had no water or light, and stores were closed. Every Saturday I went to the market to supply the refrigerator. That Saturday I could not go because of the war. On Tuesday afternoon we baked, and after selling all the bread, I thought we had to leave. Antiguo Cuscatlán still had power and water, and you could find food. I thought of going to my mother's, but where she lived was too small. I was closer, like family, to the priests. I had more confidence in them. We could not get to Jorge's family because of the war.

Jorge did not want to leave. We had a lot of supplies, and at first he refused. But we did not have light, and no candles and no electricity. I was not worried for myself; I was worried for the child. If I must fast, I do not care. But for my child, especially for her, I wanted to go find somebody to help us. I had confidence in the priests to give us shelter. I had hope that the war would be gone soon. I didn't have time to watch TV or read the newspaper.

I still remember Jorge standing in the front door. I was telling him, "Let's go, let's go, don't stay alone." He stood there with his arms folded, looking at the house. I had our daughter by the hand. "*Vamonos*," let's go.

"I don't want to," he said. "The priests do not know me. I can't go with you. Go with the child." Jorge did not know the priests but had only seen them on TV interviews. "Maybe they do not trust me."

"I won't leave you," I said. "Come. I will talk to Father Nachito, and he will give you shelter."

Finally he accepted. When we left that morning, Jorge did not completely lock our home. He only pulled the door closed. We hoped the war would be over soon, no more guerrillas in our *colonia*, and then peace. We left our home in Soyapango at 6 o'clock on the morning of November 15. We walked and walked, maybe twenty kilometers [more than twelve miles]. It is quite far. We left our home, everything, everything! I only took the money in my purse; it was heavy with the coins. I put all our wages and all our bakery money in my purse to carry with me. I also had all the keys to the UCA and to the provincial office, maybe thirty-five keys.

I held a white flag high, very high. Some soldiers were still shooting, and it was scary. Jorge carried Geraldina on his shoulders all that way. When we got into the city, I called Padre Nacho from a telephone to his private number. I asked him if he could give us some days of shelter, to stay at the UCA for food and water. For me, it was not difficult to call, because I had enough confidence with them to talk about anything. Padre Nacho said yes, come. A man came driving by in a truck. He yelled, "One *colón* for each person." We paid and had a ride almost to the UCA.

I went looking for the Jesuits because they had a good supply of food. My intention was to help their cook and to work until the battles in Soyapango stopped. The UCA had a cistern, so there was water. I had faith in them as a family. The reason we did not go to be with my mother was that she was living in just a small room with a patio. There was not room enough for the three of us. We went to the UCA for protection, for water and food, waiting for the war in Soyapango to finish.

When we came to request shelter on November 15, the Jesuits were living in a new house. About two weeks earlier the priests had moved into a new house inside the campus. This left the twin houses at numbers 15 and 16 Cantábrico empty. When they moved, Father Saínz and Father Ibisate went to live at Casa Cinquenta, the provincial house. Father Cardenal lived at the new campus residence. Just days before the massacre, soldiers had come to examine the house. From then Father Cardenal decided to stay in Santa Tecla for a while and came to UCA only to teach classes. I thought Father Ellacu was still in Spain. I just cleaned his office very well because he was away and I could clean everything and not disturb him. Houses number 15 and 16 Cantábrico were left empty.

Father Nacho took us there to stay. He met my husband that day. My husband did not know the priests that I worked with at the UCA, but he met Padre Nacho that day. My daughter, Geraldina, and I went with him to the guest room in the new house to bring sleeping mats for us to borrow. They had mats for when visitors came. Father was very happy with Geraldina because he enjoyed children. She was four years old then.

The house was empty. Geraldina asked, "Are there ghosts here?"

"No," Padre Nachito told her, "we do not have ghosts here." And we went with him to the guest room, where he took two mats for us. He carried the mats for us back to the other house. Father Nachito was excellent, a very good man. Was it Providence that we were in the old house for that night?

"Our cook did not come today," he said. "I don't know who will cook tonight." Their regular cook lived in Santa Tecla, and she could not get to the campus because of the war. That is what Father Nacho commented to me.

"I can cook tonight," I said.

"Okay. Fine, thank you," he said, and he left.

After some minutes Father Nachito came back. It surprised me when he came back. He said, "Lucía, the wife of the guardian will come to cook tonight. You stay here and rest."

"It is okay. I can come."

"No, *mujer*. You stay here. You are tired."

I asked myself, who is it that is coming? Father said the wife of the guardian, the *vigilante*, but he must have meant gardener. I never thought it was Elba Ramos. Her husband, Obdulio, was a gardener, not a guard. Elba was the regular cook at the philosophy house. The Jesuits also had a house for the study of philosophy. It was not far, in Antiguo Cuscatlán.

Jorge went out to buy something to eat and drink. He found some bread and cola for us, but he forgot to bring a match. I went to Casa Cinquenta, the provincial house, to ask the cook there for a match. I was friendly with that cook, and now she also knew we were in 16 Cantábrico that night. We had no lights, just a candle. Before we lay down we took a shower. Then we lay down to rest. The shower was important, because in Miami, when we said we were witnesses, they did not believe we were there. There was evidence of us in the shower. They found hair. And that proved that we were there.

After the priests had their dinner, about 7 o'clock, I heard Father Nachito playing guitar. I told Jorge, "Listen," and I went to open the window to hear better. Father Nachito was playing his guitar in the dining room, and he was singing. They sounded like they were having a good time.

"Let's go to join them," I said to Jorge.

"No, Lucía, remember he told you to lie down. You are tired. Leave them. They are enjoying themselves."

I remembered Padre Nacho said to sleep early because I was tired. We lay down to sleep on the mats he provided us. But I left the window open. I went to sleep to Father Nachito playing the guitar and singing.

Mary Jo Ignoffo

Some decisions, made in a moment or a day or a week, change a life. Lucía's determination to leave Soyapango came out of roaring helicopters and exploding grenades. It came out of three nights spent crouching under a mattress with her child. It came out of an empty refrigerator and a dry faucet. She had a child, and as she joined thousands streaming out of war-torn neighborhoods toward San Salvador's city center, strips of white fabric held high overhead. Lucía had a destination in mind. She would not go to the Walter Thilo Deininger School for shelter with many neighbors. She would go to the UCA.

But for Jorge it was a different story all together. He did not want to leave, and in fact felt quite strongly that he should not leave. It would be better to stay with the house and business to protect them. The priests at the UCA did not know him. Of course they would take Lucía and her child, but why should they accept him? The moment when Jorge unfolded his arms, hoisted his daughter onto his shoulders, and joined Lucía and the other refugees changed that family's life forever.

Both he and Lucía freely admit that if he had not been at the UCA with her, if he had not seen what she had seen, it would have been very difficult for this little family to remain together. He would not have understood his wife's compunction to give witness or been sympathetic to the psychological trauma she felt. Would she have gone into hiding alone, turning her daughter over to Cecilia? The civil war that had raged for almost a decade came to Soyapango. How had this happened?

Two major political factions arose in the civil war years in El Salvador. The FMLN emerged as a coalition of leftist groups in opposition to El Salvador's military-controlled government. The FMLN took its name (Farabundo Martí National Liberation Front or Frente Farabundo Martí) from Farabundo Martí, a communist leader of *La Matanza*, the peasant uprising in 1932 in which an estimated thirty thousand Salvadorans were killed by government soldiers. Martí was shot for inciting the uprising, becoming a martyr for the people. The FMLN or guerrillas, who sought to carry on in the 1980s the tradition of Martí, were led by Joaquín Villalobos, a one-time student activist who turned out to be a remarkable military strategist. He and a small circle spent most of the civil war directing guerrilla attacks from a secret hideaway in the mountains. During the course of the war guerrillas managed to take control from the military in some of El Salvador's departments or provinces, including Chalatanango and Morazán. In what became known as the final offensive, which began on November 11, 1989, the guerrillas secured a significant portion of the capital city of San Salvador, including Soyapango.

The FMLN was opposed by ARENA (Nationalist Republican Alliance or Alianza Republicana Nacionalista), a right-wing political party founded after the start of the civil war in response to the growing guerrilla movement. Its founder, Roberto D'Aubuisson, promulgated an appealing platform of democratic and representative government, family values, and protection of private property. Rhetoric never matched reality. D'Aubuisson had ordered the death of Archbishop

Romero and directed countless death squads for the better part of a decade.

ARENA and its military subsisted on U.S. military aid, and it was a generous diet—in 1980 US$5.7 million. President Reagan urged Congress to raise that amount, and a year later it was US$35.5 million. By the end of the decade the United States had sent almost US$4 billion in economic and military aid to fight leftists.[1] In doing so, the U.S. government turned a blind eye and financed incomprehensible brutality in order to fight communism.

El Salvador was a pawn in the Soviet–United States Cold War power struggle. American foreign policy, partially articulated by the Truman Doctrine after World War II, theorized that if poorer nations fell under communist rule, their peoples would suffer repression. Furthermore, Soviet influence would present an unacceptable threat to U.S. security. Each president from Harry S. Truman to Bill Clinton approved intervention in foreign countries, often supporting despotic leaders (Syngman Rhee in South Korea and Ngo Dinh Diem in South Vietnam, to name two for whom the United States went to war) because they were anti-communist. U.S. officials chose what in their eyes was the lesser of two evils. They opted to support anti-communists, overlooking brutal atrocities committed with U.S. dollars.

An intense fear of communism lies deep in the psyche of contemporary Americans. The very word often elicits a knee-jerk reaction, and strident voices decry left-leaning governments or political movements as a cancer spreading around the globe. The fear has some basis in reality in the tactics of Vladimir Lenin or Joseph Stalin. Yet the post–World War II urgency with which President Truman pushed the American Congress to fund anti-communist governments in Greece and Turkey in 1947 was specifically designed to "scare the hell out of them." The scare tactic worked better than even Truman expected, the aid packages were approved, and the Cold War was on. Containing communism became a foreign-policy imperative for almost a half century and was rarely nuanced for the particularities of a changing world.

Both President John Kennedy and President Lyndon Johnson approved funding to El Salvador in hopes of democratic and humanitarian reform. "We have today recognized the government of El Salvador," Kennedy said at a press conference on February 15, 1961. "It

---

[1] America's Watch, *El Salvador's Decade of Terror: Human Rights Since the Assassination of Archbishop Romero* (New Haven, CT: Yale University Press, 1991), 10, 119.

has announced its determination to bring about free and democratic elections in that country, and it seeks solutions for the economic and social difficulties which that country has faced." Seven years later, in 1968, President Johnson and his family visited El Salvador. The fortress-like style of the U.S. embassy took him by surprise, but he acknowledged it had been built to withstand an earthquake and that it sits in the shadow of a volcano. "Back in Washington we sit right on top of one," he quipped, referring to Congress. Then, on a more serious note, he said:

> We in the United States, as a concerned neighbor and friend, will continue to do our part to help the nations of Central America shape their futures. We will try to provide both assistance and incentive:
>
> - assistance by contributing know-how and dollars—when they are wanted, needed, and used wisely;
> - incentive by conducting ourselves as a neighbor in such a way that we can continue to warrant the respect and friendship of the nations around us.[2]

Johnson's 1968 visit came at the height of the Vietnam War. Over and over again, the official rhetoric coming out of governments—in the United States and El Salvador in this case—does not match reality. Sometimes the disconnect is the result of out-and-out lies. At other times it seems as if we hope our words turn into reality. At some point we must look to actions to define ourselves, not only words.

The government of El Salvador in the late 1970s and early 1980s was quite unstable. A 1979 coup of center-left Social Democrats was fairly short lived. One of its leaders was a UCA political science professor, Rubén Zamora. He resigned from the government a year later after his brother was killed by a right-wing death squad. Zamora has maintained a presence in Salvadoran politics, running for office and serving as an ambassador.

Roberto D'Aubuisson ran for president in 1984. He was opposed by the United States, and former U.S. Ambassador Robert E. White once called him a "psychopathic killer."[3] The more moderate and United States–educated (University of Notre Dame) José Napoleón Duarte won the election in 1984. Later, it was determined that during

---

[2] Lyndon B. Johnson, remarks at the U.S. embassy in San Salvador, July 7, 1968, available on the presidency.ucsb.edu website.

[3] See Margaret O'Brien Steinfels, "Death and Lies in El Salvador: The Ambassador's Tale," *Commonweal* 128, no. 18 (October 26, 2001).

the 1980s he was on the payroll of the Central Intelligence Agency. Duarte's eldest daughter was kidnapped by guerrillas in 1985. Although Duarte never acknowledged it, Ignacio Ellacuría negotiated for her release along with an exchange of prisoners between the government forces and the guerrillas. Duarte was president until June 1989, when Alfredo Cristiani came into power.

Of all the U.S. presidents to embrace the Truman Doctrine—and they all did—President Ronald Reagan's approach was the most simplistic. He framed his anti-communist agenda like a Hollywood movie script, giving the director's role to his secretary of state, Alexander Haig. Both Reagan and Haig decided to hold the line on communism in Nicaragua and El Salvador, positing those nations as case studies because of their relative proximity to the United States and their ties to Cuba and the Soviet Union. When the leftist Sandinistas in Nicaragua overthrew dictator Anastasio Somoza in 1979, it appeared that El Salvador might also slip left, an unacceptable eventuality for Reagan and Haig. They came up with a plan that would be very costly in cash, human lives, and political careers.

Although the U.S. Congress had specifically prohibited funds going to the civil war in Nicaragua because it feared "another Vietnam," the Reagan Administration had another view. It secretly shipped military hardware and weaponry to the embargoed Iranians in exchange for American hostages and money. The money went to fund the opposition (the Contras) to the left-wing government in Nicaragua. In this way the president did not need to inform Congress. Even after the scheme was exposed and President Reagan went on national television to admit that his administration had "exchanged arms for hostages," he did not address nor did the press report much about the illegality of funding the Contras. In most political arenas in America, an attempt to subvert communism in Central America was simply taken as a good. The fact that the Sandinistas had popular support in Nicaragua was lost on the Reagan Aadministration and most of the American public.

Another way that the United States exerted influence on internal affairs in Latin American countries was by training parts of their militaries. An American military installation called the School of the Americas (SOA) operated in Panama from 1946 until 1984. American military officials wished to ensure that Latin American fighters would stand by the United States and fight communism wherever it might crop up. The Latin American trainees were instilled with a mindset of freedom fighters, helping America fight communism and enabling their own countries to clear a path to democracy.

Fearing another war like Vietnam, though, the U.S. Congress strictly limited the number of U.S. military personnel stationed in El Salvador. Ambassador Deane Hinton explained:

> Part of the problem about a recruit center in El Salvador arose from the congressional limit on the number of American trainers you could have in El Salvador. Congress wouldn't budge. . . . It was like a football team that had 45 or 55 players, and you must shuffle them in and out (of El Salvador) of the lineup. There were days when we had to stay within the ceiling, to send trainers out so we could get people in, because we needed even more. Peculiar way to run a ball game.[4]

It became expedient to fly the Salvadoran soldiers to the United States for training. By the 1980s, the School of the Americas had been relocated to Fort Benning, Georgia.

In 1983, a Maryknoll priest who was also a U.S. Navy veteran of the Vietnam War, Father Roy Bourgeois took issue with the philosophy and training that happened at Fort Benning. Moreover, he had been friends and colleagues with two of the church women killed by the Salvadoran National Guard in 1980. Along with another priest and a woman Army reservist, he penetrated Fort Benning, and the three set themselves up high in a pine tree behind the barracks housing Salvadoran military trainees. After lights-out, they activated a loudspeaker that broadcast the final homily of Archbishop Óscar Romero. The archbishop's Spanish rang out in the night, now addressed to the recruits: "No soldier is obliged to obey an order contrary to the law of God. . . . In the name of God, in the name of our tormented people whose cries rise up to heaven, I beseech you, I beg you, I command you, stop the repression!"[5] As the soldiers tumbled out of the barracks into the black night, armed MPs and guard dogs apprehended the intruders. But not before Romero's disembodied voice pleaded for the armies to stop the killing. The two priests and woman reservist were sent to prison.

Dozens of Salvadoran military officers attended training at the School of the Americas. The elite Atlacatl Battalion emerged out of the SOA. Most officers involved in the UCA murders, including

---

[4] Deane Hinton, in Max G. Manwaring and Court Prisk, eds., *El Salvador at War: An Oral History of Conflict from the 1979 Insurrection to the Present*, (Washington, DC: National Defense University Press, 1988), 235.

[5] Óscar Romero, final homily, in James Hodge and Linda Cooper, *Disturbing the Peace* (Maryknoll, NY: Orbis Books, 2005), 3.

Emilio Ponce, Manuel Rivas, and Guillermo Benavides, had trained at the school. A non-profit organization called School of the Americas Watch (SOAW) was established in 1990 to expose crimes committed by graduates of SOA. It sponsors an annual protest at Fort Benning on the anniversary of the UCA murders, drawing upward of twenty thousand protestors from around the country. The Pentagon closed the School of the Americas in 2000 after considerable public outcry about the atrocities committed by its graduates. It promptly reopened with the new name Western Hemisphere Institute for Security Cooperation (WHINSEC) and presently carries out the same work as the School of the Americas.

The United States sent US$4 billion to the government of El Salvador, including US$1 billion worth of military weaponry and equipment, hoping it would defeat the leftist guerrilla movement. The civil war in El Salvador, which claimed more than seventy thousand lives, would have come to a conclusion years earlier if it had not been for American dollars. The Reagan Administration was completely convinced of the necessity to thwart any leftist activities in Latin America for the security of the United States. The tragic irony is that those efforts to combat communism managed to derail democracy, and the majority of the people of El Salvador could not participate in any way in the government of their own country.

At least two U.S. generals, interviewed in 1987, had a broader view than that of the Reagan Administration and its State Department. General John R. Galvin noted that "the U.S. policy (in El Salvador) is basically anti-Communist. It ought to be, basically, pro-democratic."[6] General Wallace H. Nutting concurred, and claimed:

> In the long run the actions that are going to make a difference are the political reform movements, the social improvements, health, sanitation, education, housing, all of that business and economic development. . . . It's a bad failing on our part. I don't think we understand, and we don't put the dimensions together effectively at all.[7]

But even these men, who had been commanders for the U.S. Southern Command, believed that leftists were necessarily the enemy. Neither they nor U.S. embassy officials during the 1980s perceived that the military-controlled government in El Salvador was undemocratic.

---

[6] Manwaring and Prisk, *El Salvador at War*, 458.

[7] Ibid.

Ignacio Martín-Baró pointed out

> the increasing tendency for nations to become satellites of the United States. This is an obvious consequence of the "national security" doctrine, according to which the countries' whole existence must submit to the logic of total confrontation against communism. What is hard is that we are mortgaging our identity and independence without getting anything in return: our problems are not being solved, and we are closing off the very possibility of a future for our peoples. The great political decisions for our countries are made according to the needs of the national security of the United States, not the needs of our peoples, with the justification that San Salvador and Managua are closer to San Francisco than are New York and Boston.[8]

Reagan used a logic of geographical proximity to justify an increased urgency and an elevated national security threat. The fact that San Salvador and Managua are closer to San Francisco than New York justified massive American funding of El Salvador's civil war and the illegal funding of the Contras in Nicaragua.

The national reality in which the UCA found itself immersed in the 1970s and 1980s was a bloody civil war. Whereas the vast majority of Salvadorans did not have enough to eat or decent living conditions, the oligarchy and the attendant military had a vested interest in keeping it that way. From its founding, the UCA's main academic journal, *Estudios Centroamericanos (ECA)* tackled real-life issues facing El Salvador, what authors called the "national reality." The language of the journal was explicitly democratic, an agenda for the majority. The school sought to be a conscience for the nation, calling attention to the majority of citizens suffering in grinding poverty. It attempted not only to educate the country's future professionals, but to encourage them to develop a social conscience. That is why by the middle 1970s, less than ten years after its founding, the UCA was viewed in prominent sectors of El Salvador as leftist, a threat to the status quo.

The voice of the UCA, through its administration, faculty, and publications, consistently and urgently demanded a negotiated settlement to the civil war. In 1980, in the wake of Romero's death, Ignacio Ellacuría wrote to U.S. Ambassador Robert White that "military aid to the current regime make the US even more responsible for repression

---

[8] Ignacio Martín-Baró, *Writings for a Liberation Psychology*, ed. Adrianne Aron and Shawn Corne (Cambridge, MA: Harvard University Press, 1994), 36.

in the country, one of the worst in the world. It is useless to try to excuse it as non-lethal aid, or that it is used just against armed groups."[9]

The *ECA* journal explored the war with Honduras in 1969, land reform, politics, and criticized labeling of priests and nuns as subversive communists. *ECA* had a broad audience; even Lucía noticed how many and how often the magazines were printed and mailed. The first bomb detonated at the UCA was at the print center in 1975.

In a memo from the American embassy to the State Department in November 1985, an unnamed official wrote about the *ECA*:

> The Jesuit University (UCA) journal "ECA" has an impact beyond what its rather restricted distribution would indicate. It is widely read in professional and academic circles, as well as by top level government bureaucrats and politicians. It is useful as a rather accurate reflection of the thinking of the left-wing intelligentsia. Its publication of articles . . . refute the charge that there is no freedom of the press in El Salvador and that there is no legitimate outlet for the printed expression of views opposing the government from the left.[10]

How very strange that an American diplomat would consider the academic journal of a private university "freedom of the press." Whatever the impact of printed material coming out of the UCA, Salvadorans then and now deserve an unbiased journalistic reporting of issues important to their nation in a public press.

By the late 1980s, and in 1989 particularly, the intransigency of the Cold War gave way as populist movements erupted across Czechoslovakia, Bulgaria, Romania, Austria, and Hungary. In Poland, candidates from the Solidarity union won seats in parliament. In Beijing, widespread protests against a repressive government brought a confrontation to a global audience as the Chinese military cracked down at Tiananmen Square. In South Africa a new leader ended apartheid and went on to free Nelson Mandela from prison. The leader of the Soviet Union, Mikhail Gorbachev, made it clear he would not obstruct independence movements in Eastern Europe. His meetings with U.S. President George H. W. Bush indicated the Cold War was coming

---

[9] Charles J. Beirne, SJ, *Jesuit Education and Social Change in El Salvador* (New York: Garland Publications, 1996), 155.

[10] American Embassy, San Salvador, to Washington DC, memorandum R 260007Z NOV 85, cited in Arthur Jones, "A Look at Declassifed State Department Documents," *National Catholic Reporter*, special supplement, "El Salvador Revisited" (September 23, 1994), available on the natcath.org website.

to a close. On November 9, 1989—incidentally Ignacio Ellacuría's fifty-ninth birthday—the Berlin Wall came down. But there was little evidence that the Cold War was winding down in El Salvador. The United States continued to pour cash into the tiny country to stamp out leftists.

When the guerrilla attack or "final offensive" broke out in San Salvador on November 11, 1989, Lucía and Jorge's neighborhood in Soyapango erupted in full-scale battle. That was the last day that Lucía worked at the UCA. She was not able to go to the market to buy food because of the artillery. All radio stations were commandeered by the government, which broadcast repeated death threats against those who opposed the government and the military. The threats specified the Jesuits, in particular Ignacio Ellacuría, who was called an enemy of the state.[11] Ellacuría embodied what the military and the oligarchy perceived as an instigator. He encouraged social uprisings, they said. In fact, Ellacuría had the ear of both the left and the right, attempting to be a bridge to greater equity and peace in El Salvador. Frustrating both sides, he would not be silenced. Ellacuría was deeply disturbed in the last week of his life that the leftist FMLN had disrupted what appeared to be the beginning of a negotiated peace process.

On that day Ellacuría was still in Spain, finishing up a month-long trip where he was awarded a humanitarian prize. The next day, November 12, the government declared a state of emergency, imposing a 6 p.m. to 6 a.m. curfew. Soldiers from the Atlacatl Battalion were in training at the headquarters in La Libertad under the direction of American Green Berets. On Monday, November 13, the Salvadoran commandos were ordered by Joint Command Director Emilio Ponce, with the approval of President Cristiani, to the city to conduct a search of the UCA.[12]

The soldiers got to the campus about 6:30 p.m. on the same day that Ellacuría arrived home from Spain. The priests recognized some

---

[11] Martha Doggett, *Death Foretold: The Jesuit Murders in El Salvador* (Washington DC: Georgetown University Press, 1993), 281; and United Nations Commission on the Truth for El Salvador, *From Madness to Hope: The Twelve-Year War in El Salvador*, report of the Commission on the Truth for El Salvador, S/25500 (1993), part IV, B, 42.

[12] Lawyers Committee for Human Rights, "The Jesuit Case: The Jury Trial" (la Vista Pública) (New York: Lawyers Committee for Human Rights, September 1991), 13.

of the 135 soldiers as being part of the Altacatl Battalion. At Ellacuría's request, Martín-Baró summarized the search and left the document on his computer. "The soldiers did not seem interested in papers or books," he wrote. This was a marked difference from previous searches in which files and documents were of interest to searchers.

Early on the morning of November 15, Jorge Cerna made his last bread deliveries as gun shots rang out, helicopters hovered, and grenades exploded. Lucía cajoled Jorge to leave with her. He was not convinced, afraid that if he left his home and business it would be vandalized or destroyed. He made his choice, and by late afternoon they arrived at the UCA. Padre Nacho showed them to the recently vacated Jesuit residence at number 16 Calle Cantábrico, just outside the pedestrian entrance to the campus. The Jesuits had moved, just two weeks before, to a new residence, named the Monseñor Romero Pastoral Center, inside the campus. Superiors of the community hoped the new location would provide better security for the priests.

Ellacuría's murder and the massacre of the others at the UCA that night were so barbaric that international attention focused on the dysfunction of the Salvadoran government and blind U.S. support of it. The official U.S. strategy refused to look beyond Cold War threats. An inflated fear of Soviet supremacy knocking at America's backdoor, even on the eve of the fall of the Berlin Wall, kept US$4 billion flowing from the Reagan Administration to the military in El Salvador at the cost of tens of thousands of civilian lives. Blame was placed on subversive Catholics, priests in particular, especially Jesuits, for offering respect and education, and for explaining civil liberties also favored by Jesus in the Gospels. What the words and actions of the Jesuits did not accomplish, their deaths did.

5

Cold, Like Ice

November 16–23, 1989

Lucía Cerna

I woke in the night, hearing a tremendous uproar inside the Fathers' home. I heard shooting, shooting at lamps, and walls, and windows. I heard doors kicked, and things being thrown and broken in the living room. I thought the war must be inside the campus. How could that be? I wondered. We saw soldiers earlier, so how could guerrillas get inside? The soldiers must be drunk, I thought. They were shouting bad words. I went to see what happened.

I got up to stop them. I wanted to say, "Why do you do this to the priests' home?" Jorge said no. Until that moment I did not think that they might kill me too. I would be dead now if Jorge did not say, "Don't go!" My God, I realized, they would kill us too. Shooting and shooting, I needed to stay and not move. There was only one wooden door between us and them. All they had to do was kick the door down and they could come to shoot us. We had no protection, but they believed nobody was there. That was our safety.

Padre Nacho was yelling—really, really yelling—on the path behind the house where we were. The shooting did not stop. It was serious. My blood went cold, like ice. I wished to go to stop the situation. I felt I had no hands, no arms, no power. I could do nothing to help Nachito, and he was yelling. My blood turned to ice, from the top of my head all the way down to my toes, and back up again. Then Padre Nacho yelled they are all *carroña* [scum] and "this is an injustice!" Now I wonder if he was yelling *carroña* and injustice because he knew I was in that room and he knows me. He knew I would hear, and I would tell. I would not let anything stop me from telling. After his words there was only quiet, very deep quiet. Then a huge bomb exploded and the garage and cars were destroyed. The house where we were shook with the bomb. Jorge put his hand on Geraldina, patting her back so she would not cry. He wanted to keep her silent. If they knew only a door separated us from the campus, they would have killed us too. In the quiet we went to look out the window again. There were soldiers there, with camouflage uniforms, and visors on their caps. I was afraid. How are the Fathers? I think I knew.

Very early in the morning, while it was still dark, I was sitting on the mat with my back against the wall wondering what could have happened, what sort of destruction? At that moment, Father Nachito came, I am sure, I am sure. He came at maybe five o'clock, and he had his briefcase for all his papers. He came through the door holding the briefcase, smiling and laughing, wearing the blue shirt and gray pants he had on earlier in the day. That is true, really true. I saw him at 5 o'clock, but now I know he had passed away a couple of hours before. But in that moment I did not think he had passed away. I was feeling my life was destroyed and my body was still cold, like ice cold! He appeared to me laughing, holding the briefcase.

When I remember, my mind feels like a tight, tight fist. It is hard, very hard, for me. Never has anything like that happened, never! Maybe I was crazy, I told Jorge. He said he did not see Father Nacho.

"I saw him! I saw him! I am sure," I said.

"No, you were dreaming," Jorge said.

"No! I was not dreaming! I was awake!" After all the destruction, I was waiting, awake, until the morning. We heard the soldiers, even whistling. The soldiers were inside the campus. The strange thing is that when I saw Father Nacho, he was happy. Very happy and smiling, and he had his briefcase.

In the morning, as I came out of the shower room, the UCA guards came to talk to us through the window. One said, "I was *so* close to the soldiers! I was quiet when they were shooting!" They saw the army too. Others besides us saw the soldiers. Jorge said to them, "Did you see what happened inside the house?"

"We did not go in," the UCA guard said, "but we saw bodies on the floor."

I asked, "Do you know what happened last night over there?"

"Yes, we know," they said. "We saw the bodies."

Those guards refused to leave the campus from the big gate because they did not want the soldiers to see them. They asked Jorge to open the door where we were to let them pass through, and he did. At that moment we only thought to let them out. Now I wonder why they did not report to Casa Cinquenta? They were quiet and did not tell Padre Chema.

I was already thinking the worst from the uproar in the night, but after the guards said it was true, oh, my gosh. I told Jorge, "Let's go, go inside (the campus)." It was just getting light, and we went to see. In the guest room I saw the women, two women hugging in the first room. I thought, "Oh, my God, they are nuns." But I turned back because I had my little daughter and I did not want her to see. I thought they were nuns because that room was for guests. Elba and her daughter must have stayed there because, after the six p.m. curfew, nobody could be in the street. You cannot go out after curfew. They stayed to sleep until the next day, but that night somebody came and killed them. Immediately I thought, oh, nuns here, but no, they were not nuns, it was Elba.

I saw the bodies of the priests on the lawn. "Ooooh, Father Ellacu," I said his name when I saw him. I thought he was in Spain. He was one of those killed. I had just cleaned his office on Saturday, and I knew he was in Spain. I did not know he had returned until I saw his body on the grass. Father Segundo never liked robes, but Father Ellacu was in a brown robe. Father López y López always slept in his clothes. There was Padre Nachito, in his blue shirt. Dead. Blood on his head. Oh, Nachito. Now I knew what was terrible, what had happened. But Padre Nacho was happy during dinner and playing the guitar for the Fathers. I think he was the last to die, because after he yelled there was silence.

Jorge kept our daughter where we had slept, and I started running to tell the priests at the provincial house what happened. I saw Teresita, a neighbor and a payroll clerk at the university. She saw me and asked, "Lucía, why are you here so early?"

"*Vinieron a noche, mataron a los padres*! They came and killed the Fathers last night!" I told her.

"Oh, my God!" she said, and went directly back into her house, not going to the university. Later, when we were in Miami and the investigators did not believe we stayed at the campus that night, I told them to ask Niña Teresita. She saw me there early that morning. I went to Casa Cinquenta because I knew the guards did not. They should have reported; they worked for the UCA.

When I got to the provincial's house, Elba's husband, Señor Ramos, was standing in the doorway talking to Father Estrada, a priest that worked with the provincial. I think the father did not understand what Señor Ramos was saying. I told Father Estrada, "The soldiers killed the priests in the campus, and they are on the ground there in the garden." I pushed past them and ran to Father Chema's room. He was standing before the mirror shaving. He dropped everything and came running to the campus, still in his bathrobe. Father Saínz ran after him, all were running to the campus, to the massacre.

At six or six-thirty in the morning President Cristiani said on the radio that the murder of the Jesuits was by the guerrillas. How did he know that? Did he see that? We saw soldiers on the campus, and we knew that it could not have been guerrillas that killed the priests. We saw guerrillas at our house in Soyapango, we saw guerrillas often, and we know how they dress. It was not guerrillas. And it was not guerrillas dressed in military uniforms. No. It was soldiers. We saw. Later Father Ibis told us the soldiers drank every beer they had in the refrigerator. Jesuits had one room complete with provisions. When the soldiers went looking for more people, they found beer and wine.

Father Estrada said to me, "Leave! Go! Run away, so no one will shut you up! We cannot protect you now, not even in the provincial house! Hide!" I was confused. Why hide? I did not do anything wrong. The only place I could think to go was my mother's in Antiguo Cuscatlán. No one was in the street in Colonia Guadalupe that morning, but as we left the house at 15–16 Cantábrico, we saw soldiers. I kept my eyes down. I had things on my head, the mats, and Jorge had Geraldina on his shoulders. It was a big, big group of soldiers. Where did they think we came from? We could not have come all that way from Soyapango by that hour.

We went to my mother's. It was tiny, and we did not fit, but I could not think where else to go. We were there from Thursday until Monday. We took the mats that Father Nachito loaned us. It is curious that for those days Jorge and I did not comment between us about what happened. We were mute. No comment. Only my brother, Óscar, told me when I saw him, "Luz, you be quiet! If you were there, you shut up!"

We expected some of our friends and neighbors from Soyapango to come to stay at the Walter Deininger School because of the war. Many people came out of Soyapango and came to that school. But that morning we did not see those we expected. But one of my cousins saw me. He said, "Didn't you work for those dead people?" Before I could answer, Jorge took my hand and gave it a tug to tell me not to answer my cousin. Jorge pulled me and said, "Don't talk." There was a soldier standing there, and he could hear my cousin. It was better to deny. At that moment I did not feel bad to deny.

I knew the funeral for the Fathers was on Sunday. I did not want to go because there were many people there. I had pain in my heart, and I could not watch a burial. I preferred not to go. The same day Jorge tried to go to our home in Soyapango. The war made that impossible. On Monday I told Jorge that I would go to work at the provincial offices because I had keys to open it. I had the key even to the provincial's office. Jorge said okay, and he would be with our daughter until I came back. When I went inside the provincial office, there were several priests and one woman. There I met María Julia Hernández, and I had confidence in her. I felt trust, and I started to talk, to talk about what I saw. I could not stop. I was crying and I could not stop. I had been mute all weekend, but now I was talking and crying about what I saw.

She asked me, "Is it true? Are you sure?"

"Yes! I will show you, I will show you!"

Together we went with a man named Brother Francisco to the empty house where we stayed and I showed her the window where we saw soldiers. They stood in the window, and they walked to where the soldiers shot the priests. They knew we could see the yard near the priest's house.

She said to me, "Lucía, you have a problem."

"What is my problem? I am telling the truth." Until that moment I was ignorant. To say the truth for me is better. It is better to be honest.

"You can't be here," she said. "Where is your husband?"

I explained that he was at my mother's patio with our daughter.

They took me to the Spanish embassy, but at that time I was still ignorant. Why are they bringing me here? I did not understand that I was in danger. The Fathers came, Father Pedroza, Father Pedraz, Father Chema, and Father Saínz. They tried to tell me that I needed to leave. "Leave to where?" I was asking. I wanted to tell Jorge what happened to me. What are they talking about? I have no place to leave to! I understand now, but many years have passed. I never thought I would go to another country. That was never in my mind. For me, to tell the truth to find the criminal who did it was a good thing. I did not think I needed to leave my home just for telling the truth.

Father Pedraz and Father Saínz went to get Jorge and our daughter at the address I gave. Jorge was very surprised to see the priests arrive. He did not know them, but they said to him, "You need to accompany us to go to your wife at the embassy. Prepare your belongings." They told him, "Right now you can know nothing." Our belongings were our clothes we were wearing, and the two mats Father Nachito loaned us on November 15.

I was at the embassy. I was *extranada*, so very upset over what had happened. For years and years after the Fathers died, I was upset. No one knew how much they meant to me or how close I was to them. I always see them as parents, because they showed things to me like parents would. They empowered me with faith and to be important—you are not alone, you are with us. It was like the family I never had. They gave me stability, confidence in myself. They had respect for me, and they taught me self-respect.

I became exhausted, and my mind was tight like a fist. What is good? What is bad? I am telling the truth, but for this they take me out of my home? How can this be? The Fathers brought Jorge and our daughter and we stayed at the Spanish embassy on Monday night. On Tuesday, a judge came to take my testimony. He asked questions, and he seemed very angry at me. The padres said nothing. On Tuesday, at about 4:30, when we finished the meeting, Jorge asked me, "What did you say?"

"They asked me if I saw something. I saw soldiers. I told the truth."

There were many people in the living room. The judge was very, very angry. I did not understand why he was angry, but I continued telling the truth. Somebody to one side was writing everything. I was only telling. At that time in the meeting, the two groups divided. One group was for the Fathers, and one group for the government. For that we had a lot of pressure.

Then they asked Jorge, "On the fifteenth of November, did you see the soldiers too?"

"Yes."

They asked how many? He told them.

We started at 2:30 p.m. telling what happened the night of the fifteenth. At 5:30 p.m. somebody came in and said, "Take her out of here! It's possible that the Spanish embassy will be assaulted." It was almost time for the curfew.

The Spanish ambassador told me, "We cannot protect you."

They took my daughter and Jorge in one car, speeding to the French embassy. When I finished, they put me in another car, speeding, speeding through to the French Ambassador's home. It is up high on a hill in San Benito, a private area. The French had a lot of security, maybe twenty-five guards, and the Spanish did not. We had to get there before curfew. No one could be out after curfew.

My eyes were blind, only thinking of what happened to the priests and of telling the truth. I did not pay attention to who was there listening. I don't remember how many or who they were. I did not have a good understanding because I did not read the newspaper or watch the TV.

We gave more testimony in the morning on Wednesday. Father Saínz said, "Jorge, Lucía, it is very important for you to leave the country, to go to another place. Soldiers will come to kill you if you stay here because you were a witness. You must go, you must go."

I was confused. "Where can I go? I have nowhere to go."

"You cannot stay. Your life is in danger."

"But I am telling the truth."

"Yes, but they want to kill you for it."

"Where can I go?" I remembered one time talking to Father Ellacu after he came back from a trip. I asked him about Miami, where is it, and what it is like. He told me Miami is close to El Salvador. He knew because he passed through there on his trips. I asked him because I am curious. He told me Miami is close, maybe four hours by plane, and everybody speaks Spanish.

When Father Saínz said I needed to go, I remembered my talk with Father Ellacu and I thought, well, when they discover the killers, then we can come back home and not stay there too long.

"What about my job?" I still did not understand. I was stubborn. "I will lose my job, and I did not do anything." The dangers for us did not reach my mind. No. "I do not want to leave my job here," I told him.

"You will get another job wherever you go," Father Saínz tried to tell me. "Wherever you go, Jesuits will help you. You can go to *España*, *Francia*, they will help you," the Padre said. "Don't worry. I will pay for everything for you. Over there are Fathers waiting for you."

This helped my faith a little bit. Wednesday night we stayed at the French embassy. We were to go to the airport in the morning for a plane to Miami. I had all the keys to the offices at the UCA. I also had the keys to the provincial, the master key that unlocks every room. I kept it, and I never lost it. I was worried about that.

In the morning we went to the airport at the right time, but the plane was gone. It left without us. The Fathers were confused and upset with this. Father Saínz sat with us at the airport, and we waited. One of the men from France, maybe the ambassador, said he was going to Miami on another plane and we could go with him. I sat waiting, holding our daughter and talking to Father Saínz. He said, "Lucía, I am worried for you because you do not deserve this."

I said, "Don't worry, Father. I spoke the truth. The truth is the truth. You don't need to worry."

All he said was I better go to another city.

Jorge was waiting with me, but he got up to walk around. He went to a room with a television to watch it. Suddenly, Father Saínz jumped up and yelled, "Jorge! *Venga*! Come over here! Come to me!" We did not notice that Salvadoran soldiers with radios approached and stood all around Jorge. He was so close he could hear their radios say that those people from the UCA are at the airport to go to the United States. When Father Saínz yelled, it made the French soldiers guarding us jump. The French told the Salvadorans, "Move away! Move back!" They went to get Jorge and bring him back to us. The French soldiers stood all around us from that moment. Father Saínz was praying, praying, praying, because he was our company to the airport. Maybe he thought the Salvadoran soldiers would get him and us all at once.

American Ambassador Walker came to the airport that day. A man pointed to us and said, "They are Lucía and Jorge Cerna." He looked at us with *desprecio*, scorn. He did not say hello or shake hands or anything. He seemed angry. A man named Richard Chidester was with him, and we learned Chidester was going with us to Miami. Everyone said Jesuits would be waiting for us in Miami.

I asked Father Saínz what would it be like to be in an airplane. He told me it is like a living room, comfortable, not scary. I took all the keys from my purse and gave them to him. I explained the job I did for the provincial and for the rectory. I gave over the keys, and he said "Okay, Lucía."

My life changed in one moment to another moment, immediately. That is fast. Big change. But I think also if we were not there, would it still be a mystery, a secret about who killed, like it was for Monseñor Romero? We were there that night, but we had just come in the afternoon before and several hours changed our life. But I never thought my life would change. I just thought to tell the truth. They were not grateful; they were angry and making enemies. I was a housekeeper. I never wrote about anything political, only telling the truth, but they did not like it.

We never saw Father Saínz again. He sent postcards when he traveled from Miami or from Spain saying he wished good things for us and that he prayed for us.

Mary Jo Ignoffo

"They died in community," said Jon Sobrino, SJ, many years later. He had been a member of that same UCA Jesuit community and had survived only because he was traveling.

> It could have happened differently; it could have been that Ellacuría, the main enemy, would be the only one killed. But there's

> an important truth—a providential one, if you will—in their being killed in community. That's how their lives and works had been, with joys and tensions, with virtues and sins, but always following a single, well-defined line. In this way the martyrs expressed how the Society of Jesus is all of its members. It is a body, not a sum of individuals, some of them brilliant and some ordinary.[1]

In ways that we non-Jesuits may not easily comprehend, the sense of community at that house, on that campus, in that province, extended around the globe to every Jesuit household and workplace. From San Salvador to Tokyo, from Rome to San Francisco, from Brussels to Lima, those who died and those who mourned were fused in that moment when the eight gave their lives and their liberty in a desperate proclamation that the poor must be heard. I believe that the most ardent prayer of the priests who died that night was for relief and respect for the people of El Salvador.

Controversy is nothing new for Jesuits. Throughout the almost five hundred years since Ignatius of Loyola founded the Society of Jesus, Jesuits have been lauded and reviled, praised and persecuted, sometimes at the same time. A widespread suppression of the order in eighteenth-century Europe lasted forty years. Often they have been suspected of manipulating popes and governments. Mostly they have dedicated their lives to education by establishing universities and colleges across the globe. Of the six Jesuits murdered in 1989, two bore the name of the order's founder—Ignacio—and one, like Ignatius, was a Basque. Jesuits work and live and die in every country, under every circumstance. Yet the assassinations that occurred at the UCA in the early morning hours of November 16, 1989, were more than anti-Jesuit. Post-assassination university vice-president Charles Beirne, SJ, wrote that the murders were an attempt to "kill the university . . . [which had] served as a creative and critical conscience for the nation and an agent for genuine democracy."[2] The murders were a crime against the majority of people in El Salvador.

Over time, the details of the events at the UCA on November 15 and 16, 1989, came to light. According to some soldiers who were on the campus that night,

---

[1] Jon Sobrino, SJ, "The UCA Martyrs: Challenge and Grace," lecture at Santa Clara University, November 5, 2009, Archives and Special Collections, Santa Clara University.

[2] Charles J. Beirne, SJ, *Jesuit Education and Social Change in El Salvador* (New York: Garland Publications, 1996), 14.

> the operation involved three concentric circles. One group of soldiers kept a distance from the Jesuit residence, others encircled the building, some climbed on the roofs of neighboring houses. Finally, a smaller group did the actual killing. After encircling the house where the Jesuits were sleeping, the soldiers began to bang on the doors. Simultaneously, they entered the lower floor of the building, destroying and burning the offices. Those who encircled the Jesuit residence yelled at the priests to open the doors. The priests rushed out the back door.[3]

Private Óscar Mariano Amaya Grimaldi had been allocated an AK-47 that had been captured from the FMLN. Amaya stood over the priests after they were ordered to lay face down on the ground. Sergeant Antonio Ramiro Avalos Vargas, the youngest of the shooters that night, just twenty-three years of age, raised an M-16 machine gun that had been issued to the Atlacatl Battalion two days earlier. "Let us begin,"[4] he reportedly said, and shot Amando López and Juan Ramón Moreno.

Amaya held the AK-47 close to his victims' heads, and shot Ignacio Ellacuría, Ignacio Martin-Baró, and Segundo Montes. The oldest of the priests, seventy-one and already dying of cancer, Joaquín López y López, had not come out of the house with the others. When he appeared in the doorway, Corporal Angel Pérez Vásquez shot him.

Deputy Sergeant Tomás Zárpate Castillo found two women in a room holding each other. He had been directed to shoot Elba Ramos and Celina Ramos. A short time later, when the women were heard groaning, Private Sierra Ascencio shot Elba and Celina again.

Amaya told investigators that he "drank a beer in the residence kitchen afterwards and stayed around to join in shooting up the building."[5] A few grenades and bombs were detonated at other areas of the campus. Some men used a flamethrower to torch offices, books, and computers. The offices Lucía had cleaned for years, bookcases and file cabinets full of archival material important to the university and the nation, were torched and reduced to ash.

---

[3] Lawyers Committee for Human Rights, "The Jesuit Case: The Jury Trial" (la Vista Pública) (New York: Lawyers Committee for Human Rights, September 1991), 16.

[4] United States Congress, Interim Report of the Speaker's Task Force on El Salvador, April 30, 1990, 23, available at www.cja.org/downloads/Jesuits_Interim_Report_on_Task_Force.pdf. Often referred to as the "Moakley Report."

[5] Lawyers Committee for Human Rights, "The 'Jesuit Case," 23.

The details of the devastating crime were really quite simple. Orders given, orders obeyed. Lucía has always maintained that soldiers act upon orders and thus higher-ranking officers must have been responsible. Her basic logic turned out to be accurate. Earlier that night Colonel René Emilio Ponce, chief of the Armed Forces, Joint Staff, with General Juan Rafael Bustillo, commander of the Air Force, and three other colonels, ordered Colonel Guillermo Alfredo Benavides to kill Father Ellacuría and leave no witnesses.[6] In turn, Benavides issued orders to his subordinates. Neither Ponce nor Benavides was at the UCA that night.

After leaving the UCA, Major Carlos Camilo Hernández Barahona and Lieutenant José Vicente Hernández Ayala reported to Colonel Ponce back at Joint Command headquarters and detailed everything that had happened. They presented a briefcase containing photographs, documents, and money that the soldiers had taken from the Jesuits' house a few hours earlier. It belonged to Ellacuría, and he had carried it back from Spain. Ponce told them to destroy it. In the meantime Colonel Benavides sought out Lieutenant Colonel Manuel Antonio Rivas Mejía, head of the CIHD (Commission for the Investigation of Criminal Acts). Rivas told him that the weapons used in the assault should be destroyed so that if ballistic tests were carried out, they would not be identified. Rivas wondered about the arrival and departure logs for the Military College and suggested that they be destroyed as well.

As Lucía and Jorge emerged from their hiding place in the early morning, so did a few others. Elba Ramos's husband had already discovered the bodies. The UCA security guards decided to absent themselves and exited the campus through a door that Jorge opened for them. Lucía's worst fears paled in comparison to reality. Here were not accidental war casualties, people caught in an unfortunate crossfire. The bloody-headed bodies lying on the ground were "destroyed." She lost her friend Nacho, "still in his blue shirt." And seeing Father Ellacuría unnerved her. She thought he was in Spain, and so therefore should have escaped the massacre.

After alerting Father Tojeira and the other Jesuits at the provincial house, Lucía was not sure what to do next. She and Jorge collected their things to set out for her mother's little room. Stepping from the safety of 16 Cantábrico and onto the street, they encountered soldiers

---

[6] United Nations Commission on the Truth for El Salvador, *From Madness to Hope: The Twelve-Year War in El Salvador*, report of the Commission on the Truth for El Salvador, S/25500 (1993), Part IV, B, 1.

of the Atlacatl Battalion. When she described how frightened she was that they might detain and question them, I asked, "Did you recognize any of them from the night before?"

"I put my eyes down," she said, incredulous that the soldiers did not wonder where they had come from. There was no reasonable explanation for why they were walking on that street at that early hour. She held her breath as the soldiers of the Atlacatl Battalion passed.

Tojeira called Richard Howard, SJ, who worked for the Jesuit Refugee Service (JRS) in El Salvador. The day before, Howard had been ferrying food and medical supplies to people in the back country. His shipment had been confiscated by the military, and on the morning of the sixteenth, as he sat writing a report of what had happened on the previous day, he received Tojeira's call. The provincial explained to Father Howard what had happened at the UCA, that six Jesuits and two women were dead. Tojiera asked Howard to go personally to tell the archbishop because telephone service was so unreliable. Richard Howard carried the news of the massacre at the UCA to Archbishop Arturo Rivera y Damas.[7]

Tojeira contacted the Jesuit leadership in Rome, informing Father General Peter-Hans Kolvenbach, SJ. His predecessor, the former Superior General Pedro Arrupe, SJ, was gravely ill when he was informed. Years later, Jon Sobrino said that Arrupe "was very sick—in bed, and barely able to say a word—when they were murdered. The nurse, a Jesuit brother, who gave him the news, said that Fr. Arrupe began to cry. It was all he could do, but in his tears, he was giving himself completely."[8]

That very day an article appeared in the *Washington Post* about the "execution-style" slayings. The article is remarkable for how close to the truth it came in the hours immediately after the massacre. Official investigations, on the other hand, dragged on. The case did not come to trial for almost two years; even then, the results were outrageously unjust. Yet that same day journalists Lee Hockstader and Douglas Farah reported: "Witnesses reported seeing more than twenty armed men in uniforms enter the house between 2 a.m. and 3 a.m., apparently through a back door blown off by an explosive device. There was no fighting in the area, which was in the hands of the army and police under the state of emergency and night-hours curfew imposed by the government."[9] If the case had been handled by the *Washington*

---

[7] Richard Howard, phone conversation with Mary Jo Ignoffo, February 23, 2012.

[8] Sobrino, "The UCA Martyrs."

[9] Lee Hockstader and Douglas Farah, "Six Priests, Two Others Slain in San Salvador," *Washington Post*, November 17, 1989.

Post rather than the Salvadoran government or the American embassy, more questions would have been answered. "Uniformed men" and "the area in the hands of the army" are two descriptors also reported by Lucía Cerna.

A quotation from an unnamed American diplomat in the *Post* article is most intriguing. "What is scaring me rigid," the diplomat said, "is that the right wing is taking over. I think Cristiani has lost control." The article says that "several analysts attributed the killings to the extreme right." If the *Washington Post* reporters were able to discern these realities within one day, and they were acknowledged by an American embassy official, it is curious that the investigations, accusations, obfuscation, inept trials, and sentencing took years. President Cristiani assigned the CIHD, headed up by Colonel Rivas, to investigate the crime—the proverbial fox guarding the henhouse. Rivas arrived at the crime scene at about 8:30 a.m. on November 16. The Salvadoran military, including the CIHD, saw any proponents of social change and realignment of land ownership or better conditions for the poor as archenemies. The enemy must be eliminated. The military carried out its mission.

While the American embassy officials mistrusted Ellacuría and believed he was a communist manipulating the FMLN from the university, there was never any indication they participated in the decision to eliminate him. They did, however, follow Ambassador William Walker's lead by covering up the crime to keep Cristiani and his government in power. Cristiani was someone the Americans could talk to. He had even been educated at Georgetown University, a Jesuit university. If he lost control of the government, the military men who manipulated death squads and stood further right on the political spectrum than Cristiani would likely take over. The United States believed it was in its interests to keep Cristiani afloat. In the wake of the UCA murders Ambassador William Walker and President Cristiani often stood side by side at the podium in press conferences, one echoing the other's perspective. From this venue both men denied that high-ranking Salvadoran military officials participated in the planning or execution of the crime. They both also publicly repudiated the testimony of Lucía Cerna.

How must the other Jesuits in El Salvador have felt? The tremendous grief must have been cloaked in very realistic fear. To be a priest in a country that announces death threats over the radio and displays signs reading "Be a Patriot! Kill a Priest!" one would already be aware of the danger. As Ignacio Martín-Baró—Padre Nacho—had reported, "There is an environment of the possibility of being killed at any moment of the day, and the possibility of being involved in a violent clash at any moment, and you have to count on that."[10] Nevertheless, the audacity and brutality of the murders must have been profoundly disturbing, the destruction of friends devastating.

In looking back Lucía recalls two episodes that remain completely inexplicable to her. In the pre-dawn hours of November 16, 1989, after the "scandal" and destruction at the campus but before morning, Lucía reports that Padre Nacho came to see her, happy and laughing, carrying his briefcase. This experience felt so real that she asked her husband if he too had seen Padre Nacho. She was sitting, she says, not lying down; she was awake, not sleeping. She experienced a powerful presence of Padre Nacho before she knew for certain that he was dead, yet hours after he actually had died. Was she comforted, I wondered, by seeing him laughing and happy? The experience did not bring comfort or consolation, just confusion.

Almost as confounding as encountering Padre Nacho was the fact that for the entire four days immediately after the massacre, Lucía and her husband did not discuss it between themselves. To this day she cannot fathom why they did not talk about it. Understandably, they would not tell her elderly mother or talk about it around their little daughter. Why did they not so much as mention it to each other? Perhaps reacting with classic symptoms of shock and trauma, pushing recollection from consciousness, allowed them to carry on through those days, finding food and taking shelter on a tiny patio.

A funeral for the victims was held on Sunday, November 19, 1989. Some foreign dignitaries flew in, and many priests and family members attended the service led by Father Tojeira and Archbishop Rivera y Damas. Other memorials were held all around the world. In New York on November 22, 1989, Joseph O'Hare, SJ, the president of Fordham University, said "The assassinations of November 16 pose, with brutal clarity, the question that continues to haunt the policy of the United States toward El Salvador: Can we hand weapons to butchers and remain unstained by the blood of their innocent victims?"[11] The question O'Hare posed is still haunting. It swirls not only over foreign policy, but also on the home front where gun control measures are debated and we seem unable or unwilling to make a firm decision in favor of the most vulnerable.

---

[10] Ignacio Martín-Baró, *60 Minutes,* April 22, 1990.

[11] Joseph O'Hare, SJ, "In Solidarity with the Slain Jesuits of El Salvador," St. Ignatius Church, November 22, 1989, New York, available on the onlineministries.creighton.edu website.

In California, at Santa Clara University a memorial mass was also held, and Stephen Privett, SJ, preached a homily, barely camouflaging his rage. "I am angry and disgusted," he said, "with the United States government's long-standing and blind adherence to a foreign policy that is misinformed and unjust."[12] Within days, SCU's president, Paul Locatelli, SJ, attended a demonstration at the U.S. Federal Building in San Francisco to protest funding of the Salvadoran military. He directed the placement of simple white crosses, each with the name of one victim handwritten in black paint, in front of the Santa Clara Mission Church. Not long after, someone removed the crosses, which in their crude simplicity are a sharp contrast to the pristine mission church and surrounding gardens. Locatelli promptly put them back, and they remain a quiet yet clear reminder of the martyrs and the people of El Salvador, and now that Locatelli has also died, of his fidelity with *los Salvadoreños*.

The day after the funeral at the UCA on November 20, Lucía reported to work at the provincial office. She did not know what else to do. At Father Tojeira's office she encountered a woman who spoke kindly to her. That woman was María Julia Hernández, the executive director of the San Salvadoran Archdiocesan Tutela Legal, a human rights advocacy of the Catholic archdiocese. Hernández had worked closely with Archbishop Óscar Romero, and his assassination galvanized her efforts to disclose the wanton violence of El Salvador. Under her directorship, Tutela Legal recorded a haunting "encyclopedia" of photographs and documentation of Salvadorans who had been victims of human rights abuses throughout the civil war. Undoubtedly, she was in Tojeira's office to record the latest atrocities. Tutela Legal became known as a highly credible source of the reality of life in El Salvador for the last twenty years of the twentieth century.

As Lucía spoke to Hernández and began to describe what she had seen the night of the murders, she found she was unable to contain her emotions. She could not stop talking, saying and repeating what she had heard and what she had seen. The story came out in a torrent of tears and sobs. Having spent the entire weekend "mute," with neither she nor Jorge mentioning to each other the events that they saw, the overwhelming emotions surprised her. The conversation with María Julia changed Lucía's life.

---

[12] Stephen Privett, SJ, untitled homily, Mass of the Resurrection, November 17, 1989, Mission Santa Clara, copy in Archives and Special Collections, Santa Clara University.

To verify Lucía's story, Hernández and one of the Jesuit brothers took Lucía back to the campus and stood in the window where Lucía said she had seen soldiers. Lucía never claimed to have seen the shootings, nor did she believe she could identify particular men. She was absolutely certain, however, that the men she clearly saw in the moonlight through an open window were dressed in Salvadoran military uniforms. Walking out to the place where the priests were shot, Hernández realized Lucía's story needed to be reported, and that doing so would endanger Lucía's life. She took Lucía directly to the Spanish embassy.

In 1991, Hernández wrote the foreword to *El Salvador's Decade of Terror*. In it she outlines the U.S. policy of funding the right-wing military and ARENA government:

> For Salvadorans, U.S. policy has represented one of the chief obstacles to improving human rights in a conflict that has already taken more than eighty thousand lives. We have had to struggle against our own problems, and in addition, we have had to carry an even greater burden: to fight the policies of the U.S. government toward El Salvador.[13]

Hernández was not a simple church worker. She had studied philosophy and law at the UCA, and she never stopped investigating, photographing, and detailing human rights crimes in El Salvador. Her records allow for a national historical memory, something that Martín-Baró insisted was so important to move a society forward. Bald-faced denials of human rights abuses are countered by Hernández's work. She was a strong intellect, with a very realistic notion of life in El Salvador. In her estimation, Lucía and her family were not safe in the country. They would be killed.

It is surprising that María Julia Hernández was not eliminated. She lived until 2007, when she died of natural causes. An obituary said of Hernández:

> Her unwavering faith in the social gospel and a liberating God of love and justice anchored her as she faced generals, presidents, ambassadors, death squads and international courts of law, politics and public opinion. Her ministry became a model, not

---

[13] America's Watch, *El Salvador's Decade of Terror: Human Rights Since the Assassination of Archbishop Romero* (New Haven, CT: Yale University Press, 1991), vii.

> just for El Salvador but for human rights advocates around the globe, from Latin America to the Middle East.[14]

If María Julia Hernández felt it was important for the Cerna family to leave El Salvador, we can be sure that it was.

The Cernas' exit from El Salvador was a circuitous series of mishaps and misinformation. Taken to one embassy then swiftly shuttled to another, it seems the family was a political hot potato. Even the commercial airliner on which they had a reservation took off without them. The understandably upset Jesuits wanted the Cernas safely out of the country. Tojeira did not trust the U.S. State Department, but he thought it could get the family into the United States. It would be another ten days before he knew that upon arrival in the United States, the family was turned over to the FBI.[15]

It was the French, though, who saved the Cernas during the week of November 20. First, when the Spanish embassy did not have strong enough security and would not be able to withstand an attack if word got out that witnesses to the UCA massacre were staying there, the better-armed French embassy took them in for the night before they fled El Salvador. Second, they secured the family at the airport as the Salvadoran military took note that the UCA witnesses were leaving the country. And finally, the French provided transport out of the country on a military plane. French Assistant Secretary of Humanitarian Action Bernard Kouchner changed his flight plan to Paris to include a stop in Miami specifically to accommodate the family.

Even from a geographical distance the murder of the Jesuits and the women had a major impact on me. I spoke to Dan Germann, and he told me what he knew of the events. Later on that November 16, I went to the regular daily mass held at the Saint Francis Chapel at Mission Santa Clara. Theodore Mackin, SJ, presided at the gathering of about twenty, some of whom had not heard the news from the UCA. Mackin was quietly resigned. "There will be more to go in their places," he predicted. And there were. By some estimates, well over a hundred Jesuits volunteered from around the world to go to the UCA. Mackin spoke of another disturbing fact. He explained that the shooters "scooped out their [the priests'] brains," a coup de grâce as punishment for their so-called role as the intellects behind the guerrilla forces.

---

[14] Eileen M. Purcell, "María Julia Hernández: Human Rights Advocate from El Salvador Dies," October 15, 2008, in Oscar Romero Faith and Solidarity Network in the Americas (SICSAL-USA).

[15] Lawyers Committee for Human Rights, "The 'Jesuit Case,'" 26.

Mackin's description stuck with me, almost as ghastly as the murders. The *Washington Post* article of that day reported, "Several had chunks of flesh gouged out, and the brains of two of the victims shot in the head lay several feet from the bodies."[16] It is curious that of all the various reports that have been generated since the crime, including the Moakley Report, the U.N. Truth Commission, and the Lawyers Committee for Human Rights, none refers to this act. The reports identify the shooters, the weapons, the officers who gave the orders, but do not describe the *coup de grâce*. If the triggermen pulled out the brains, it is not included in their descriptions of that night. If others besides the shooters removed brain matter from the victims, it is not documented.

The murderers could take the brains, and hearts for that matter. Nothing can silence their spirits and souls, crying out as Padre Nacho did, "This is an injustice!" As the soldiers followed orders and killed the priests and the women, they destroyed some of the best intellects in the country. In the brutal violence they also succeeded in generating international revulsion. Now the Salvadoran government and its U.S. ally would have to explain how its rhetoric of democracy, freedom, and human rights got turned inside-out and justified cold-blooded murder.

As an American, I felt partially responsible. There is no getting around the fact that the U.S. Congress signed the paychecks of the Salvadoran military officers who acted with impunity against their own people for more than a decade. Foot soldiers, receiving training from the United States, saw themselves as freedom fighters on the frontlines of America's war on communism. We underwrote many of those atrocities in María Julia Hernández's horrific encyclopedia in hopes of a communist-free and democratic El Salvador. When, I wondered, will we reexamine policies so that our hands are not stained, as Joseph O'Hare's memorial said, "by the blood of their innocent victims"? Reflecting on the events and listening to the words of Dan Germann, Theodore Mackin, and Stephen Privett invited me to embrace Lucía and her family when I met them. I was also drawn in by her ability simply to speak the truth.

---

[16] Hockstader and Farah, "Six Priests, Two Others Slain in San Salvador."

Lucía Cerna cleaning the office of Ignacio Martín-Baró, SJ, at University of Central America José Simeón Cañas (UCA), 1988. Photograph by Ignacio Marín-Baró. Courtesy of the Cerna Family.

Baptism Geraldina Cerna, 1991. Jorge and Lucía Cerna, Dan Germann, SJ, and Geraldina, in Nobili Chapel, Santa Clara University. Courtesy of the Ignoffo Family.

James Torrens, SJ, at Mayer theatre, Santa Clara University, 1996. Photograph by Charles Barry. Courtesy of the Santa Clara University Archives.

(left to right) Geraldina Cerna, Mary Jo Ignoffo, Lucía Cerna, Dan Germann, SJ, Patrick Ignoffo, Jorge Cerna, 2000, at a celebration for Dan's fifty years as a Jesuit. Courtesy of the Ignoffo Family.

Fidelia Amaya, the daughter of Rufina Amaya, demonstrating how her mother escaped the massacre at El Mozote in 1981. Rufina died in 2007, and her daughter, despite her own health problems, carried on her mother's witness so that the people of El Mozote are remembered. 2011. Photograph by Lisa Ignoffo.

Paul Tipton, SJ, circa 1989, President of the Association of Jesuit Colleges and Universities and former President of Spring Hill College in Mobile, Alabama. Courtesy of the Cerna Family.

The clothing worn by Padre Nacho when he was killed. Students from Notre Dame San Jose are reflected in the photo. 2011. Photograph by Lisa Ignoffo.

The likeness of Archbishop Óscar Romero on a mural in Santa Cecilia. 2011. Photograph by Lisa Ignoffo.

A representative of the ARENA party met with students from Notre Dame San José in 2011. He explained that he believed it was better to forget what is in the past, and to move ahead. The background portrait is Roberto D'Aubuisson, founder of the ARENA party and one-time presidential candidate. He formed death squads to eliminate adversaries, and he ordered the assassination of Archbishop Romero. D'Aubuisson is still revered in some quarters in El Salvador. Photograph by Lisa Ignoffo.

Geraldina Cerna helping in her father's bakery at home in Soyapango, 1989. This is one of the few photographs from life in El Salvador that the Cernas have. Courtesy of the Cerna Family.

Lucía Cerna, circa 1984. Courtesy of the Cerna Family.

Santa Clara University President Paul Locatelli, SJ, interviewed by the press after a memorial mass, November 17, 1989. Photograph by Charles Berry. Courtesy of the Santa Clara University Archives.

Ignacio Ellacuría, SJ (right) receives an honorary doctoral degree from Santa Clara University President William Rewak, SJ, 1982. Courtesy of the Santa Clara University Archives.

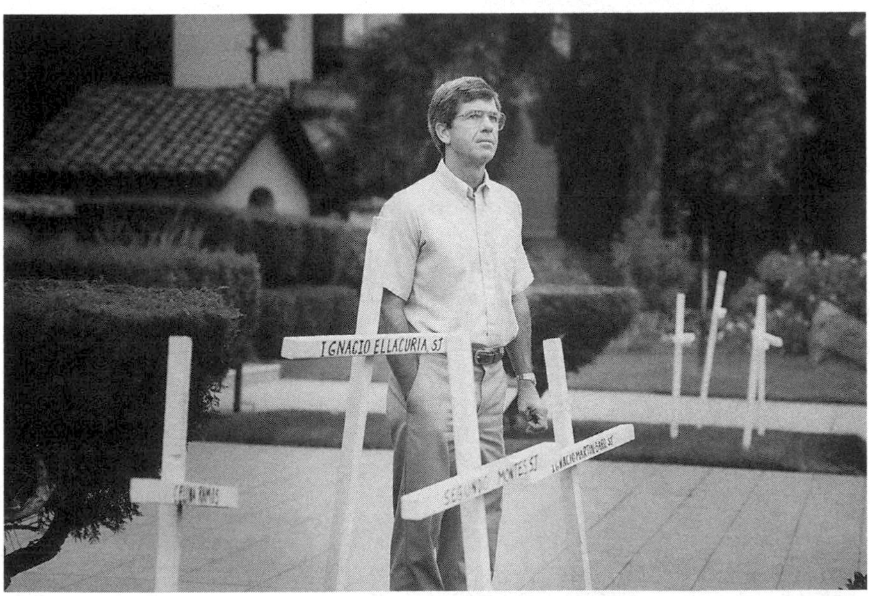

Stephen Privett, SJ, with memorial crosses at Mission Santa Clara, 1993. Photograph by Charles Barry. Courtesy of the Santa Clara University Archives.

Jon Sobrino, SJ, at the UCA, 2013. Photograph by Edward Fassett, SJ.

José María Tojeira, SJ, at the UCA, 2013. Photograph by Edward Fassett, SJ.

A 2013 photograph looking from the window where Lucía and Jorge stood toward the site of the murders. Lucía never claimed to have seen the actual shootings. However, she was certain that the men she saw from the window were Salvadoran soldiers. Photograph by Edward Fassett, SJ.

A 2013 photograph of the window from which Lucía and Jorge Cerna saw Salvadoran soldiers on the campus on the night of November 15 and 16, 1989. They stood inside the louvered window. From this spot, Lucía clearly heard the shouts of Ignacio Martín-Baró. The landscape is far more dense than it was in 1989. Photograph by Edward Fassett, SJ.

Contemporary photo of the site of the murder of five of the Jesuits. The area was planted with roses by Obdulio Ramos, the husband of Elba Ramos and father of Celina Ramos. Photograph by Edward Fassett, SJ.

Monumento a la Memoria y la Verdad, Antiquo Cuscatlán. 2011. Photograph by Lisa Ignoffo.

Memorial to Elba and Celina Ramos at the UCA. Photograph by Lisa Ignoffo.

6

Sacrificed

November 23–December 3, 1989

Lucía Cerna

Early in the morning of November 16, President Cristiani told the people through the radio that the guerrillas killed the Fathers. I knew that was not true because I saw the men in uniforms. I thought the president and investigators wanted to know the truth. After the days in Miami I knew they did not want truth. They did not want to have witnesses. Nobody knew we went to the UCA on the afternoon of November 15. Twenty-five years have passed since that incident, but I do not forget. Step by step, I remember everything. The president and the investigators did not like it. But here is the truth.

A French diplomat allowed us to go with him on a French airplane. I do not remember his name, but he spoke Spanish. He was kind, and I could tell he had a beautiful education. He had very fine manners. We went to Miami on Thanksgiving. We did not know what Thanksgiving was. When we went on that airplane I could not call my mother, Jorge could not call his parents. Nothing. But soon our families knew everything because it was on the radio and in the newspaper there. It was announced that Jorge and Lucía went to the United States because of what they saw at the UCA.

Mr. Richard Chidester told us that U.S. Ambassador Walker instructed him to give us protection. Another man named Rivero was with us too. He said he was stationed in Mexico with the American DEA (Drug Enforcement Administration). He had been called to El Salvador one day before to accompany us. We never thought to ask why a drug agent would accompany us. An FBI agent named Sánchez was also told to stay with us. I was quiet and did not talk on the airplane. A man from Colombia approached me and asked me something. Chidester came and said, "Don't ask her anything." I thought in my mind, why does he not want me to talk?

When we landed in Miami the French diplomat said goodbye and went on to France. We were with Mr. Chidester, Agent Rivero, and Agent Sánchez until more people came and spoke to us in a little office. I think one was a reporter, and there were two priests and two more FBI agents. "*Hola, que tal*?" they asked. The two priests were Jesuits from Cuba, and they talked to the FBI agents in English. After they said hello and asked how the flight was, they told us to go with the FBI. "They will care for you," the priests said.

The FBI took us to the Radisson Hotel, and we spent two days in the same room under their supervision. From the first day, everything was unplugged. The television did not work. Jorge tried to let our daughter watch a cartoon, but it did not work. When he asked, the guard said "No TV for you." There was no telephone. I wanted to call one of those priests we met at the airport. We never asked why we could not have a telephone. We were mute. We did not know how to be with American police. On the third day they moved us to another floor. We were in a room, and a guard was in an adjoining room with an open door. I didn't know if maybe it was a special room for the police and criminals like us. I was still trusting. I had never been in a hotel before. I remember the long, dark hall; for me, it was ugly. I did not know about hotels.

On Saturday evening a priest from Miami gave us clothing. It was a big, big dress and a shirt. Immediately I saw they were too big. "Can you bring me a needle and thread?" I asked him. "Then I will make the clothes smaller to fit us." He spoke in English to the FBI agents, but I do not know what they told him. He promised to come to see us. He never did. Still I had nothing warm I could put on my daughter. I do not know, even today, why that Father never came back. He only gave the clothes and left.

The agents came for us early on Monday morning to take us to the FBI offices for questioning. I was willing to tell what happened. Sincerely, I thought they wanted my testimony. They did not allow Jorge and me to be questioned together. When they questioned me all morning, Jorge was in the waiting room with our little daughter. Then the agents went to lunch and left us for a long time in that waiting room. They brought back hamburgers for us. We never had American fast food before, and especially not a hamburger with thin potatoes. There was a McDonalds in San Salvador, but it was so expensive. It would cost seventy-five *colónes* for our family to have lunch. We could not afford that. In America they gave us fast food.

In the afternoon they questioned Jorge, and I stayed with our girl. She was wearing the same tank top and shorts that she wore when we left El Salvador. She had never been in an air-conditioned office before, and she was cold. She was good and quiet and did not jump on the furniture. She sat close to me or close to him. Sometimes she said, "Papi, I want to eat," or "Papi, I want to drink." We were careful with the girl and never let her be without one of us.

On Monday evening Chidester told us: "Jorge, Lucía, tomorrow a doctor from El Salvador is coming. Whatever he asks you can answer, no problem. You can say anything to him." I wondered why a doctor was called. Maybe because I had high blood pressure and they thought I might die. Don't they have doctors here? I wondered. When we were alone, I asked Jorge, "Who is sick here?"

"I don't know," Jorge said.

Breakfast at the hotel was a scrambled egg, bread, and coffee, and milk for Geraldina. We ate breakfast in the hotel and came back to the hotel to eat dinner in the room. We were not accustomed to bothering people to ask for food. We never asked for food, especially if we had breakfast. But it was important for my daughter to have lunch. They gave us fast food to eat in the waiting room of the FBI office. Then at night they had food brought to our room. I thought that must be how Americans eat. I did not know there was a dining room we could go to. They did not allow us. But then I did not even know how to push a button in an elevator. They opened the door and closed the door; we never opened the door.

The doctor came with us to the FBI offices so that he could question us too. He talked to Jorge first, and he said rude things to him. He told Jorge I must have provided favors to the priests. When he spoke to me he did not ask medical questions. He asked me about the Jesuits, what kind of men they were. Humble, I said. Good men. He argued with me, "I don't believe it! They are bad men, and they have guns."

"You must be confused about them," I said. "They are philosophers and psychologists, intelligent men, they do not have guns. I clean their offices, and I know them. No guns." I knew them.

On Tuesday, I had to explain again, step by step, what happened and what we saw on November 15 and 16. But they had in mind that the priests were communists. They asked the question again and again, "Why were you with communists?" I told them no, they are not communists. They are philosophers, psychologists, geologists. They have a lot in the mind and talk to you, but no guns, *no armas*, nothing they defend, only with talking with the person. They did not believe me. The doctor insisted again and again that they had guns in the UCA. I know they do not have guns. I cleaned the house. I cleaned the offices. I know, I know, but they did not believe. The word is stubborn. Those people were stubborn!

They did not believe me. They accused me of being a communist and guerrilla. I am not. I don't know what that is. I kept saying, "I am a housekeeper." I couldn't stop crying, explaining, and they did not believe my explanation. I was totally upset because I felt like I lost my family. The agents and the doctor did not care that I had a deep, deep loss. They did not want me to tell. I know that the guards and some neighbors at the UCA also saw what happened, but they did not come forward. In El Salvador many people do not tell the truth because it is very scary. I told. I kept repeating and repeating, like a crazy woman. The doctor and the agents became more and more angry with me. They said I must have been a prostitute for the priests. I cried again. "Doctor," I said, "you should ask the guards, because they saw and they were closer." He said no, even President Cristiani was saying that the men who came to the residence wore short pants like the guerrillas. I said no, that is not true. The men wore complete uniforms. He said I was *una communista*.

They continued with questions, but this time they said that I did not even work at the UCA. I told them to check the payroll books because my name appeared there for many years. Then they did not believe that Jorge and I stayed in Casa 16 the night of November 15. "How do you know?" the doctor shouted and hit his hand on the table. "You are not telling the truth!" He jumped from his chair, he was so upset. He put his hands on his waistband and pulled at his pants. "You must be Superwoman to hear and see so much! I don't understand how you were there. You are not telling the truth!" I told him to ask Niña Teresita, the neighbor and payroll clerk at the university who saw me that morning as I was running to the provincial to tell the bad news.

It was from 7 a.m. to 7 p.m., twelve hours each day of telling the truth always, but they did not believe. They laughed when I was talking and they said, "The priests don't like you anymore." They insulted me, they did not believe me, they offended me horribly. One man touched his gun as he was talking to me, laughing at me and saying I must be a prostitute.

I tried not to cry when I had my small daughter with me so she would not worry. I looked at her, and I wanted to talk to her, to keep her comfortable and keep her with me. My heart was very tight with emotion, and I felt very alone. Why did the Jesuits not send someone with me? I am sure, I am absolutely sure if Father Ellacu or Father Nachito or Father Segundo Montes were alive in that moment, any one of them would have been with me, behind me. I am sure of it. According to my thinking, I was helping. They would not leave me alone to be sacrificed.

The doctor demanded, "If you were scared why would you look out the window that night?"

I explained that I heard fighting against the priests, and I wished to go help. How [could] I stay sleeping? I was close to those priests, every day. "I am sincere," I explained. Later that day, Jorge overheard one of the men refer to the "doctor" as "colonel." He understood from that moment that this was not a doctor but a Salvadoran officer. Now we know it was Colonel Rivas. Jorge told me, "They do not want the truth." He thought the colonel came to put pressure on me for saying the soldiers killed the Fathers. More hostile questions came for Jorge:

"If you had your own house in Soyapango, why were you at the university?"

"To be safe from the war."

"How could you see the soldiers?"

"Through the window."

"What color was the uniform?"

"Some green, some black."

"Why do you say it was not the guerrillas that killed the priests?"

Jorge said, "The area was surrounded by soldiers. Do you think they were sleeping? How could guerrillas get in?" Those investigators did not like that answer, and they were even worse to Jorge after that.

Colonel Rivas asked about my family, and I told the truth. He asked if my brothers were guerrillas, and I said no. They are a carpenter and a brickmason. "Where do they live?" he asked me. I told. I never thought he would send soldiers to find and beat my brother, but he did. Even while we were still in Miami, he sent the soldiers. I did not know this for many weeks. My brother was beaten by the soldiers after they found him at the small room where my mother lived. She had to watch, and she was old. It was terrible, terrible. When I called her after several weeks, she cried and cried, "Lucita, *ay* Lucita, I don't know what happened but the soldiers beat your brother! They came looking for guns." Even today he blames me and does not speak with me. We were children together, always together. But no more.

My family was split apart by the injustice, injustice! If you are telling the truth, they should be grateful. They did not want to hear the truth, but we did not understand that. It was confusing to us because we kept thinking they wanted the truth. "*Loca, vieja loca*," the colonel told me. "You are a crazy old woman."

I think that Richard Chidester wished us to say we saw nothing. "Do you know how much we are paying for this hotel?" he asked my husband. By then we had been in that hotel about six days.

"Do you know how much we are paying and how much the food costs?"

"I don't know and I don't care," Jorge told him.

"Why do you not cooperate with us?"

"We are cooperating with the truth."

Colonel Rivas told me, "Well, you know the priests hate you now, don't you? They will not let you work for them ever again."

"That is my problem," I said, "not yours. I will cook *pupusas* and set up a stand in the street to make money."

He shook his hand at me and said if we did not say what he wanted he would send us back to El Salvador.

"Fine. Put me back in my home there," I said. "I don't want to be here anyway." He thought we wanted to be in America. I just wished to go home.

Then something curious happened. He started to insist that "the priests are not dead. You are crazy. All this is in your head."

I said to him, "If you do not believe me, why did you take me out of El Salvador? I would have stayed. Why am I here if I am not saying the truth?" He kept saying I had gone crazy. I could not understand. I asked Jorge, "Am I crazy?" "No," he said.

Colonel Rivas was worse with Jorge. "They'll kill you," he told my husband. But Jorge has been threatened before, and he knows how to use a gun.

"I'll be okay, send us back," he told the colonel.

After that the colonel spoke in a low voice, menacing, to Jorge and said, "If you were in El Salvador now, I would cut your balls off!" Jorge was shaken when he came out of the interview room. I thought he was going to be sick. They said awful things to him. Torture happens to many Salvadorans. We know about the torture. They will kill you, they told Jorge again and again.

Jorge said quietly to me, "It's okay. I will wait with a .38. I will show you how to use a gun. We will be safe."

One of the days at the Bureau, a janitor came near collecting the trash. He spoke Spanish quietly to us. "Why are you still here?" he asked. All I could say was I don't know, I don't know. This is America, and we thought they wanted the truth. In fact, we never, never thought that they would not like us. We were cooperating to help find the assassins who committed the massacre. And they told me the Jesuits hate us. I had to believe I would be okay. I thought, okay, fine, I will work someplace else. But the investigators, the Americans and one Salvadoran, were liars. They threatened us and did not allow us to have any outside communication. For one week we were abused. What happened to freedom in the United States? Now since we are citizens we have learned about the Constitution. What happened in Miami? It was a big abuse. That's it.

On Wednesday the colonel gave the order "*no comer ahora*," no food today. They did not allow us food all day, and we had a small child with us. I had a packet of powdered milk in my purse, and I prepared the milk with hot water from the faucet for our daughter. As adults we can survive with only drinking water, but not the child. The powdered milk needed a bit of sugar, so Jorge asked Chidester to bring sugar when he came from lunch, and he said he would. The men went out to lunch from 1 p.m. until 3 p.m. and left us in the FBI office. When they came back, they did not mention sugar or that we were hungry. Now we know that it is very easy to get a small packet of sugar in any restaurant, and even so, they did not bring it to us. We had explained step by step, repeating the same story again and again. After that day, when they didn't give food all day with our hungry four-year-old, I told Jorge, "I do not want to continue it! I will tell them I don't know!" After three days I had enough.

Jorge is serious, and when something is true, that's it. I was serious too, but for me three days was enough. Monday, Tuesday, Wednesday, I told [the truth]. On the third day, I wanted to try to escape. I told Jorge to keep our daughter and I would climb out the window of the hotel. I thought I would find somebody, anybody walking on the street, who would tell me where there was a church or a priest. Jorge did not like this idea.

"What I think is that we need help. I'll go. You take care." I was so desperate that I didn't even think about how high the building was. I thought that my body was strong enough to try to escape. I had faith to walk on the street and go to find somebody and find a church. I wanted to leave there. We were looking through the window, and I was telling Jorge how I would go. Then one of the guards, Rivero, came in and said to move away from the window. "Stand back, for your protection."

That night we spoke quietly so the men in the next room would not hear. "I am exhausted. I don't want to say the same thing again. I want to go home. I want to say that I don't know anything, that I did not see anything. Please tell them that I will say I did not see anything." I told Jorge that now I would say I did not see anything.

Jorge said to me that these men do not like that we say soldiers killed the Fathers. They want to hear that we don't know anything. Tomorrow we will both say we don't know anything about that problem.

"Okay, Jorge," I said. He asked me to practice. "Now, what is our answer?"

"How can I say that I was not there? We were there! We were there!"

"No. You tell you were not there. Say you were not there. Then we will be set loose, we will be free."

I agreed. "I did not see."

"You tell you were not there, you did not see anything."

"I was not there," I said. "I am retired from telling that story."

Jorge went to talk to Richard Chidester, who was in the next room guarding us that night. He told him that we would say we were not there. Chidester came and sat down on the bed next to me. "*Está segura, señora*?" Are you sure? When I said yes, he hugged me and said, really? He was very happy.

Next day we went again in that office and [they asked], are you sure you [were] not there? Yes I am sure, I don't know nothing. Are you sure again, are you sure you don't know? Yes, I don't know. Send me home, send me home. I hoped they would now send us back to El Salvador.

Thursday we went to the office, maybe at 7:30 in the morning. I went first. They hooked me up to the machine. I told them and the machine that I did not know anything. I did not know what the machine was, and they did not tell me. Now I understand that it is a lie-detector machine, but then I did not know. The man began to ask me questions, and all my answers were "no, no, *no sabemos nada*." The man left the office and went to talk to the other guard. He came back [saying], "Ahhh." He was upset. He yelled at me more questions. He did not like what the machine was doing. I did not care. I yelled back, "I did not see! I did not see. I do not know!" It was hard to figure out. They were angry if I told the truth and angry if I did not.

Then I waited, holding Geraldina while Jorge went to tell the same. "Did you and your wife stay in that house that night?"

"No."

"Did you see anything?"

"No. *No sabemos nada*." We don't know anything.

After those three days I finally discovered the truth. They did not want to hear about what I saw. They thought I was wishing to stay here, in the United States. I thought they would say, "Okay Señora, I understand what you say. You can go back home now." But they did not, and that worried me.

We got to go back to the hotel early. Even though the man with the machine was not so happy because now it said we were not saying the truth, Chidester was very happy. He slapped Jorge on the back, "Good man, Jorge," and was so happy, like he wanted to be Jorge's friend. "Thank you, Jorge, thank you. Today we will call for somebody to come for you."

Later Jorge told me he was worried about what they would do with us after that. At that time Jorge did not tell me that he was worried that we might be killed.

One hour after that in El Salvador they put on the radio that the Cernas are liars. President Cristiani said Jorge and Lucía Cerna are *mentirosos* (liars) and *guerilleros* (guerrillas). They accused us so that nobody would believe what we say. They accused us so no one else would be a witness. Finally, they were happy when we decided to say we were not there.

We had to go to the offices on Friday again, and they cut a bit of our hair and took pictures. I don't know why and I did not care. I just wanted to go back home. When they finished their questions and started to speak in English, I left the chair and said, "If we are finished now I would like to leave." I got up to leave.

It was a big mistake that the Jesuits did not send a priest with us. I think they trusted the Jesuits in Miami to help. They were no help. For me, still it is a deep, deep loss. Finally, I just said I did not see. My problem is in that time long ago I trusted people. Now I think even if I see, I will say I did not see. But then I felt no choice. How could I be quiet? I could not be quiet. How would I live knowing the soldiers killed them?

While I was in Miami I couldn't stop crying and explaining, and they did not believe my explanation. I was totally upset. We are in the United States, and they do not like to listen to the truth! Where is the freedom? They never wanted my help to discover who killed the priests. They sacrificed me to hide the truth. The priests were destroyed, and they also killed me but left me alive.

Mary Jo Ignoffo

As millions of Americans sat down to Thanksgiving dinner in 1989, a French military jet taxied toward the Miami International Airport terminals. The Cerna family had weathered its first plane trip. For better or worse, other firsts awaited—the first time in a hotel or an elevator, the first experience of air conditioning, the first meal in a restaurant, and the first time eating American fast food. The adventure of it all was lost on the couple, stunned at being pulled out of their home, work, families, and culture. And Lucía grappled with the brutality of the deaths of her employer friends.

In the Miami terminal the French diplomat bid *adieu* and relinquished his role as protector to Richard J. Chidester, the legal advisor at the U.S. embassy in El Salvador, who escorted the couple at Ambassador Walker's direction. Also along on the trip at the behest of the U.S. government was Agent Fred Rivero, a DEA investigator who had been called in from Mexico to join Chidester, and FBI Agent Sánchez.

Two Jesuit priests from the Miami area greeted the small entourage in a room near the customs checkpoint at the airport. The priests asked the Cernas about their flight, then spoke English to Chidester and the agents. The Cernas thought it odd that the priests switched to English when everyone in the room spoke Spanish. After about ten minutes the priests said goodbye. Paperwork was completed, and the agents transported the family to a Radisson Hotel near the airport. The Cernas stayed at the hotel from their arrival on Thursday, November 23, until Sunday, December 3. They visited briefly with one of the Miami Jesuits on Saturday, and he gave them a few pieces of used clothing.

Lucía expected, as Fermín Saínz had explained, that the Americans wished to have her testimony in order to investigate the crime. She believed that upon giving her testimony, she would be met by Jesuits who would find a job for her. She would try to be patient until returning to El Salvador.

Beginning on Monday, November 27, the Cernas were rousted from their bed at the Radisson in order to have a light breakfast before arriving at 7:30 a.m. at the offices of the FBI. The couple was not questioned together, and when one was being questioned, the other sat in the waiting room with their daughter, most often for about four hours at a time. Either Lucía or Jorge was ushered into a private office to answer questions. No accommodations were made for the child. This routine went on through Thursday of that week.

On that first day of questioning the couple gave complete testimony, exactly the same as they had given in El Salvador on November 21 at the Spanish embassy. That evening, Richard Chidester explained that in the morning, a doctor from El Salvador would be part of the questioning, and they could freely discuss anything with him. Lucía thought that perhaps they had called a doctor because of her high blood pressure.

"*El Doctor*" joined them in the morning for the early session of questions. The Cernas presumed the doctor wanted the truth, but they were confused by his angry demeanor.

"*Estas una guerillera?*" he demanded. "Are your brothers *guerilleros*? Where do they live?" The information she provided about her brothers was transmitted to El Salvador, and within days, her younger brother Óscar was located in the room where his mother lived. He was beaten, in front of the mother, almost to death, as the soldiers continually demanded to know where his stash of weapons was located. Lucía did not know this took place for several weeks. From that time her relatives quit speaking to her. If she called them by telephone, they indicated that they did not want to hear from her. She has not spoken to her beloved Óscar since.

As the doctor hurled insults, threatened torture, used foul language, and demeaned them, their confusion changed to raw fear. Lucía Cerna knew rich and poor. When she was accused of being a communist, she explained that she did not read the newspaper, did not watch TV, and was not interested in politics. She was a housekeeper.

As James Torrens reported in his 1990 interview of Lucía, the interrogators insisted that she repeat the details. "Tell it to me again." Torrens quotes her as saying: "Every time they themselves wanted to say anything they shut off the recorder. They had a lot of things *(un montón de cosas)* to tell me."[1] The doctor accused Lucía of providing sexual favors to the UCA Jesuits, of guerrilla and communist affiliation, of abandoning her older children, and of being an unfit mother. He did not believe her when she insisted that there were no weapons in the rectory and that the priests were good people. Dumbfounded that the investigators did not believe she was telling the truth, Lucía repeatedly said: "I am sincere. I am saying what is true." What she did not understand was that they already *knew* the truth. They were not after the truth. Their task was to make sure that a simple housekeeper did not stop the flow of billions of American dollars to the Salvadoran

[1] James S. Torrens, SJ, "U.C.A.—The Witnesses Talk," *America* (November 24, 1990), 398.

military. Rivas set out to break her, and break her he did. These many years later she is still recovering from the inquisition.

The investigators presumed Jorge was a guerrilla. In their mindset, anyone who was poor was necessarily an insurrectionist. Rivas threatened him, in no uncertain terms and in graphic detail, with torture and castration if he returned to El Salvador. All the while the Americans sat and allowed this treatment to proceed uninterrupted except for occasionally accusing the couple of being communists. As Jorge was being questioned and Lucía sat in the waiting room with her daughter, she noticed a telephone. As she picked it up to dial, one of the agents said: "What are you doing? Hang it up."[2]

On the third day, November 29, the couple realized that the "doctor" was in fact a Salvadoran colonel. At that moment, more than at any time since the murders at the UCA, they knew their lives were in jeopardy. That was the day that the colonel announced, "*No comer ahora*"—no food now—and neither the couple nor their daughter was given food or water, at the colonel's command, for the entire day. Lucía seriously considered climbing out the hotel window in search of some kind of help.

The colonel was Lt. Colonel Manuel Antonio Rivas Mejia (Colonel Rivas) of the Commission for the Investigation of Criminal Acts, an agency established with and funded by American dollars to investigate human rights abuses. By the time he interrogated the Cernas, he had already counseled the Atlacatl commander Benavides to destroy the weapons used in the murders. Rivas had been at the military headquarters the night of the massacre and knew full well that the assassinations had been carried out by the Salvadoran military and not the guerrillas.[3]

Rivas, like many in the Atlacatl Battalion, was a graduate of the School of the Americas. His interrogation tactics appear to be a page right out of the SOA's training manuals. One of the manuals has instructions to follow if there are two interrogators, for the "questioners" to play "good cop, bad cop." Throughout the manuals the term *questioner* appears in quotations, implying that the so-called questioner may be something quite different. Intended as a technique to be used on a suspected enemy or criminal, in Lucía's case it was used on a woman seeking political asylum. The manual directs:

---

[2] Ibid., 400.

[3] United Nations Commission on the Truth for El Salvador, *From Madness to Hope: The Twelve-Year War in El Salvador*, report of the Commission on the Truth for El Salvador, S/25500 (1993), 43.

> The two "questioners" display opposing personalities and attitudes toward the subject. For example, the first "questioner" displays an unsympathetic attitude toward the subject. He may be brutal, angry, or domineering. He makes it plain that he considers the subject the vilest person on earth. His goal is to alienate the subject.

The role of the second "questioner" was played alternately by the FBI agents and Richard Chidester. The latter kept a low profile, did not use foul language, but implied that he could turn the family over to Rivas. The SOA manual continues:

> At the height of alienation, the second "questioner" takes over, sending the first out of the room. The second "questioner" displays a sympathetic attitude toward the subject. . . . The second "questioner" can state that he cannot afford to waste time on sources who fail to cooperate and imply that the first "questioner" might return to continue the "questioning." . . . This technique . . . works best with women.[4]

The tactics were successful in pushing Lucía to the emotional brink and intimidating her into recanting her previous testimony.

The Cernas were directed to take polygraph tests after they changed their story. Lucía explained to me that she was afraid of *la machina*, the polygraph. Would it be painful? The administrator of the test became increasingly frustrated, indicating that he expected their story of having seen nothing to be true. Perhaps in the only moment when she was strong enough to respond, Lucía returned his consternation by shouting back at him. She told me she thought these Americans were crazy. First, they asked for the truth and didn't believe it when they heard it. Then they wanted lies, which the machine identified. What did they want? She just wanted to go home. Both Jorge and Lucía failed the polygraphs. This allowed Colonel Rivas and President Cristiani to proclaim that the Cernas were liars. Jorge explained to me that within an hour of recanting their story, radio broadcasts in El Salvador, heard by his parents and brothers and sisters, labeled him a liar and a communist guerrilla.

---

[4] Manuelas de la Escuela de las Américas, "Interrogacion," J10–11, available on the soaw.org website, SOA Manuals.

On December 9, 1989, President Alfredo Cristiani offered $250,000 as a reward to anyone offering information about the killers' identity.[5] Needless to say, the Cernas never collected the reward. At the same press conference Cristiani stated that Lucía Cerna had admitted lying to the Salvadoran inquiry the day before she flew out of El Salvador. Lucía did not lie to the inquiry, and she did not say that she had lied to the inquiry. Cristiani is the one who lied. This would not be the last lie from his lips.

The next day, on Sunday, December 10, Archbishop Arturo Rivera y Damas, while giving a homily at the Cathedral in San Salvador that was broadcast on the radio, gave explicit details of the mistreatment of Lucía Cerna at the hands of U.S. officials in Miami. The *Los Angeles Times* reported that Bishop Rivera y Damas, "quoting an American attorney who has since interviewed Cerna, described the interrogations as 'aggressive and violent.'" The bishop went on, "Instead of being protected, as officials of the U.S. Embassy in El Salvador had promised, she was subjected . . . to a veritable brainwashing and to the blackmail that she would be deported if she was not telling the truth."[6] The bishop had learned details from the human rights lawyer R. Scott Greathead, who interviewed Lucía in the meantime. Her elderly mother and aunt, who had not yet heard from Lucía, listened, horrified, to the radio broadcast of the bishop's words that morning. The two women wondered what had become of Lucía.

Back in El Salvador, Colonel Rivas, accompanied by "U.S. embassy personnel," went to the Military Academy and met with Colonel Benavides. In Salvadoran court in 1990, Rivas denied having this meeting, but facts proved otherwise.[7] The U.S. embassy under Ambassador Walker had offered protection to any witness to the Jesuit murders who would come forward. One did, but her story did not align with the political agenda of the United States and the Salvadoran military. Unfortunately, Lucía discovered that she was not under protection, she was under arrest. When word got out about how Lucía had been treated by U.S. officials, other would-be witnesses kept silent.[8]

---

[5] Martha Doggett, *Death Foretold: The Jesuit Murders in El Salvador* (Washington DC: Georgetown University Press, 1993), 281.

[6] Tracy Wilkinson, "Archbishop Assails U.S. on Murder Probe," *Los Angeles Times*, December 11, 1989.

[7] Lawyers Committee for Human Rights, "The Jesuit Case: The Jury Trial" (la Vista Pública) (New York: Lawyers Committee for Human Rights, September 1991), 35.

[8] Doggett, *Death Foretold*, 221.

Father J. Donald Monan, president of Boston College, underscored the fact that after Lucía's treatment, other witnesses would resist coming forward. He explained in an interview for *60 Minutes:* "If we are ever going to get to people who authored the crime, even though they didn't pull the triggers, we are going to have to have informants come forward to talk about what they know. And in this case the only people we know who came forward [the Cernas and U.S. Army Major Eric Warren Buckland] came to the United States and suffered the consequences of having provided their information. That discouragement of people to come forward with information is fundamental to this case."[9] Father Monan saw the Cernas and Buckland facing similar treatment by U.S. officials.

The case of Major Buckland is one that has never been fully explained. He had been a military advisor in El Salvador and had befriended Colonel Carlos Avilés, a special assistant to Colonel Emilio Ponce. Major Buckland reported on about December 15, 1989, that his friend, Avilés, told him he knew that Colonel Benavides carried out the military operation to kill Ellacuría. Buckland's statements caused an uproar in the Army, the State Department, and the Salvadoran military.

Buckland underwent questioning, just as Lucía had, by the FBI. After the interrogation, like Lucía, he recanted his story. Buckland was subjected to polygraphs, just as Lucía had been, after he changed his story. The polygraphs indicated that he was lying when he recanted. Avilés denied the conversations and even the friendship with Buckland. Ultimately, each insisted he knew nothing of the murders. Major Buckland's version of events means that Colonel Rivas, to whom Benavides first confided, was heavily involved in the coverup. Officials at the American embassy had befriended Colonel Rivas and "consistently protected" him.[10]

Notwithstanding the FBI tactics used on the Cernas, the most egregious offense was that the Department of State allowed a Salvadoran colonel to threaten and intimidate them. Richard Chidester lied to the couple, telling them that the Salvadoran man was a doctor, one with whom they could speak freely. Later, after the Cernas told human rights lawyers and the Jesuits about the days of questioning, they discovered that the FBI never reported the presence of Rivas. When the Moakley Commission investigated, FBI documentation makes no mention of Rivas's presence in the interrogation of the Cernas.

---

[9] *60 Minutes,* April 22, 1990.

[10] Doggett, *Death Foretold*, 221.

In an interview for *60 Minutes* in April 1990, Ambassador William Walker was called to task by commentator Ed Bradley for the way the Cernas were treated. Walker defended the procedures even as Bradley asked why Lucía Cerna was treated more like a criminal than a witness. Neither Walker nor Chidester explained why Rivas was introduced as a doctor. Neither acknowledged that under their watch, Lucía was accused of prostitution and Jorge was threatened with dismemberment. And when the United Nations Human Rights Committee identified Rivas as a participant in the coverup of the crime, neither Walker nor Chidester ever admitted it was a mistake for the Americans to allow Rivas to interrogate the Cernas. The only possible purpose for Rivas, who already knew the perpetrators, to interview the Cernas, was intimidation.

What happened during that time period is a shameful episode where witnesses were interrogated as criminals because the scene that they described did not support the political agenda of the United States and the Salvadoran military. Their treatment violated the most basic civil rights afforded anyone arrested for a crime in the United States They were not allowed counsel, by attorney or priest; when they asked to telephone family members, they were denied. The telephone and television in their room were disabled, leaving them unable to make any outside contact or hear any news. They were threatened, bullied, and denied food.

The speaker of the House of Representatives, Thomas Foley, established the Moakley Commission, named for the committee chairman, Congressman John Joseph "Joe" Moakley, to look into the murder of the Jesuits. The committee's interim report, issued on April 30, 1990, said that it had made a request to the FBI to interview the agents who questioned the Cernas. The request was denied, the report stated, but the concerns of task force members were alleviated with assurances from the director of the FBI that the Cernas "were treated in a courteous and professional manner . . . great care was taken to ensure that the witnesses were comfortable . . . and FBI personnel took the Cerna family to sightsee various parts of Miami."[11] The report concluded, "Given the limited nature of what Mrs. Cerna actually saw on the night of the murders, there would have been no motive, even under the most cynical of circumstances, for the U.S. Embassy or others to have sought to discredit her statement."

---

[11] United States Congress, Interim Report of the Speaker's Task Force on El Salvador, April 30, 1990, 23, available at www.cja.org/downloads/Jesuits_Interim_Report_on_Task_Force.pdf. Often referred to as the "Moakley Report."

Father Tojeira, the Jesuit provincial of Central America, had a different view. "The U.S. Embassy made a commitment to accompany the witness to Miami and to hand her over there to the priests of the Society of Jesus. Instead, the witness was handed over to U.S. police agents for eight days under the pretext of watching out for her security and with no attention to the wishes which had been expressed here."[12]

What motivated Rivas? Why would he leave El Salvador when he himself was a leading investigator? The couple had already been deposed in El Salvador and had given full testimony. Why would he travel to the United States? As head of the CIHD (Commission for the Investigation of Criminal Acts), shouldn't he have been directing the investigation at the scene of the crime? Perhaps in being out of the country, he removed himself from contact with his guilty colleagues. It gave him a role to play to elevate himself in the estimation of the Americans. It allowed him to play investigator but at the same time be out of the explosive environment of El Salvador.

Furthermore, why did it take three twelve-hour days to interrogate the Cernas when they had already given and signed sworn testimony? Even the janitor was surprised at how long the Cernas were detained, and presumably, as he cleaned the FBI offices, he had seen many people come and go, few being detained for such a long period.

The truth of the matter of the Cernas stands more solidly on Tojeira's interpretation than the Interim Report. Tojeira understood quite clearly that no one in Miami was interested in Lucía's security. While the report lists the inappropriate behaviors and missteps of the investigators, it does not take into account how personally costly the experience was for the Cernas. The report was issued in April 1990, perhaps too early to assess the damage done to them.

What became of Walker, Chidester, Cristiani, and Rivas? Walker and Chidester went on to a long career in the U.S. Department of State. In a *New York Times* interview in December 1989, Chidester said, "I find it appalling that these kinds of accusations have been made"—accusations that the Cernas were lied to, mistreated, bullied, and harassed. Chidester claimed, "We took every possible action to make sure her concerns and needs were met." He concluded that "Lucía never had anything." He continued, "There was no reason for her to leave

[12] Ibid., 24.

[El Salvador]."[13] Did he believe she could live in safety in San Salvador and go back to cleaning offices at the UCA? He must have discounted the fact that Lucía's younger brother had been beaten almost to death after she had given his address to Rivas.

A legal brief submitted for trial in 1991 by the Lawyers Committee for Human Rights (today's Human Rights First, a not-for-profit international human rights organization) succinctly states that the treatment of Lucía Cerna "served to define public perceptions of the police investigation and the U.S. role in the case." It goes on that she

> was the first witness to provide testimony placing soldiers on the campus at the time of the murders, fled the country under the protection of the Jesuits and European diplomats. U.S. officials [including Chidester], who said they wished to accompany Ms. [Cerna] to help her through immigration procedures at Miami airport, actually turned her over to the custody of the FBI. Belatedly apprised of what had transpired, the Jesuits felt deceived by U.S. officials, who had not mentioned the possibilities of FBI questioning, though they arranged for an FBI agent [Rivero] to be on the plane with [Cerna] out of El Salvador.[14]

Rivas was promoted to a full colonel a year after the Jesuit murders and then to second in command of the National Civilian Police (PNC) in 1992 after the Chapultepec Peace Accords. Rivas has never been held accountable for destroying evidence, obstruction of justice, or intimidating witnesses. He has slipped through the hands of prosecutors and is not on the list of defendants in the current court case for the Jesuit murders being held in Spain.

When the peace agreement called for the establishment of the PNC to replace the former security forces in El Salvador, it outlined requirements for commanders in the national police:

> Personnel of the National Civil Police must have a vocation of service to the community, a capacity for human relations and emotional maturity, and the conduct and physical condition required to serve as a police officer. They must also be suited to serving in a police force which is designed, structured and operated as a civilian institution with the purpose of protecting

---

[13] Elaine Sciolino, "Witnesses in Jesuit Slayings Charge Harassment in U.S.," *New York Times*, December 18, 1989.

[14] Lawyers Committee for Human Rights, "The Jesuit Case," 26.

> and guaranteeing the free exercise of the rights and freedoms of individuals.[15]

Colonel Rivas qualified!

The peace agreement also established a Truth Commission under the jurisdiction of the United Nations to investigate human rights violations by both sides during the civil war. Those investigations turned up conclusive evidence about the UCA murders and wartime atrocities. Ultimately, it maintains that 85 percent of the acts of violence in the civil war were committed by government forces, 10 percent by death squads, and 5 percent by the guerrillas.[16]

Cristiani finally conceded, on January 7, 1990, that "some elements" of the military may have been involved in the massacre, but he withheld an incriminating report from the Salvadoran court hearing the case. In July 1990, the president stated that guerrilla weapons had been found at the UCA the previous November. A year later he acknowledged that no weapons had ever been found at the UCA. On September 7, 1990, President Cristiani admitted in court that he had been at the Joint Command headquarters during the raid on the UCA on the night of November 15 until the early morning hours of November 16, 1989.[17] If Lucía had not come forward and sounded the alarm, that concession would most likely have come much, much later.

Where were the Miami Jesuits? Why did they not insist on seeing the Cernas? Could they not have extended more than some ill-fitting clothing? Richard Chidester gave one clue when he claimed the priests he met in the airport at Miami told him they "were not like the Jesuits in El Salvador."[18] The Cernas clearly remember that the priests were Cuban. When Lucía was interviewed in 1990 by James Torrens, she said when she met one of the Cuban priests, "he sweated a lot and seemed very nervous. He talked very little with me."[19]

Did the priests believe that the Cernas were communists, and did their antipathy to Castro's Cuba cause them to be less than sympathetic?

---

[15] El Salvador Peace Agreement, Chapter 2, Chapulapec, 1992. See United States Institute of Peace at www.usip.org.

[16] United Nations Commission on the Truth for El Salvador, *From Madness to Hope,* Part IV.

[17] Lawyers Committee for Human Rights, "The Jesuit Case."

[18] Whitfield, *Paying the Price*, 264.

[19] Torrens, "U.C.A.—The Witnesses Talk," 398.

Did they object to the writings of the Jesuits in El Salvador who had been assassinated? Or worse, could their own lives have been in danger? Death squads in El Salvador were known to have been directed out of Miami. Whatever the case, the Jesuits of Miami did not offer meaningful assistance to the Cernas.

What about other Jesuit leadership? When the Jesuit Conference in Washington DC inquired of the State Department several times over the course of the week of November 27, 1989, as to the whereabouts and well-being of the Cerna family, the conference was told that issues of Lucía's safety were being evaluated. In short, the Conference was lied to.

From November 17, when news of the massacre broke, through the week of the Cernas' interrogation, memorials for the slain victims were held around the world. It is not surprising that the Jesuits in El Salvador and in the United States were preoccupied and presumed that the Cernas were safe and as comfortable as they could be. On November 29, the same day that the Cernas were polygraphed, the UCA got a new president. Miguel Francisco Estrada, SJ, was appointed rector (and therefore president) of the UCA. One of the FBI agents demanded of Lucía, "Is that Estrada a guerrilla or not?"[20] He had not even started his job, and already the accusations had begun.

Undoubtedly, if the Cernas had fled to Spain or to France rather than the United States, they would have avoided the treatment meted out in Miami. The scars have not completely healed, even twenty-five years later. It is difficult for Lucía to separate the trauma of losing some of the people she held most dear to horrific violence from the interrogation in Miami. Healing from the first ordeal would have proceeded more quickly if she had not been subjected to the second. Lucía Cerna has not fully recovered from the tactics used on her and her husband by the State Department, the FBI, and the Salvadoran colonel who was invited to the interrogation. Her powerful words resound to this day: "The priests were destroyed, and they also killed me but left me alive."

---

[20] United States Congress, Interim Report of the Speaker's Task Force on El Salvador, 23.

7

Rescue

December 1989–1990

Lucía Cerna

Father Tipton rescued us from those police.

I knew Father Berra from the provincial's office in San Salvador. I did not know Father Tipton, but I knew if Father Berra was with him that we would be safe. Immediately when I saw Father Tipton and Father Berra, I told them, "I denied. I denied. The police did not want to hear what I saw, so I told them I did not see." I explained why I said that. After three days of interrogation, after telling the truth again and again, they just did not want it. "I understand now that they do not want the truth. I will not tell it. I have no money. I have nothing, but I want to go back to my home. Please help us!"

"Lucía, *paciencia*—patience," Father Berra said. "You come with us. We will keep you safe."

Father Tipton was very angry at them. He was yelling. He yelled a lot of things at the FBI agents about unplugging the TV and unplugging the telephone. He was a strong man with a big voice. We could not understand everything he said. "Take them away!" he yelled. "We will shame these people!"

Father Tipton did not speak Spanish, but Father Berra did. I remember the reaction after Father Berra and Father Tipton came to our hotel room. They ordered food for us. We had not eaten since breakfast. Now I know there was a lot of food in that place, but then I did not know, and we did not ask for food. We wanted to be polite. But we worried that our daughter did not have enough to eat or drink. I only wanted a little coffee and bread. I was too upset to eat.

When the priests came to our hotel, the guard was still in the adjoining room with the door between the rooms open. Father Berra spoke to us in Spanish, and we explained everything. He had a laptop.

I had seen big computers that the priests at the UCA had in their offices. I had never seen a laptop. Father Berra typed everything we said into that laptop. "Tell me what happened, tell me what happened," he said.

"*Tengo miedo*," I am afraid, I told him. Now that I denied, what would they do to us? Are we to be killed too? "Please stay here with us," I asked him. "You sleep in the bed, and I will sleep in the chair." That night, Father Berra stayed with us in the hotel room.

"Talk low and don't make noise," he warned me. He did not want the guard in the next room to hear us talking. As he wrote on the computer, I explained what happened three days back. I explained to Father Berra what happened, step by step.

The Fathers asked us to be interviewed by human rights lawyers. They spoke Spanish. The first thing I told the woman lawyer was that I denied, I denied. I could not go on like that. She said, "Don't worry, Lucía. Relax, relax."

"I want to go home," I told her.

"Right now it is not safe for you. You must stay here."

The next day we flew on an *avioneta*, a small airplane. The pilot was a friend of Father Tipton's. The priests did not ask permission of the FBI to take us. They just took us.

"Where are we going?" Jorge asked. Father Berra told us Alabama, and it was a place that looked like the UCA.

"I want to go back to my home," I told Father Berra but he said, "No, you cannot go." Everything was new for us. Even in the small airport in Miami. I saw someone get a can of soda from a machine. I asked Father Berra, how is it possible to have a soda from the machine?

"Here, you do it, Lucía. You have to learn," Father Berra said. Put in a dollar, push a button, and bring out one soda. I was amazed. For me, it was strange. He carried our daughter to the airplane and helped her into a seat.

Everything was new. We walked through a grove of big trees to get to an isolated house where we were staying. The house was solitary. I did not know it then, but Jorge—he was expecting someone to try to kill us in the night. Now he tells me, but then he did not comment on it. He did not tell me that he was waiting for somebody to come. No, when I went to the room, I did not want to leave that room. I was very cold. Miami is not cold, but Mobile was cold. The big sweater and socks and hat that Father Christopher Viscardi gave were a blessing. I did not want to change the clothes, just keep them on day and night. Even though they were friendly, I could not believe in those people.

When we were in Alabama, I was afraid to look at American people because of the bad experience in Miami. I thought everybody was the same, and I did not want to speak. Alabama was colder than Miami. Father Tipton asked a woman from Mobile to take us to buy coats. We had never worn a coat. We did not know about coats. We never even had a sweater before. That woman spoke Spanish and helped us buy coats. Father Tipton's mother brought clothes for Geraldina. She brought thermal pants and overalls with a pink sweater. Now our child was warm. His mother did not speak Spanish, but she was so sweet, a nice lady. I know she was worried about her son for his association to us. At that time I did not understand a lot of things, but I did understand that she thought someone would bang, bang, bang, to her son because of our trouble. She was not angry. She was worried. He was not worried.

I was totally depressed. I stayed in the room in Alabama, in that sweater with a hat pulled over my head, and I was crying, crying, crying. Suddenly I was very, very sick after the bad experience in Miami, after the FBI pushed and pushed emotionally. It is terrible what they do to people. Jorge tried to get me to come out and go buy some tea or something. I did not want it. I only stayed in that room. I did not want to leave that room. I would stay there and not go out. The refrigerator was full, but I did not want it and I did not want to cook.

Father Viscardi said, "Tomorrow I will take you downtown."

"No! Please! I do not want to go." I refused to go. I felt better hiding in the clothes. Father Viscardi was very good with us.

One night we went to a restaurant with beautiful round tables and tablecloths. Then Father Viscardi came and in Spanish told the cook, a very big woman, give anything to these people that they would like. All I wanted was a little coffee, only a little coffee, and a piece of bread. Still I could not eat.

"Where is here?" I asked the cook. "Where are we?" She did not know our past, and the Fathers did not tell her. She laughed that I did not know where I was.

She told me, "The Jesuit dining room in Mobile." Those big round tables! I thought it was a restaurant! I don't know how I survived, because when I came to Mobile, everybody was friendly, but nobody explained to me where Mobile was or that this was a university. But they offered friendship, and I understood that.

Jorge did not want to stay in the house. He went out and found a retired priest who was planting a garden. The priest did not speak Spanish, but he let Jorge help. Jorge told me the priest kept saying "Okay, okay, okay," but he did not understand Spanish. After Jorge helped, the father gave him a five-dollar bill. Jorge wondered whether to accept the gift. Finally he did and said thank you.

Father Tipton asked if we would agree to go to Washington DC to the Capitol to give the testimony. Yes, we would go. But I had a big conflict in my mind. I was worried and depressed, and I did not want to see American people. I didn't want to have more problems because I felt sick, really sick. We already gave testimony, and no one believed us. Father Tipton said we would fly to Washington. He would meet us there.

One of the secretaries was assigned to take us to the airport in Mobile. She came very late and when we got to the airport the plane almost left without us. We had to run, run, run through that airport. I was the last one, and they closed the door quick and said, "Sit!" The plane was full but for our three seats.

Father Tipton met us at the airport, and took us to the Capitol and we went to give our testimony again. He asked us to talk to Mr. Moakley. I did not know he was a congressman, or even what a congressman is. I was afraid, very afraid. How do I speak to Americans? Once I began to speak I was surprised. When I started to tell, I felt very fluent and the fear went away. I spoke in Spanish, with human rights lawyers translating. When I started to talk about the Jesuits, I forgot I was in America, and I talked and talked. There were many men there and some women, a lot of people writing. Ahhhh, a lot of people, but I do not remember the faces. I was asking myself, who are these people? because it was a lot of people, and all those statues in the hall! They listened and did not interrupt like in Miami, just asking questions. When I finished, Mr. Moakley said he had a question for Jorge.

"Why do you say that Salvadoran soldiers killed the Jesuits?" Jorge answered that he saw the soldiers through the window, and that he could clearly see that they were wearing the uniform of the Salvadoran solders. The uniform of the guerrillas is different, he explained, and we had seen many guerrillas.

Jorge and I answered Mr. Moakley even though at that time we did not know who he was. Later, Jorge told me he was nervous too, because he thought they would be like they were in Miami and refuse to listen. When we finished, Mr. Moakley said to everybody there, and I understood because of a translator, "These people are humble, but they say the truth." He said to us, "Take care," but I was disoriented and I did not know where I was. Mr. Moakley shook our hands. To us, that was respect.

We went to Father Tipton's home. He took us there and we stayed for maybe for four days. It was a big house in Washington DC. It had many rooms and a very large dining room. One night he came home to have dinner with us. He said that he just came from talking with the FBI and Mr. Chidester. He told us what he shouted at them: "You! You! You treated them badly and you are guilty of injustice! You put pressure on these people to hide information!" Father Tipton was a powerful, tall person with a very strong voice. I hope the FBI was afraid of him.

At dinner there were things I had never seen. They cooked a whole side of an animal—I don't know if it was lamb or beef or veal, but it was really, really big. As everyone came in with a plate, a man with a tall white hat cut one part and put it on the plate. It was delicious, but new for me. I was so serious at that time, looking at everything and everyone. I was not enjoying, just still sick. But I remember that meat.

The next day we went to the store and bought supplies for Jorge to make sweet bread for the priests. And I was to make *pupusas*. I stayed in the kitchen. I think there were many people there, but I was still afraid. I made *pupusas*. For me, it is strange to try to remember exactly. I remember that house, and a black priest who had a model train in the house. Maybe it was his hobby or he had worked before on a train. I don't know, but it was very realistic, very nice with little figures. I remember Father Tipton's big car, and going in the car, but I did not really look at Washington. Jorge remembers things in Washington, but I was not feeling happy. I lost all sense of humor or fun. We met with some people in the living room, and they spoke to Geraldina.

The house had very big stairs, and Geraldina wanted to run up the stairs, but she was afraid because at the top it was dark. Outside it was very cold, colder than Alabama, and there was ice on the ground. We had to be careful not to slip. This was very strange for us. My daughter was amazed by the ice. "Look, Mommy!" and she was laughing. Father Tipton sent his friend to take us to a museum. Jorge remembers well, airplanes from World War I and World War II, but I could not pay attention. I only wished to be alone, safe in the room. My heart was very upset. Jorge is different from me; he was not depressed. But I was, and I was feeling sick. We were both very serious to never leave our daughter alone, to lose her over there.

Father Tipton also had another house that was his own home where he lived alone. It was beautifully decorated but smaller than the other house. One day I saw that he was taking his laundry to the machine. I was so surprised. In El Salvador the priests do not do laundry. I thought to myself, a priest can't wash his clothes. I told D.J., his friend who was an interpreter for us, to tell Father Tipton that I would wash his clothes. I was doing nothing; I would like to wash his clothes for him. When D.J. told Father Tipton of my offer, he started laughing. He did not let me do his laundry. I was confused. Where are the servants? People have so much in America, but no servants? The life is so different.

Sometime in December, I don't remember what date, Jorge called his mother from Washington.

"Ah, *hijo*, son, where are you?" She asked. She was so upset to lose Jorge, her youngest son.

"I'm here," Jorge told her. "We are okay."

"Take care and be careful!" She said. "Be careful."

But what we can do?

Father Tipton decided to send us to San Antonio.

He wanted to mix us up with other Hispanic people. After Miami, Jorge never thought it was dangerous for us. But Father Tipton had experience and he knew that it was, so he changed our names. Our little daughter was Teresa; Jorge was Mario; and I was María. We were with those names, I am not sure how long.

After finishing in the Capitol and in San Antonio, I called my mother to tell her we were okay and don't worry. She was crying and crying, my mother. She told me, "Lucita, *aye* Lucita, I don't know what happened, but the soldiers came here to fight your brother!" They said he was a guerrilla, and they had a big fight with guns. He was upset and scared. When I called my aunt, she told me what happened and they blamed me for the situation of the soldiers fighting him. How did the soldiers find him? Then I remembered that I told Colonel Rivas where my mother lived. I never thought he would send his soldiers to hurt my brother! My mother had to watch her son get beaten in her home.

I felt myself against a wall. I never thought my mother's home would suffer from the soldiers. I told my mother and my aunt it was not my fault. My life changed so much. My brother has not forgiven me even today and does not speak to me. I told the truth and my family was destroyed. I lost my brother because he is still so angry with me. We were together always.

We stayed in San Antonio about two weeks in a convent. There was a nun there, Sister Diana, who spoke Spanish. We talked to the parish priest, but he could not help. He found one place for Jorge to work, but it offered only food, no pay. We knew we could not stay in that convent very long. Jorge was worried to find a job for pay. We needed to rent a place to live. At that time I did not understand renting because in my country it does not work that way. People do not rent their houses. Here I learned about rent. And we knew we could not live in the convent forever. No.

Father Berra came to visit us, and we went to a restaurant to eat. They brought us a big bowl of chips. It was a really, really big bowl! Jorge said, "Well, this is Texas, so the bowls are big." I told Father Berra that I wanted to go home. I told him it is better for us at home, please, please, just send us there.

"*Lo siento,* Lucía," I am sorry. "You cannot go. It is too dangerous for you in El Salvador. You and your family will be in danger." By now I knew my brother was beaten, so I thought Father Berra must be correct.

One night Sister Diana received a visit from her brother, and he spoke Spanish. Jorge was in the kitchen and said, "Hi, Sir." Jorge likes to talk to people. And there were never men in that convent, so he talked to the one man he found. When the brother asked Jorge what he was doing there, my husband explained our situation. He said, "I am looking for a job." The man said in San Antonio it was impossible to find a job. Maybe there were more jobs in California. Then Jorge talked to Sister Diana about California. And she called Father Tipton in Washington and arranged for us to come to California. Father Tipton, I think, talked to Father Daniel Germann, and between them they decided to send us here.

Father Tipton was a very special person.

I am telling you, he was busy, busy, busy! And even so, he took us into his life. Not everybody does that, even the priests. Ah, yes, he was a very good man. In Spanish we gave an expression of our gratitude. But after I learned to speak English, I wished to talk directly to him. I wished to buy a plane ticket to visit him and be able to speak in English. I called Washington asking for him, and only then did I learn that he left [the Jesuits]. He became the president of a big school, but I never knew the address or more information. We wished to go to visit him and show our gratitude to him because he was great with us. Then my daughter found information on the Internet that he had died. It hurt my heart that I could not say thank you in English. He was very, very good to us.

I think my mind was disturbed by the big shock of the murders. I was mute. For several years I couldn't speak and explain without crying from that night. I missed my job. I missed my friends, my people, my family. For me to work in the rectory and in administration at UCA was familiar. I felt that my whole family was in that rectory, and it instantly disappeared. The secretaries were very close to priests, they were very good women, very good. That disaster upset the secretaries too, I think. Years later, Father Luís Calero gave me the telephone to speak to one of the secretaries, but I couldn't. It was too hard to remember.

Finally, what happened? The criminals got amnesty. The same president that gave amnesty accused Jorge of being a liar. But in El Salvador they do not like to know the truth. They kill somebody and nobody talks about it. That is the law in El Salvador. Here, the United States invites the Salvadoran witness, but it is the same. Why does the FBI invite Salvadoran witnesses if they already knew who killed the priests? At that time I could not discern. My mind was closed like this. I was afraid and depressed. I was not able to have a diversion, to eat, or to enjoy. No.

Where can we go, with a child alongside? I was so afraid. Sister Diana told us that Padre Daniel would be waiting for us. When we arrived in San Francisco, Padre Daniel Germann and Father James Torrens were waiting for us.

Mary Jo Ignoffo

The murders at the UCA sent a shudder through the U.S. House of Representatives. On November 20, 1989, it adopted a resolution condemning the violence in El Salvador and reevaluated its commitment to military aid:

> *Resolved by the House of Representatives (the Senate concurring),* That the Congress—deplores and expresses its strongest revulsion at the heinous murder of six Jesuit priests and two women and demands that those responsible be brought to justice and punished for their crimes; and states unequivocally that a satisfactory resolution of this case is a pivotal test of El Salvador's democratic and judicial institutions and will be instrumental in determining continued United States support for the Government of El Salvador.

Passed the House of Representatives November 20, 1989.[1]

When House Speaker Thomas Foley asked a congressman from Boston to head a task force to search for truth in the case of the Jesuit murders, the choice appeared an unlikely one. Congressman Joe Moakley (John Joseph "Joe" Moakley, 1927–2001) did not have a record in foreign affairs, and as he told Speaker Foley, he had no intention of going anywhere south of Miami. "Mr. Speaker," Moakley said, "if you'd put a list—if you'd put a request on the bulletin board, you'd have 434 members on it, but you wouldn't have me on it."

"I know," Foley said. "That's why I'm calling."[2]

Despite a self-deprecating style, Moakley did have a connection to El Salvador. Early in the 1980s during the Reagan Administration, a group of Salvadoran immigrants in Massachusetts sought Moakley's help. The Salvadorans were about to be deported to El Salvador, where they were marked for death. By visiting the congressman, they risked exposing themselves as undocumented aliens. But it appeared better than the alternative—returning to El Salvador to assured death. They asked Moakley for some kind of reprieve for the deportation order. Congressman Moakley directed his aide, James McGovern, to look into the matter, and the result was the Moakley-DeConcini Bill of 1983. It allowed the Salvadorans another eighteen months in the United States to work out their legal status.

The plight of the Salvadoran immigrants focused Moakley's attention on the U.S. policy toward El Salvador. When the congressman learned that Salvadoran military personnel were being trained in the United States, he wrote to President Reagan. "It seems to me," he wrote in 1982, "that by militarily supporting the present Salvadoran government and, now, by training Salvadoran soldiers in the United States we are contributing to the oppression that already exists. We are, in essence, training Salvadoran troops to oppress their own people."[3] Moakley's entreaty to President Reagan was sadly prescient.

So when Speaker Foley asked Moakley to lead a task force to investigate the UCA murders, he did so knowing that the congressman had

---

[1] Congressional Resolution 236 1989, 101st Congress, 1st Session.

[2] Moakley, John Joseph. Interviewed by Robert Allison and Joseph McEttrick, John Joseph Moakley Oral History Project, OH-001. 2 April 2001. Transcript and video recording available. John Joseph Moakley Archive and Institute, Suffolk University, Boston, MA. Available at www2.suffolk.edu/files/Archives/oh-110_transcript.pdf.

[3] John Joseph Moakley to President Ronald Reagan, February 1, 1982, John Joseph Moakley papers, MS 100, Suffolk University.

some background on the country. Foley spelled out what he wanted from the committee:

> The committee should employ the resources of the relevant House committees and of its members to gather all available information about the murders, those responsible and the process undertaken to apprehend and bring them to justice. Since the murders were preceded by other unsolved political killings and deteriorating human rights conditions, and by the failure of the Salvadoran judicial system to offer either remedy or redress, the committee should examine the way in which these factors contributed or are relevant to the murders. I would expect the chairman to keep me informed of all developments in the case and that the committee would make periodic reports to me as well as to the [Central American] Task Force.[4]

The task force was made up of nineteen members of Congress.[5] One of the first orders of business was to interview the Cernas.

Paul Tipton, SJ, then president of the Association of Jesuit Colleges and Universities and former president of Spring Hill College in Mobile, Alabama, arrived at the FBI offices in Miami to find the whereabouts of the Cernas. At the hotel where they were being detained he got into a loud and angry altercation, mostly lost on the Cernas because it was all in English. Although Tipton did not speak Spanish, he made his outrage at the treatment meted out to the family perfectly clear.

A chain-smoking, hard-drinking, charismatic, big, brash Southerner, Tipton stands tall, literally and figuratively, in the Cernas' narrative. He swept in to rescue them, feed and clothe them—his mother purchased the only change of clothing their little daughter had in the eight days since they fled Salvador—and most important, Paul Tipton was the first American to believe them. He did not speak Spanish, but with an interpreter named D.J., followed every nuance of the Cernas' odyssey. Also accompanying Tipton was Joseph Berra, SJ, a

---

[4] Thomas S. Foley to John Joseph Moakley, December 5, 1989, John Joseph Moakley papers, Suffolk University.

[5] The members of the Speaker's Special Task Force on El Salvador (the Moakley Commission) were Joe Moakley, David E. Bonior, George W. Crockett, Jr., Dan Glickman, Lee H. Hamilton, Steny H. Hoyer, Barbara Kennelly, H. Martin Lancaster, Mel Levine, Frank McCloskey, Dave McCurdy, Jim McDermott, Matthew F. McHugh, George Miller, John P. Murtha, David E. Obey, Lawrence J. Smith, John M. Spratt, and Gerry E. Studds.

younger American Jesuit who had lived in El Salvador in the Jesuits' philosophy house and whom Lucía had known from working at the provincial offices. Berra's familiar face and quiet kindness began what would be a very long healing process for Lucía.

Outraged that they had not been allowed out of their room to eat, the priests took the family to the hotel dining room—a luxury never experienced by the Cernas. "Fine plates and silver, with beautiful food," Lucía recalls. She had no appetite, but welcomed the chance to speak with the priests. All the while an FBI agent sat at an adjacent table. Lucía was frightened that now that she had changed her story that she would be killed by the Americans. She begged Berra not to leave them, so he spent the night in the Cernas' hotel room, quietly taking down Lucía's long story on his laptop. "Speak only in a low voice," he urged, so the FBI agents in the adjoining room would not hear.

Berra and Tipton arranged for human rights lawyers to interview the couple, and the priests sat in. The lawyers compared what the couple reported of the massacre with their deposed testimony in El Salvador of November 21 and 22, and concluded that it was the same. The lawyers proceeded to interview them about their days in FBI custody. This was a new story, and one that deeply disturbed the Jesuits in the United States and in El Salvador.

On Sunday, December 3, Tipton arranged for a flight out of Miami. Tipton, Berra, and the Cerna family took off by private jet from Miami to Mobile, Alabama, where the family had several days' rest. They met Christopher Viscardi, SJ, who arranged for a shopping trip to buy warmer clothes. They met Tipton's mother, who purchased clothing for their daughter. Lucía was unable to manage her fear and refused to go outdoors and or to go out in public. Tipton made an appointment for her to see a doctor.

Tipton asked if Jorge and Lucía would testify before the Moakley Commission in Washington. Filled with trepidation, the Cernas agreed only because they trusted Tipton. His presence, authority, and even his physical stature reassured them. They flew to Washington and were taken to Leonard Neale House, a Jesuit residence in the District, where they stayed for a few days. Tipton drove them to the Capitol to give testimony. After Lucía relayed her story, and after a few questions directed to Jorge, the Cernas were surprised by Moakley's statements to the task force. Through a translator Lucía understood him to say "these people are humble, but they speak the truth." When Moakley shook their hands, it startled them. This was quite a departure from the attitude of the Americans in Miami.

Moakley got in touch with Ambassador Walker while he was in Washington DC over the holidays. The ambassador insisted: "Anyone can get uniforms. . . . The fact that they were dressed in military uniforms was not proof that they were military."[6] Walker kept denying participation by the Salvadoran military and pointed out that Lucía's version of events could be flawed.

Later, when Moakley was asked about Lucía's story, he replied:

> So we had her in the office. We got her in, and I asked her I said, "How come you told one story one time, and the other story?" So she says, "Well, the FBI brought me into Miami. They asked me to tell the story, and I told the story. Then after I told the story—a colonel from El Salvador came into the room, and says, I hope you know what you're saying. You know, you still got your family down there." He intimidated her. Now there was no report and no activity that this fellow walked in the room. But he was telling her, so then she changed the story. But nowhere did it appear on the FBI records that this happened.[7]

Moakley never knew that the Salvadoran colonel made good on his threats and that Lucía's brother had been beaten within an inch of his life. The brother was forced to flee El Salvador with his wife and children. Lucía was concerned about her mother and her older children. Jorge had a very large family to worry about. Moakley was very clear that the FBI was stonewalling. "The FBI tried to suppress it. Okay? I mean we were fighting our own country on this one,"[8] he said.

Early in 1990, Father Tipton sent the Cernas to Texas, to place them in an environment with a larger Hispanic population. They changed their names and stayed in a convent, but it became apparent that finding a job would be impossible. The work ethic of the Cernas is significant. As soon as they possibly could, they sought out paid employment. Some discussion and phone calls to Tipton had them heading to California.

Paul Tipton, with the approval of U.S. Jesuit college presidents, pushed Congress to designate ten million dollars of its aid to El Salvador to pay down UCA's debt. The cash was crucial to the survival of the institution in the post-assassination years. Yet, as many victims experience, money is no substitute for the ones we love. Tipton later

---

[6] Quoted in Guy Gugliotta and Douglas Farah, "12 Years of Tortured Truth on El Salvador," *Washington Post*, March 21, 1993.

[7] Moakley, Oral History, Suffolk University, 49.

[8] Ibid.

left the Jesuits, eventually became president of Jacksonville University for a few years, and died of lung cancer in 2008. Lucía learned of his death when her daughter found an online obituary for him. Over the years they had attempted to locate Tipton, because Lucía wished to go visit him and thank him in English.

In February 1990, the Moakley Task Force traveled to El Salvador. Committee members were met at the airport by Ambassador William Walker and his staff. The U.S. Congress had never sent such a large contingent to examine a criminal case. The committee members may have also recalled the disturbing bit of history when Congressman Leo Ryan led an investigative trip to Guyana in 1979; he lost his life when he and his staff were gunned down on the tarmac at the airport. The ambassador certainly understood the gravity of the case, and the powerful presence of congressional representatives only underscored it. Despite the fact that the ambassador was at the airport and offered strong security measures for the high-ranking officials, all were very much aware that there were no guarantees. Moakley later explained: "The embassy kept putting us on the sanitation road, you know, didn't want us to get near anything. And it was very, very awakening. I'll tell you, frightening at times. I mean a couple of times I thought I was going to get killed, because we ended up in the car with big machine guns, and I wasn't sure who they were."[9]

The Moakley Commission issued its interim report on April 30, 1990. Its findings determined that high-ranking Salvadoran military officers were involved in the UCA murders. Moakley recalled, "They [U.S. State Department officials] just were stalling, because they just couldn't tell the American people that we've spent six billion dollars to a military group that killed priests, sodomized churchwomen, you know, and did all these terrible things."[10] The U.S. House of Representatives voted to reduce military aid to El Salvador by half.

In March 1990, Santa Clara University sent a delegation to El Salvador. Dan Germann, SJ, was part of that group. By this time he had met the Cernas and helped them get settled. For him, the trip offered insights not only on the culture of his new friends, but also on the impact of U.S. foreign policy in Central America. And in an even more significant way, he talked about how it personalized a Jesuit theme

[9] Ibid., 48.
[10] Ibid., 50.

of "faith doing justice." He admitted to being "in process," reaching for a broader understanding of faith connected with actively seeking justice. He said for him it was "somehow being able to enter the world of poor, to listen to the poor, to walk with the poor as did Jesus, to begin to see with their eyes, to experience reality as they do. We cannot really become poor ourselves. But through friendship, through listening, through compassion and solidarity with the poor we can ourselves begin to see reality with new eyes."[11] Dan had a unique capacity to develop true and lasting friendships across the full social and economic spectrum.

The Chapultepec Peace Accords, signed by President Cristiani and representatives of the FMLN on January 16, 1992, called for an end to El Salvador's civil war. The UCA murder victims gave their lives to bring worldwide attention to the atrocities in El Salvador. Sadly, their names are added to the tens of thousands of others mowed down by gunfire. The Cristiani government of El Salvador announced it would provide protection for Archbishop Rivera y Damas. The *National Catholic Reporter* said that at a meeting of Cristiani, Tojeira, and Rivera y Damas, the bishop made a personal request to President Cristiani for government soldiers to stand guard at his residence. "Don't get me wrong," Rivera reportedly told the president. "It's not that I trust the soldiers. But if I'm killed, I want it clear who did it."[12]

The United Nations Commission on the Truth for El Salvador (the Truth Commission) was established as part of the 1992 peace negotiations. It was instructed to report on human rights crimes committed during the civil war by all sides. The Truth Commission ultimately confirmed the findings of the Moakley Commission. It concluded that Colonel René Emilio Ponce issued the order to kill Ellacuría and any witnesses, provided the arms to carry out the order, and later destroyed evidence. The United Nations Truth Commission also stated:

> That same night of 15 November, Colonel Guillermo Alfredo Benavides informed the officers at the Military College of the order he had been given for the murder. When he asked whether anyone had any objection, they all remained silent.
>
> Colonel Manuel Antonio Rivas Mejía of the Commission for the Investigation of Criminal Acts (CIHD) learnt the facts and

---

[11] Daniel Germann, "South Bay Response to the Provincial's Talk," August 13, 1991.

[12] Quoted in Gene Palumbo, "Peace Architect Rivera Damas Dies at Seventy-One: El Salvador Mourns Óscar Romero's Successor, *National Catholic Reporter* 31/7 (December 9, 1994).

> concealed the truth and also recommended to Colonel Benavides measures for the destruction of incriminating evidence.[13]

In 1993, the same year that the United Nations came out with its report, the Clinton Administration ordered the release of twelve thousand previously classified documents from the State Department, the Department of Defense, and the CIA, and their association with El Salvador from the Carter presidency through the Salvadoran civil war and the Jesuit murders. Pressure from Congress, particularly Congressman John Joseph Moakley, brought about this unprecedented disclosure. Author Teresa Whitfield specifically points out that the released records confirmed "the extent to which the U.S. government mistreated the witness Lucía Cerna."[14] Since 1993, however, thousands of these released documents have been reclassified by the U.S. government as threats to national security.

By 1994, it was clear that the U.S. State Department had protected Colonel Ponce, the one who issued orders to Benavides. "The United States knew that Salvador's defense minister, Col. René Emilio Ponce, was directly implicated in the deaths of the six Jesuit priests and their two housekeepers," said a 1994 article in the *National Catholic Reporter*, "but the United States thought Ponce was worth protecting in the hope he could reform the armed forces."[15] Ponce, with the U.S. State Department's support, negotiated the peace in Chapultepec in 1992 and covered up the crime at the UCA at the same time.

---

[13] United Nations Commission on the Truth for El Salvador, *From Madness to Hope: The Twelve-Year War in El Salvador*, report of the Commission on the Truth for El Salvador, S/25500 (1993).

[14] Teresa Whitfield, *Paying the Price: Ignacio Ellacuría and the Murdered Jesuits of El Salvador* (Philadelphia: Temple University Press, 1994), 391.

[15] Arthur Jones, "El Salvador Revisited: A Look at Declassified State Department Documents—Some of What the U.S. Knew—and When It Knew It," *National Catholic Reporter*, special supplement (September 23, 1994).

8

Exile

1990–2012

Lucía Cerna

Father Daniel and Father James were waiting for us at the airport. We had not met these priests before. They were new to us. We also saw Father Richard Howard at the airport. I was very surprised to see somebody that I knew from El Salvador. Now he is married, but then he knew me from working as a housekeeper in the provincial offices.

"What are you doing here?" I asked him. He was flying back to El Salvador.

"*¿Estás bien?* Are you okay?" he said to me.

Immediately I told him what happened to my brother. I told him my brother had been beaten by the soldiers and that my mother's little room had been searched for guns. I explained that Óscar was hiding and very angry against me, saying I had handed him over to the soldiers. The soldiers were searching for guns, I told him.

"But my mother is old. She does not have guns. My mother is crying and crying for my brother."

Mr. Howard told me he was going to El Salvador. He gave me a small business card with his number on it. He was working with refugees in San Salvador. He said to send it to my brother, and I did. My brother called Mr. Howard, who helped with the whole family. He had a big family and wife, and together they got out of El Salvador safely. But he is still angry with me.

It is curious. Many, many years later, when my young daughter went to high school, Richard Howard was teaching at the same school. He invites me every year to speak to his class about El Salvador and the massacre. I speak to the students in Spanish, and some of these students go to visit El Salvador.

From that time, we began to get to know Father Daniel and Father James, and they were very good to us. Father James interviewed me in Spanish, and he wrote an article for a magazine. He still calls and visits us.

Padre Daniel helped us find a place to rent. It was small, and we called it the *casita*, but we were comfortable. He took us to English classes. He taught Jorge to drive, how to put gas in the car, how to change a tire. We did not know these things. When the American television show *60 Minutes* wanted to interview us, Padre Daniel was with us to help. He also helped with writing the immigration papers, and he took us to Catholic Charities. When our little daughter needed to start school, he found her a place in a Jesuit parish school.

After I came to the United States, I remember, maybe even two or three years later, when I was talking with Father James or Father Daniel, I couldn't stop crying because still I missed Father Nachito and Father Ellacu. They gave me stability in my life, confidence in myself. They talked to me as a person, even for very short time, but I missed them. It took a very long time before I could speak of them without crying and becoming very upset. Even now, sometimes I cry when I speak of what happened to them.

The first job I got in the United States was cleaning houses for a company that hired several maids. Padre Daniel helped me get that job. But when I told him the truth, I left that job. Here is what happened. I went as a helper for a housecleaner lady, for maybe two months. The company paid us to clean two houses in one day, but we cleaned three. I got paid to clean two. The lady kept the money from the third house. We always had to rush, because we had to report back to the company office by 5 p.m., so there was no time to eat lunch. Another coworker also knew this, but she needed the job and could not quit.

The houses were very big houses for people who had a lot of money. The lady gave me the job to clean the bathrooms, and she chose only to dust or vacuum. I did not know at that time, because I was new to the job, so I just did it. I never thought the manager lady was not good until I noticed that the homeowner several times gave a bag of clothes for us to share. But the woman never shared; she kept everything. Little by little I learned that she was not honest. I told Padre Daniel this and said I want to quit. He said "Okay, do what you need to do." I found work at a childcare center.

He helped Jorge get a job at the university in the cafeteria. Not long after, Jorge went to work in a small bakery. It did not work out because other workers there did not like Salvadorans. Padre Daniel helped him get another job. At the beginning our jobs did not work out. But now Jorge retired from the same job after more than twenty years. Before I retired, I was at my job as a certified nursing assistant (CNA) for sixteen years.

We tried to understand the American system. There are many differences between life in El Salvador and life in America. For example, in our country a car is not required. It is not possible to live here without a car. Jorge went to buy a car from an auto auction, and I think maybe it was for six hundred dollars. The man selling the car said, "Here is your paperwork to take to the DMV to get signed." But when Jorge brought the paperwork back, the seller would not give him the car. It was a big problem. We paid six hundred dollars, but no car. Three times we went back, and no car.

We called Padre Daniel and told him what happened. He called a friend who went with Jorge to the auto auction, carrying a briefcase and wearing a suit. The man asked "Who are you?"

"I am his friend," said the woman Padre Daniel introduced to us. Jorge thought the man believed she was a lawyer, and suddenly the paperwork was in order and we got our car. They were taking advantage of immigrants who do not know about life in the United States. Jorge wanted me to learn to drive that car. I was afraid. I thought, oh, what if I get into an accident and have to speak to American police? Ayyeee, no, no. I do not want to have problem with police. But how could I tell Jorge I did not want to drive that car? I do not want any problems with police. I have never learned to drive. I prefer the bus.

Finally we were working and did not need financial help from the Jesuits anymore. They had been helping us with expenses, but now we were on our own with our wages. We wrote a letter to show our gratitude to them for helping us so much. We saved our pay, and we bought a condominium. It was farther away, and we did not see Jesuits very often, but our daughter continued in the same school. She got a very good education. Later we sold the condominium and bought our house, where we have lived now for many years.

One day I told Padre Daniel I would like more education to become a CNA. He said, "Okay, do what you need to do." I went to the community college and took the classes for certification to work with older people. My English was not good, so I had to study long hours. I studied at the kitchen table, sometimes all night. Even today I am surprised I passed because now my English is so much better.

In my mind I knew that Padre Daniel had Parkinson's disease, and I wished to help him because he helped us in everything. I completed the classes and got a certificate. I found work at the [Sacred Heart Jesuit Center] retirement facility as a CNA. I wanted to work there because I thought, when Padre Daniel gets more sick, I will be there to help him.

He laughed and said, "I don't want to live there, and I don't want to be sick."

But I could tell Parkinson's is a very bad disease. It was a couple of years before he went to live there.

I took the bus from home to downtown Los Gatos, and then I walked up the steep hill to the facility. There are no sidewalks on that street, just a narrow road. This was fine until one day, walking down the hill, a car went speeding by and I fell and I broke my leg. After my leg healed, it was very difficult for me to walk up the hill. Going down was okay, but up was terrible. Finally I got better, but I needed my husband or daughter to take me to work.

For a time I worked nights. For some it is difficult to stay awake at night. I can do it because I feel it is my responsibility. One night at Sacred Heart we were only two CNAs on duty, no nurses, and together we were in one of the Father's room, changing his bedding. At that time they did not lock the main door. One priest, one with dementia, went out to the mountains at midnight when it was raining and the wind was blowing. I went to his room, looking around, and he was not there. And it was midnight! Where is he, where is he? At that time they did not have an alarm on the leg. Now it is required for dementia patients to have an alarm on the leg. I took the flashlight and went out into the raining night, looking everywhere. I never thought to call the police. We did not have instructions to call the police. I thought, I must find him! He cannot spend the whole night in the rain where anything can happen, sickness or suffer an animal bite, or he could die out there!

My coworker said, "How can you go out there? It is too scary!"

I crossed the parking lot and went down many steps in the dark to the provincial office, looking, maybe he was down over there. I was calling his name, calling and calling out his name, and yelling his name. Then I went all the way around the property to the mountain trail, still calling and yelling, and finally I heard, "Oooo, over here, over here." I found him sliding in the mud, spread on the ground and he could not get up himself. I picked him up with all my strength,

"Come, come, and we'll get you back inside!" I did not care that my uniform got muddy. My coworker was amazed.

She said, "Weren't you scared?" I did not think about danger. I just went. "Where did you find him?" she asked.

"All the way out on the mountain trail. He fell out there."

We brought him in to have a hot shower and to be comfortable in bed. In the morning I reported to the head nurse everything that happened. After that they started to lock the doors at night.

My interest in being in that facility was someday to be of help to Padre Daniel. That was my priority. When Parkinson's disease brought him there, I wished to give special care for him. I was happy to see him, but I knew he preferred to be living his life as he was when he was healthy. One of my coworkers did not like that I took special care of Padre Daniel. They moved me to another hall to care for others. They said that I was spoiling Daniel. So I said okay and gave my special care to other Fathers.

I said, "Please take care with him so he does not fall." From then I could only talk to Padre Daniel and help with some things that he needed. It was very hard for me because I wished to help him. Padre Daniel told me, "*Ella es la jefe*," she is the boss, and that we should do what she says. "Don't worry, Lucía," he told me. "I am fine."

Padre Daniel was very comfortable. Anything was okay with him. He did not get upset with things. But not me. I told him that I was thinking of quitting the job because it was not possible to attend to him. "I am here for you, not for other priests."

He was laughing because he was one saint. I was grateful to him, and I wanted to give my good service for him, especially in that location where he needed somebody. When family is not there, you need someone to attend.

I talked to Jorge about bringing Padre Daniel to our house to take care of him. I copied the menu of what food he could eat so I would know what to cook for him. When I asked Padre Daniel, he said they would not permit him to come to our house to live. He knew we would be happy to bring him to our home, and give good attention, like family. I was working there maybe five years, and I explained to Padre Daniel why I thought I could not work there anymore. He said, "Okay, do what you need to do." He was always comfortable, easy, easy to talk to. I told the head nurse I could not work there anymore.

After that, Jorge and our daughter went with me to visit Padre Daniel, and we tried to bring something he might need, a new shirt or pants. One day he told us that he fell from the bed in the night. But when he told it, he was laughing. He was surprised no one checked, but he was not angry. With Parkinson's he was moving, moving, and he fell out of the bed. He said the CNA did not come at 2 a.m. to check, and he lay there from one until six in the morning. I thought, oh, my God, she should check every moment, every moment! They do not pay you to go to sleep. They pay for you to pay attention! I was heartbroken when he told how he fell and had a long night on the floor. When nobody came he pulled blankets off the bed to not be cold. It is far from the bed to the floor. I was so upset about this!

"Maybe they thought I went for a walk," he was laughing. I was more upset than him. I would not let this happen. Now I have worked in several facilities, and I know that is not a difficult place to work. The patients there are easy, easy. It was terrible when Padre Daniel was telling us, and my heart, ahhhhh, I was in pain, like this. I know he told the head nurse, but nothing happened. In another facility somebody would get fired. That was negligence. To leave him on the floor all night and not check! We need to know every moment.

Padre Daniel was like a father for us. Like a father, always. We remember him with love. He is in heaven because he was a very good man. Not only with us, but I think with everybody he was a very good man. We do not have the words to say thank you, because he was excellent. Even when he was very, very busy, he was helping us. Not everyone would do that, not even priests. But he did. When Padre Daniel had Parkinson's, Jorge asked, "Why does God permit this? He is only a good man." When he passed away, I was upset with God because Daniel was for the people, helping everybody. Why does God permit that? I do not understand. I pray and I think God listens. But sometimes God does not answer fast.

All the time I was working, I put money in *cuchubal.*

I do not know if there is an English word for it. Each month I give some money that I earn to one woman who holds it until the end of the year. She does this for many people. This way each has a large amount to pay for something. I paid for my older daughter in El Salvador to attend school. For example, you give maybe one hundred dollars every month. After twelve months the woman returns your money. I took the *cuchubal* money and paid the school for my older daughter.

Both my son and daughter from my first husband came to the United States. We sponsored them. My older daughter came to the United States with one son and a baby on the way. When she first came, she needed a job. I like to pray a lot. Sometimes I sit in the Cathedral in the quiet, beautiful church to pray. I talk to God, and God gives me ideas and gives me support. I found support in that circumstance, that situation, and I found I could help my daughter. I got the idea that I might be able to help her to get a job. I did the same for the boy when he came here, giving money to help. He did not like the jobs he found here, so he moved to the East Coast.

I knew a residential care facility, and I thought I could introduce my daughter there. So I took an extra job there to be able to introduce her. I worked nights for six months after working the day too. For the days, I started at 7 a.m. until 4 p.m. Then I went directly to the other job to begin at 4:30. After the night shift I slept only for a little while and came back to work. I went to talk with the head nurse, and I asked if it was possible to help my daughter and give her a job. I explained that she was becoming a CNA, but she spoke only a little English. Well, she said, she should bring her certificate when she finished and a teacher recommendation. Then she could have a job. I did not have much sleep for six months. Finally I reached the goal. My older daughter got the job there, and I left the night job.

But there was trouble getting to the goal. I pushed her into the CNA program, but she was against it. I told her she would get a better job and have good advantage with good benefits, especially health insurance. I also told her she must learn English. It was difficult, and she was very angry with me. Her anger confused me, because I thought I was helping. Maybe she was still angry because of the hatred her father had for me. She is okay now and enjoys her work. She has said, "Thank you, Mama, for introducing me to work when I had no experience." At first she was upset—and now she enjoys two jobs. She is happy with a house to live with her two kids and she is free. That's what she wants. I told her, "You are beautiful." I wish the best for her future.

There are a lot of nurses in El Salvador, but no jobs, so they come here. But many are illegal. Some facilities for the elderly accept illegal people, but they are not supposed to. Many work as CNAs, even though in El Salvador they are nurses. When the state officials come to inspect, all the illegals have to rush to go home. They call all the others on the phone to stay at home. These people have a lot of stress. They want to buy a house in El Salvador and try to save money. Once you have a house there, it is cheaper to live.

My patients were my company. I did the best for them. I recommended the best for them. It is not spoiling them; it is normal to work like that. Most people I observe go to work for money. They do not have compassion.

I trained new CNAs for several years. I asked, "Why are you here?"

They'd say, "For the money."

I told them not to say that. The money is passing, but you must have compassion, compassion. I showed how to manage the bodies. I wish the best for my people.

One day the supervisor was walking the hall and a patient was out of control and wanted to jump out of bed. The supervisor went to talk to the lady, but the patient ignored her. I came in and the patient knew my voice, and I talked quietly to her and calmed her down. "How did you do that?" the supervisor asked. We need to know how to manage that situation when it is like that. The supervisors are in the office all the time, and they do not know the patients or how to talk to them. I lean close to them to talk. "Mrs. Rose, this is Lucía, it's time to get up for dinner, let's go." And they cooperate. I know the system, joking with patients, talking softly to them. "You are sweet," one says to me. One man is a veteran, and sometimes I sing the "Star Spangled Banner" to him or salute him. He smiles and laughs. He appreciates hearing this from a Spanish lady.

I was given a certificate of the Circle of Excellence. Now I have been employee of the month two times. The first time I said thank you, and they took my picture. Then some years later I was told, "You are employee of the month." I said to the manager, "There must be an error. I already had that." She said, "Lucía, you deserve it because you give your life for the patients." I have known that manager a long time, because she is the one who first hired me sixteen years ago.

A court in Spain wants justice for those who killed the Jesuits.

El Salvador's government only punished the soldiers with three years in jail and afterward invented amnesty. Now Spain is pushing El Salvador authorities to re-catch the soldiers who killed the priests. They want to make justice, repatriate them to *España*, Spain. Jorge and I were interviewed by Spanish lawyers. They asked us to go to Spain to testify to bring justice. I was not sure what to do. I called Mr. Howard and asked for advice. He called Father Dean [Brackley] at the UCA. Father Dean called me and we talked for a while. He was healthy then.

"Do I go?" I asked him.

"Lucía," he said, "you have been responsible in everything. You gave your own life in this case. If you want to talk about the Jesuit case, go. If you do not want to go, do not feel that you must. Do what you want to do. Especially I do not recommend that you speak to the

FBI." Then Father Dean told me that he works in Nachito's place at Jayace on the weekends. Padre Nacho always went there on the weekends. Not long after, Father Dean got sick. He was not sick very long.

One day I received a phone call from the FBI. He spoke in Spanish. He said, "I am from the FBI." I don't remember his name. He said he would like to come to our home and talk to us about the trial in Spain.

"Excuse me sir," I said, "with respect, but I do not believe in the FBI."

"You don't believe in the FBI?" He was surprised. "Well, I will talk to your husband, and he will understand why he should talk to me."

I was not happy with that comment.

They asked us to go to Spain. Human rights lawyers called us, and they had talked with Padre Esteban [Stephen Privett]. If Padre Esteban sent them, I knew they were okay. But I did not want to go to Spain, and I did not want to testify again. Jorge wanted to go. Not me. I refused to go. We agreed to be interviewed, and the solicitor made an appointment to interview us in a building downtown on satellite with the judge in Spain. The judge wanted to hear our voice and our testimony. We don't like *venganza*, revenge. We told the truth always. But they want to take those soldiers to *España*. Those soldiers have families now. If they had to go to jail in Spain, it would leave kids abandoned. In El Salvador women usually do not work, only the men. If the soldiers leave, the wife has no protection, the children are abandoned. It does not do any good to harm some children.

They do not want to point to who gave the order. The one who thought up the crime was Emilio Ponce. He passed away some time ago. For that, we are against forcing the soldiers to go to Spain. It is very easy for the president and the colonel to give an order. For example, you are my boss, I live under your orders, and you tell me you tear down that wall. I tear it down because you are my boss. That case is similar. The soldiers were told, "Go kill the priests." And the ones who gave the order were not brought to justice. Now the reports say that Ponce and Cristiani were that night having a meeting at 9:30. They knew. Jorge does not think they made that order without the United States. At that meeting they decided now is time to go to kill the priests, finish with no witnesses. Everybody go home. Tomorrow nobody knows anything.

Jorge pays attention to the trial in Spain, but so far the men are still in El Salvador.

We would like to be in our home in El Salvador, but that is impossible.

Life has changed. Jorge had good work as a baker then, making fresh sweet bread, and *pan francais*. Now it would be so different because we are old. We cannot start again. We only wish to stay near our daughter. I wish we could all be in peace back home, but we will not leave our daughter. She is our whole family. She is so good, and my heart is full and grateful when I think of her. So very, very good.

After we were here maybe ten years, we sold our home in Soyapango. It is good we did that then, because now there are so many gangs and delinquents that it is not a safe place to live. But when we sold, we went back, and it was sad. When we first left, we had asked a relative to sell the things, all the bakery equipment and supplies, and give the money to Jorge's mother, who needed it. He sold everything, a lot of sacks of flour, sugar, *manteca*, he sold everything. I had a sewing machine, a refrigerator, supplies for a home, a few clothes. Padre Nacho had given me copies of the books he wrote and that Padre Ellacu wrote. All those are gone. The relative did not make an inventory and sold everything. He only gave Jorge's mother one hundred *colónes*. Jorge was so disappointed at that. The relative emptied the home.

When we went back to sell, we cleaned. The new buyer did not want the stove, the one Jorge built and used for business. The buyer wanted a clean patio. We had to destroy the stove. All our good memories and our life we had to abandon. We had ten years already in the United States. Jorge said, no, we will not come back. We will not come back to war like this.

My life is so different. Before I liked to listen to music and be happy and lively. Jorge had a big warm family. I feel depressed sometimes. Before Miami my character was so happy. It changed totally. I think and pray to God. I think and after only praying, he gives me comfort. I tell God thank you for job and family and friends, but here I do not have many friends, but that's okay. I tell God, if Jorge had stayed in Soyapango that night, if he had been away from me, he would not understand. But he was with us that night, and he understands why I am different and suffered. He has been with me in this, and I talk to God and say thank you. Sometimes I even thank God we were there that night, for believe it or not, we were there. We told what happened. If they do not believe, it is on their conscience.

Deep in my heart I feel complete because I acted for the priests. They deserved help from somebody. They were very good bosses, for more than just me. When they first gave me respect, I appreciated it, and I used my work to show my appreciation. They deserved the best from service because of all the work they were doing. If something happens in your home to your family, you go to get help. You tell. They were my family, and I told. I told.

MARY JO IGNOFFO

Upon arriving at San Francisco International Airport, in a strange coincidence, the Cernas ran into Father Richard Howard. Besides being a familiar and friendly face, Howard could offer real help. His work with the Jesuit Refugee Service (JRS) in El Salvador enabled him to help people who were in danger get out of the country.

The JRS had been instituted in 1980 by the superior general of the Jesuit order, Pedro Arrupe, SJ, in reaction to the predicament faced by the Vietnamese "boat people" who were displaced by politics and hunger in the years after the end of the Vietnam War. The desperate refugees, by some estimates well over a million people, set out to sea in vastly inadequate and overloaded vessels in an attempt to get out of the country. While many emigrants were accepted in the United States, Australia, Britain, France, and Canada, tens of thousands were lost at sea. Father Arrupe put out a call for help, and in response came personnel, cash, and resources. The JRS grew to include helping people forcibly displaced around the globe. In the case of El Salvador, the civil war in the 1980s not only displaced people from the land, but also created thousands of political refugees.

When Howard returned to El Salvador, he facilitated the safe emigration of Lucía's younger brother and family, among hundreds of others. Sadly, Lucía's brother has never been able to understand why his sister bore witness, and he cut any communication with her. In 1992, Howard left the Jesuits, and in a happenstance that Lucía refers to as "curious," was later a teacher at the school her daughter attended. They have maintained their friendship.

The investigations into the massacre at the UCA proceeded in fits and starts, and continue to this day.

President Alfredo Cristiani insisted that his own military was not involved until overwhelming evidence forced him to admit that high-ranking military officers ordered the murders. U.S. Ambassador

William Walker insisted that the Salvadoran military was not involved until insurmountable evidence forced him to admit that it was.

The Moakley Commission issued the first and most comprehensive report of the crimes at the end of April 1990. It laid out a damning series of events leading up to the massacre and the steps taken to cover it up. The report concluded, however, that "the investigation and preparations for prosecuting the case have come to a virtual standstill."[1]

The language of the report took a tone of incredulity when it asserted that

> literally hundreds of military personnel were deployed in the area around the University on the night of the crime. . . . Despite this, not one member of the Salvadoran armed forces has voluntarily provided information of real value. . . . Even the head of the SIU, Lt. Col. Manuel Antonio Rivas Mejia, has refused to give a formal statement concerning the allegation that Col. Benavides confessed to him his guilt.[2]

This is the same Colonel Rivas who questioned Lucía in Miami.

In more conciliatory words, the report leans toward exonerating President Cristiani, who it said "has made a sincere effort to encourage a professional investigation into the murders."[3] The president's obfuscation became more apparent as investigations continued.

How did the Moakley Report address the situation of Lucía Cerna? The commissioners had listened to her firsthand in Washington DC. They believed her. Yet, "while the Task Force believes that U.S. officials should have acted with greater sensitivity, we do not have the basis for concluding that their actions were abusive or part of a conscious plan to discredit Mrs. Cerna's testimony."[4] The treatment of her was "regrettable."

"Given the fact that she [Lucía Cerna] was not a criminal suspect," the report stated, "and given the grisly nature of the crime she was testifying about, it is disturbing that she was interrogated for so long, and especially that she and her husband were subjected to polygraph examinations, without being offered access to an attorney."[5]

---

[1] United States Congress, Interim Report of the Speaker's Task Force on El Salvador, April 30, 1990, 23, available at www.cja.org/downloads/Jesuits_Interim_Report_on_Task_Force.pdf. Often referred to as the "Moakley Report."

[2] Ibid., 10.

[3] Ibid., 7.

[4] Ibid., 26.

[5] Ibid.

In El Salvador a trial to prosecute the UCA murders began on September 26, 1991. Lucía's testimony was irrelevant to the case. By this time it was clear that the Salvadoran military carried out the killing. What was not clear was whose idea it was, or who gave orders. Two men were convicted—Colonel Guillermo Alfredo Benavides Moreno, a member of the *tandona* or 1966 graduating class of the Military Academy and the only man charged who was not actually at the UCA that night; and Lt. Yusshy René Mendoza Vallecillos, who did not shoot anyone and whose role that night remains quite murky. Each was sentenced to thirty years in prison. A few men who confessed to participating were not convicted. The defense attorneys were paid, according to the February 23, 1990, *Miami Herald*, by "influential military friends of Benavides."

Peace Accords for the civil war were signed by the warring parties in Mexico City at Chapultepec Castle on January 16, 1992. Part of the agreement called for truth. The United Nations formed the Commission on the Truth for El Salvador, which issued its report on March 15, 1993. Its task was more far-reaching than that of the Moakley Commission. The U.N. commission was tasked with finding the truth in hundreds of instances during El Salvador's civil war, from El Mozote to death-squad assassinations. It searched out documentation of atrocities committed by both sides.

Within less than a week after the issuance of the Truth Commission report, the Salvadoran Justice Department established an Amnesty Law giving amnesty to anyone convicted of crimes during the civil war, including the only two men sent to prison in the UCA murders. The two were released, and the Amnesty Law is still in effect, even though in 1999, the Inter-American Commission of the United Nations ruled that the Salvadoran Amnesty Law violated international law.

The case as tried in El Salvador was a sham. In frustration that standard legal practices were not followed, human rights advocates sought alternative jurisdictions to bring the perpetrators to justice.

The case of the UCA murders was opened again as an international case of crimes against humanity in November 2008. A lawsuit was filed in Spain by the Spanish Association for Human Rights (APDHE) in conjunction with the California-based Center for Justice and Accountability (CJA) on behalf of the victims, their families, and the Society of Jesus. Spain's National Court in Madrid, acting under the principle of universal jurisdiction, indicted twenty former Salvadoran military officers and government ministers for crimes against humanity, coverup of crimes against humanity, and state terrorism.

Spain has enacted laws of "international obligation," which stipulate that for the sake of justice, nations have an obligation to prosecute crimes like genocide, terrorism, or piracy—regardless of where they were committed. The Spanish court has pursued these kinds of cases of universal jurisdiction, including the prosecution of former Chilean dictator Augusto Pinochet, and the Guatemalan genocide, when whole villages were wiped out during the 1980s.

During 2009 and 2010, evidence in the Jesuit case was presented to Presiding Judge Eloy Velasco. New evidence has come to light since the publication of the U.N. Truth Commission in 1993. Two previously unidentified witnesses have come forward, one who participated in the killings and is a protected witness, and another, also testifying as a protected witness, who provided new and highly credible details on the conspiracy to kill the priests. Additional evidence came from the testimony of two Spanish attorneys who observed the original trial in El Salvador, and the testimony of two public prosecutors in El Salvador, who had resigned in protest when their government shielded the perpetrators of the crime. The prosecutors also enlisted expert witnesses, one of whom is Stanford University Professor Terry Karl, who have examined thousands of pages of documentation in the case, much of which was not available to the Truth Commission in 1993.

The CJA searched out Lucía and Jorge Cerna through Stephen Privett, SJ, currently the president of the University of San Francisco, whom they had known since 1990. An attorney visited the Cernas and asked them to go to Spain to testify in the trial. Jorge was tempted; Lucía was not. The request caused Lucía some anxiety, so she consulted Dean Brackley, SJ, at the UCA. Ultimately, the Cernas agreed to testify via satellite from offices of the FBI in the United States to the judge in Spain. According to the CJA website, "For the first time, the U.S. government cooperated with a Spanish National Court investigation of a human rights case, by facilitating the Cernas' testimony through video-conference." The CJA reported that "even these many years later, Lucía Cerna expressed great trepidation about testifying." Her unease extended not only to Salvadoran officials but also to American ones. When an agent from the FBI contacted her about the trial she startled him by saying, "I do not believe in the FBI." She has not forgotten what happened in Miami.

Jorge and Lucía's attitudes about the new trial are somewhat surprising. "*No queremos venganza*"—we don't want revenge—they say. They explain that El Salvador has its own laws and judicial system, and even though that system is terribly flawed, it saw fit to give the triggermen amnesty. She refers to El Salvador's Amnesty Law, which was issued amid political skirmishing five days after the U.N. Truth Commission issued its report on March 15, 1993.

Lucía points out that the men charged have families now, children, and what good would it do now to have them put in prison? They should have been punished long before, she says. She reiterated that she believes the real men responsible were Emilio Ponce and Alfredo Cristiani. Both are dead. So why pursue the others?

It is possible that her perceptions are stuck in time. By now, those men are not fathers of young children, but grandparents. Even if this were pointed out, though, she identifies the root problem as the fact that the instigators, those who issued orders to men in their commands, were not prosecuted. The real perpetrators should have been brought to justice. They were not. Why pursue the triggermen yet again? The international court, however, sees the crimes as so heinous that all who participated in any way ought to be brought to justice.

Judge Velasco issued extradition requests for the defendants from El Salvador and from the United States, where one resides. The Salvadoran Supreme Court violated its own treaty with Spain by denying the requests. As of this writing, the outcome of the extradition requests is uncertain. The case in the Spanish court regarding President Cristiani is unsettled. The judge has held off but reserved the right to charge him posthumously with covering up crimes against humanity.

Every November 15, thousands descend on the campus at the UCA for an outdoor Eucharist to remember all the Salvadorans, including the UCA martyrs, killed during the civil war. Dean Brackley, SJ, reported that music and singing, sharing food and remembering, carry on until dawn.[6] Brackley had been a theology professor at Fordham University who volunteered to go to the UCA after the murders "for a few years," until the university could recover from the devastation of the massacre. Instead, Brackley found a home in El Salvador.

He took over Nacho's service at the parish in Jayace. He authored books and articles and hosted hundreds of pilgrims from around the world who came to the UCA to pay their respects and to learn. For me, his book *The Call to Discernment in Troubled Times*, articulates a path toward hope in the worst of circumstances. He even converted

---

[6] Dean Brackley, SJ, "Remembering the UCA Martyrs: Ten Years Later," *Conversations on Jesuit Higher Education*: Vol. 16, Article 3 (1999), available at: http://epublications.marquette.edu.

its copy editor, Ellen Calmus. In a highly unusual foreword, she writes about finding faith in Brackley's Ignatian wisdom.[7]

My daughter, Lisa, was one of those pilgrims traveling to El Salvador. She went in 2011 with a small group from her high school, Notre Dame San Jose. Sending high school juniors to El Salvador fills a parent with trepidation. The crime rate is not imaginary. Lisa sought advice from Lucía.

"Do not carry much cash, and then only in small bills. No twenties," she warned. "The people there are too poor and cannot change a twenty." She also said, "Enjoy the people—it is a very simple life. But do not leave your group. Go nowhere alone."

The Notre Dame students visited Archbishop Romero's tomb, and they went to the UCA. Lisa said she tried to imagine the stories she had heard from Lucía, seeing the house at 16 Cantábrico and the place where the priests and women were killed. A small museum exhibits the clothing the martyrs were wearing when they died—the blue shirt, the brown robe. The chapel of Jesus Christ the Liberator holds the remains of the priests and women. The students traveled to El Mozote and spoke to Rufina Amaya's daughter, who carries on her mother's mission to report on the massacre of that village. The group also met with a representative of the FMLN and the ARENA political parties. The portrait of Roberto D'Aubuisson hanging behind the ARENA speaker angered many of the students. When they questioned the speaker, he suggested it would be better to forget the past and to move ahead.

More important than any historical or political presentation, though, was the group's visit to Yoncolo. The Notre Dame students were driven by van to the village of just under two hundred a few hours from San Salvador. Yoncolo has been adopted by Notre Dame San Jose as its sister community, and when its students travel there, each year they are welcomed and housed for a few days. The students were taken in by families who have no running water and no electrical power. But Yoncolo shared its love and its life with its friends from California. Lisa purchased a Yoncolo-made hammock that our whole family has enjoyed since.

I saw from Lisa's itinerary that the group was scheduled to meet with Dean Brackley, and I explained how much I had appreciated his writings. When she got home, I asked what she thought of his

---

[7] Dean Brackley, SJ, *The Call to Discernment in Troubled Times: New Perspectives on the Transformative Wisdom of Ignatius of Loyola* (New York: Crossroad, 2004).

presentation. She said, "He was sick, and he could not meet with us." Sadly, Brackley had been diagnosed with pancreatic cancer; at the time of her visit, he was not well enough to carry on his work. He came to the United States for treatment, but when all options ran out, he returned to his home at the UCA, where he died in 2011, just months after the Notre Dame visit.

The affinity between the UCA and Santa Clara University in California predates the massacre. In 1982, Ignacio Ellacuría was awarded an honorary degree from Santa Clara, and he delivered the commencement address, although some on the board of trustees objected, claiming that they had heard Ellacuría was a Marxist.[8] Misunderstandings about Ellacuría's theology and politics extended well beyond El Salvador. Over the years of civil war in El Salvador, some at Santa Clara were friends or collaborators with the UCA Jesuits and faculty.

In 1989, Jon Sobrino was also awarded an honorary degree and gave the homily at the baccalaureate mass. On November 10 of that year, SCU's president, Paul Locatelli, wrote a letter to the board of trustees, inviting members to be part of a delegation to travel to El Salvador to mark the tenth anniversary of the assassination of Archbishop Óscar Romero. Dan Germann was part of the delegation.

Just before the murders of November 16, while Ellacuría was in Spain, Jon Sobrino stopped again at Santa Clara on his way to give a retreat and lectures in Thailand. When the news of the massacre broke, SCU President Paul Locatelli invited Sobrino to return and to stay for a time of healing and support in the aftermath of the loss of his community. Twenty years later Sobrino recalled, "I was welcomed like a brother."

The delegation formed by Locatelli a few days before the murders confirmed its travel plans and left for El Salvador, accompanied by Jon Sobrino, on March 18, 1990.[9]

SCU's academic vice president at the time, Charles Beirne, SJ, volunteered to go to the UCA. During his time there, from 1990 to 1993, he researched and wrote *Jesuit Education and Social Change in El Salvador*, a history of the UCA since its inception in 1966. Dedicated to Congressman Moakley, the book is an analysis of the evolution of the

---

[8] From a conversation with Francis Smith, SJ, who was on the board of trustees at the time.

[9] The eleven members of the SCU delegation to El Salvador were Paul Locatelli, Charles Beirne, Daniel Germann, Arthur Liebscher, John Mallen, Thomas Farley, Sheri Sager, Creaghe Gordon, Lois Gordon, Stephen Privett, and Jon Sobrino.

institution and its leadership.[10] Later, Beirne worked as an administrator in a number of Jesuit institutions, including ones in Guatemala, Africa, and New York. He died of cancer in 2010.

James Torrens, SJ, had taught for many years at Santa Clara University, but in 1990 he was an editor for *America*, a national Catholic magazine published by the Jesuits. In August of that year, only months after the Cernas arrived in California, Torrens interviewed Lucía, and her account of the massacre was published in *America* in November of that year. The article remains important for a number of reasons. It offers Lucía's perceptions within the first year of the UCA murders. While that account provides a few more details than her current recollections, the two demonstrate notable consistency. Torrens's interview was the most comprehensive one to focus on Lucía. Torrens managed to underscore the importance of her observations and her feelings, creating a timely historical record. He also helped Lucía's healing process by his careful listening and respect for her story. He has remained a friend to the Cernas from the day of meeting them at the airport. His work today in Fresno includes prison ministry and spiritual direction.

Dan Germann, SJ, had been a Santa Clara University theology teacher and director of campus ministry for most of his career. In the mid-1980s he enrolled in summer language schools in Guatemala and Mexico to learn Spanish. For the next several years he worked as a university liaison to poor communities, linking SCU students with community organizers, day-worker centers, and soup kitchens. He was a co-founder with Sonny Manuel, SJ, Stephen Privett, SJ, and SCU staff member Laura Jiménez of what was then called the Eastside Project. It is currently called the Arrupe Partnerships for Community-Based Learning.

By 1989, despite an advancing case of Parkinson's disease, he moved into a low-income neighborhood. He helped found a day-worker center so that the mostly undocumented workers would not be exploited and so that those needing workers had a safe and reliable way to hire. Working with Spanish-speaking immigrants put Germann in a good position to guide the Cernas as they adjusted to a new country and culture. He helped them, and many others, find work, navigate immigration hearings, and go to language classes.

The Cernas had a unique immigration status because the Jesuits had pushed for political asylum. The couple's path to citizenship was long, about ten years, yet throughout the process they had proof that

---

[10] Charles J. Beirne, SJ, *Jesuit Education and Social Change in El Salvador* (New York: Garland Publications, 1996).

they were in the United States legally. This allowed them to get good jobs. Jorge joined a union. The family had healthcare benefits. Their legal status allowed them to succeed financially where many of their illegal counterparts cannot.

Two days after the one-year anniversary of the UCA martyrs, on November 18, 1990, Germann gave a homily at Mission Santa Clara in which he related a passage from the Gospel of Matthew to the work and life of the victims. "In today's Gospel the patrón disburses thousands of silver pieces to his servants, expecting them to make good use of this wealth," he said. "These Jesuits had taken the risk of using their silver pieces, their own abilities, their educational expertise, their perceptive insights, their passion for justice, and they dedicated all these abilities to the service of the poor. . . . Elba and Celina trusted these men. . . . In El Salvador to side with the poor is to be a threat to the established power." When Dan traveled to El Salvador earlier that year as part of the SCU delegation, he saw firsthand what Lucía had been up against.

Lucía forged a strong bond with Padre Daniel, deeply grateful for how much time and help he had given her family. From the early weeks after they met through the first several years resettling in California, she relied on his advice, counsel, and good humor. It is difficult for her to imagine how the family would have gotten through the early years without Dan's friendship. She went so far as to plan how she could be of help to him as his disease progressed. She got herself hired as a CNA at Sacred Heart Jesuit Center in Los Gatos, a retirement community and assisted living facility, in anticipation of his arrival three years before he moved there. He was jovial about her wish to help him but realistic about his health and his living situation.

Declining health forced him to Sacred Heart in 1997. For the next ten years he struggled with the effects of Parkinson's, trapped not only by disease, but also by facility regulations that kept him from work, ministry, and socializing. About two years after he moved there, Lucía quit in frustration that her time with Padre Daniel was limited. It is not difficult to understand that Lucía's plan to "care for him like family" would not work very well in an institutional setting. She quickly found work in another facility.

Dan Germann died in 2007. Perhaps the most poignant expression of the impact of his values and work was an honor guard of white-clad Hispanic day workers lined up at the entry of Mission Santa Clara when his casket passed.

The terrible legacy of El Salvador's civil war—besides the ghastly indiscriminate killing, the ruination of the countryside, and the decimation of villages—is an imprint of impunity on the culture. Today gangs or *maras* rove the neighborhoods, markets, and villages, maiming, retaliating, and exacting revenge with as much impunity as the military did a generation ago. Jorge claims, "For ten dollars, bang, bang, they'll kill you dead." A warning to travelers from the U.S. State Department confirms his assertion.

> The State Department considers El Salvador a critical-crime-threat country. El Salvador has one of the highest homicide rates in the world; violent crimes, as well as petty crimes are prevalent throughout El Salvador, and U.S. citizens have been among the victims. Central America has been identified as the most violent region in the world, with El Salvador reporting the highest death rate due to armed violence. According to a recent study, El Salvador has the highest rate of violent fatalities, with over 70 deaths recorded for every 100,000 inhabitants.[11]

In the national election in 2009, FMLN candidate Mauricio Funes won the presidency, the first presidential victory for the left wing. Funes had attended the UCA and worked as a correspondent for CNN. As expected from a left-wing candidate, he reestablished ties with Cuba. More unexpected was a friendly attitude toward doing business with the United States. He welcomed President Barack Obama in 2011, and official placards saying *Bienvenidos Presidente Obama* hung from street lights in San Salvador. Funes and Obama held a joint press conference, but Salvadoran journalists were frustrated when they were limited to just two questions predetermined by the U.S. Secret Service.[12]

The Salvadoran president said, "I want to thank President Obama when he recognizes the importance of . . . the presence of more than 2 million Salvadorans that work and live in the United States, and the importance that this population has in the development of El Salvador through the remittances that they send year by year."[13] The "more than two million" Salvadorans, legal and illegal, living in the United

---

[11] travel.state.gov website (El Salvador selection), managed by the Bureau of Consular Affairs, U.S. Department of State.

[12] Roberto Lovato, "America's Grisly History Haunts Obama's El Salvador Visit," Colorlines News for Action (March 25, 2011), available on the colorlines.com website.

[13] Quoted in "El Salvador: Onwards and Upwards," *Our World* (October 24, 2011), available online.

States that year sent nearly $3.6 billion back to their homeland.[14] Segundo Montes was still correct in his assertion that El Salvador is addicted to remittances, which come in at more than 15 percent of its GDP. The poor of El Salvador may go unrecognized in that country and in ours, but in terms of economics, at least, they are monumentally important.

Funes indicated that if Salvadorans could remain in their native place and find work and peace, then the country would be better off. Countries like El Salvador need a partnership with U.S. immigration laws and procedures. "We agree that migration is a painful expression of a world that has not been able to establish accessible parameters of justice and inclusion. I have expressed to President Obama my pleasure when I heard in his speech in the State of the Union the commitment of pushing an agreement of both parties, bipartisan agreement for comprehensive immigration reform and present it to the Congress of the United States."[15] Managing immigration will remain an issue of great complexity in the United States, and weaning El Salvador from remittances may prove untenable.

As of 2011, according to UNICEF statistics, the population of El Salvador was 6.2 million people, and the capital city of San Salvador has more than 1.5 million. Forty percent of the population lives below the poverty line—living on US$2 a day or less. Almost 30 percent of the population is under the age of fourteen, and only slightly more than half of those of appropriate age attend secondary school. Of children under age five, more than 6 percent are chronically underweight. If the problem of hunger for El Salvador's children has improved since Lucía's childhood, it is only a marginal improvement. The urgency of the challenge for El Salvador to grow, import, and distribute food has never been greater.

On his visit President Obama and his family visited Romero's tomb, but the visit had a perfunctory tone. Obama was clearly distracted by the airstrikes on Libya by a coalition of nations that occurred the same day. He cut short the visit, did not make it to the UCA, and announced US$200 million of U.S. aid for "regional security," sending a shudder through memories still too fresh. Was Obama's visit yet another

---

[14] David Kaufman, "Why Obama Is Placing His Hopes on El Salvador," *Time* (March 21, 2011).

[15] The White House, Office of the Press Secretary, March 11, 2011, remarks of President Mauricio Funes of El Salvador in Joint Press Conference with President Barack Obama, National Palace, San Salvador, El Salvador.

episode of the United States dangling its wallet to manipulate its own goals? Protesters' posters reading "El Imperialismo" contradicted the official welcome by the government.

In the immediate aftermath of the murders at the UCA, Lucía was in shock. Over the years she has fought depression and anxiety. Work sustains her as she focuses intently on the patients at hand. As she describes how she attends to her patients, it is clear that for her, her work is a vocation. She ministers to the infirm, aging bodies, "massaging the legs, cleaning the face, holding the hand," conscious of speaking in a quiet and comforting voice. Lucía admits she does not have many friends and that her daughter has sometimes thought her not very sociable. The massacre and her life in El Salvador are so much a part of who she is that it is difficult to develop friendships without speaking of the past. Yet she does not want to speak of it and burden others with sadness. "I feel depressed sometimes," she said. "Before Miami my character was so happy. It changed totally." The interrogation in Miami exacerbated the trauma of the murders, and in many ways, recovering from it has been more problematic.

As Lucía and I talked about her life and El Salvador and what has happened since, we encountered many curiosities. It is curious, for example, that in reviewing Lucía's life and Elba Ramos's life that both had connections to the Regalados. Elba had been a coffee picker on the Regalado estate at the time of Don Ernesto's kidnapping. If their paths crossed at that time, Lucía does not remember.

It is curious that Ignacio Martín-Baró, Dan Germann, and Rutilio Grande, all deeply pastoral men, had done their studies in Lumen Vitae and at Louvain in Belgium in the 1960s.[16] Did their paths cross in Europe? Could it be that Nacho's kindness to the children of Jayace, Dan's deep friendships with SCU students, and Rutilio's commitment to the poor of Aguilares came out of the academic framework offered in Louvain? Most assuredly these three envisioned and worked for the "transformation of the world according to the plan of God, to

---

[16] Nelson Portillo, "The Life of Ignacio Martín-Baró: A Narrative Account of a Personal Biographical Journey," *Peace and Conflict: Journal of Peace Psychology* 18/1 (2012): 80; *Rutilio Grande, Mártir de la evangelización rural en El Salvador* (UCA, 1978); Daniel Germann did post-graduate studies at Lumen Viae, then earned a doctorate from Saint Albert's College, Louvain.

make it more and more balanced, more comfortable, more human and more just."[17]

It is curious that a gift Dan brought from Central America and presented to my husband and me before the UCA murders, before any of us knew the Cernas, resembles them so closely. It is a weaving, a scene from Latin America, of a woman seated at a fire making a meal, a man standing nearby, and a little girl walking away. It is, frankly, eerie that this scene looks so much like the Cerna family.

It is curious that, given Lucía and Jorge's unpleasant associations with soldiers and with U.S. officials, today their daughter is a nurse for the Veterans Administration. She is charged with tending to the injuries sustained by U.S. service personnel in wars ranging from World War II to Afghanistan and Iraq.

Where is hope?

The father general of the Society of Jesus at the time of the murders, Peter-Hans Kolvenbach, SJ, was experienced with living in war zones. "He noted that while living in the midst of war emphasizes the fragility of human life, the sound of a bird singing after a night of terror announces that 'death will never have the last word in the Creator's will.'"[18] We hope that the people of El Salvador can forge a way to their best selves, that they will not be impeded by outside forces, and that they determine their future in peace and in justice. As Joseph O'Hare, SJ, implored within days of the murders, "We pray that the irony of that tiny tortured country's name, El Salvador, will be redeemed by the resurrection of its people."[19]

There is hope in El Salvador's very name. The humble country's name sounds a call to humanity, to compassion, to justice, to listen to the poor—30 percent of the world's seven billion people. The day after the massacre, Stephen Privett, SJ, in a homily at Mission Santa Clara, said, "I have been trying to do what Jesuits have been doing since the time of Ignatius of Loyola: to place myself before the broken body of our crucified savior—*Cristo, El Salvador*—and ask myself the

---

[17] Father Idoate, quoted in Beirne, *Jesuit Education and Social Change in El Salvador*, 78.

[18] See "Peter-Hans Kolvenbach, SJ (1928–)," ignatianspirituality.com, a service of Loyola Press.

[19] Joseph A. O'Hare, SJ, "In Solidarity with the Slain Jesuits of El Salvador," homily, memorial mass, St. Ignatius Church, New York City, November 22, 1989.

unsettling questions: What have I done *por Cristo, El Salvador*? What am I doing now *por Cristo, El Salvador*? And what am I going to do henceforth, *por Cristo, El Salvador*?"[20]

The crucified Jesus as Savior was an embarrassment and profound disappointment to his contemporaries who were looking for a politician messiah. The surprising truth perceived in the days after Jesus' death by Peter, Mary, and John, and even the doubting Thomas, was that the wounded, tortured, murdered Jesus had triumphed over death—for them and for us.

Attorneys for the CJA who brought this case to the courts in Spain have found hope that the important work of Martín-Baró and Ellacuría may now find a wider audience. The attorneys noted that in Spain the priests' work "has long been ignored by the press, the TV, and the general public. Their work and their commitment to the poor, however, is timeless. The hope instilled by their words and acts—for the still-suffering people of El Salvador and for all of us, seeking justice for the victims of human rights violations—is a priceless gift that they left us."[21]

In his book *Where Is God?* Jon Sobrino suggests that hope can emerge if we allow ourselves to be affected by suffering. "To let ourselves be affected, to feel pain over lives cut short or endangered, to feel indignation over the injustice behind the tragedy, to feel shame over the way we have ruined the planet . . . letting ourselves be affected by tragedy can generate solidarity."[22] The mysterious reality of the presence of God reveals itself in the love and hope expressed by such solidarity.

There is hope when schools facilitate "immersion" trips to the developing world to do service or to seek information. My daughter was able to go to El Salvador. My son, through Bellarmine College Prep in San Jose, went to Guaymas, Mexico, to work in a soup kitchen, and also spent time on skid row and at Homeboy Industries in Los Angeles. Those trips educate a new generation in compassion and active justice. The memorial fund set up at Santa Clara University in honor of Dan Germann upon his death in 2007 is specifically designated to finance immersion experiences for students. The young people who go

---

[20] Stephen Privett, SJ, homily, November 17, 1989, Mission Santa Clara.

[21] Almudena Bernabeu and Carolyn Patty Blum, "The Road to Spain: The Jesuit Massacre and the Struggle Against Impunity in El Salvador," American Psychological Association, *Peace and Conflict: Journal of Peace Psychology* 18/1 (2012): 100.

[22] Jon Sobrino, SJ, *Where Is God? Earthquake, Terrorism, Barbarity, and Hope* (Maryknoll, NY: Orbis Books), 7.

out into the world to learn, and see, and help, are hope and inspiration for us all.

There is hope when we share meals, Eucharist and everyday meals, like that personal memorial on the twentieth anniversary of the massacre when Lucía's family and mine shared food and love and stories. There is hope in all those meals around our table over the years, with grandparents who are now gone, aunts, uncles, friends, and colleagues. On one occasion when Dan Germann joined us and several families, he looked around at the quite chaotic meal and commented that this is what our world needs to be—where the more able take care of the less able; where we make sure everyone has enough to eat; where squabbles are negotiated, and when one is hurt, we pick him up, dust him off, and send him off again. It is loud, and messy, and non-stop—and that is life. That was his blessing for us. He translated our crowded, noisy meal into sacramental language.

Hope depends on truth.

The Cernas' experience makes that truism only too clear. It is often difficult to get at the truth. José María Tojeira, SJ, provincial of Central America at the time of the murders, declared in 1991, "Only by establishing truth can justice be done, the first step toward reconciliation for El Salvador's bitterly divided people."[23] In a country so mired in lies, it has been difficult to dig out. Congressman Joe Moakley tried to explain that "truth is not the enemy."[24] In many quarters it still is. The massacre and its pseudo-investigations have been travesties.

It seems as if it is in El Salvador's DNA to have priests call out injustice, from the earliest, José Cañas and José Matías Delgado, to Father Alas, Rutilio Grande, Óscar Romero, and the UCA martyrs. Many women, church women and lay women, have added their voices to the call for truth. Jean Donovan, Dorothy Kazel, Ita Ford, and Maura Clarke have left imprints of integrity and courage for those who work for justice in El Salvador. María Julia Hernández along with her staff, not long before she died of a heart attack in 2007, successfully scuttled the ARENA party's plan to declare Roberto D'Aubuisson the posthumous winner of a coveted national award. And on the twenty-year anniversary of the deaths at the UCA, El Salvador's President Mauricio Funes awarded the nation's highest award, the Order of José Matías Delgado, posthumously to the six martyred Jesuits. These are tentative steps toward honesty.

---

[23] José María Tojeira, "Perspective on El Salvador, Tipping the Scales of Justice: A Civil Court Is Ready to Try Soldiers for the 1989 Jesuit Massacre; The U.S. Must Stop Shielding Key Witnesses," *Los Angeles Times*, April 26, 1991.

[24] Joe Moakley, remarks at UCA, quoted in Whitfield, *Paying the Price*, 288.

Lucía asks—and answers—the fundamental question, "Why did we have to leave? We did nothing but tell *la verdad*, the truth. The authorities did not want the truth. They had that. They wanted something else. The truth required us to leave everything—our parents and families, our home and country. The truth required it. That's it."

Epilogue

"Telling the Truth"

Jon Sobrino, SJ

I was asked to write a prologue about the *value* of truth, but I feared that what I wanted to say would seem too theoretical if the reader didn't already know Lucía's story. So I decided to write an epilogue, instead, and to speak, more specifically, about *telling* the truth, because I think that focus will help us better understand Lucía's greatness.

Karl Rahner liked to say that reality "doesn't want to stay silent forever." I would add: and truth wants to be communicated. That's what happened with Lucía when she saw that some Jesuits had been killed: she told the truth about who they were and, especially, about who had killed them.

When she said what she had seen and heard, Lucía became a *witness* to the truth and also its *defendant*, since she spoke the truth against those who fought it. She became a heroic *servant* of the truth in highly dangerous circumstances. She was also a faithful *servant* of the truth, threatened from without by powerful people, and from within by her anguish. She obeyed a higher voice: her conscience. She risked all that she most loved: her life, her family, the possibility of living in her country. She did this with dignity and with fidelity to the Jesuits with whom she had worked.

She received no official recognition for her honesty and firmness. On the contrary, the powerful did everything they could to make her seem like a liar. She quickly became yet another victim of what had happened on November 16, 1989. But she would become a symbol of the struggle against murder and lies. In her case, "telling the truth" was a victory over powerful enemies.

Others came to her defense: the Jesuits in El Salvador, Archbishop Rivera y Damas, María Julia Hernández of Tutela Legal (the archdiocesan human rights office), some members of the diplomatic corps, and some of the U.S. Jesuits.

Those who were lying were frightened because Lucía wouldn't let them get away with hiding the truth. And her truth was a far-reaching condemnation that established the fundamental fact: in El Salvador there were criminals, important members of official classes, who murdered defenseless and innocent people—many of them, and massively. There were also people who, after killing, lied unscrupulously and arrogantly, and with government support; people who tried to manipulate and cover up the truth; and if someone like Lucía dared to state the truth, the liars threatened them and tried to silence them—a powerful sign of sin in the world.

They didn't lie to punish Lucía for doing something wrong. They lied because she did something very good—but it wasn't good for them. Structurally, their power—military, political, imperial (the United States was involved)—was exposed. Personally, their ill-gotten wealth was in danger.

Without naming names, Lucía was saying that the government, military men, politicians, and some diplomats were liars. Many of those criminals lied to evade the words of a simple worker at the UCA. The killers had placed a sign near the rose garden where the Jesuits were killed: "This is what the FMLN does to traitors." President Cristiani and his government sent two groups—one to countries in Europe, the other to the United States—to say that the FMLN had murdered the Jesuits. Bishop Romeo Tovar Astorga went to the Vatican, saying publicly, as was published in European newspapers, that the FMLN were the killers. And when he was asked for proof, he replied, "*¿Qui prodest?*" That is to say, who benefited from the killings? According to him, it was the FMLN. All of them invented hallucinating lies.

Archbishop Romero said, "They kill those who get in the way." We want to add something similar: "They eliminate—or try to eliminate—those who tell the truth." They wanted to eliminate Lucía—if not physically, then, as Father Tojeira explained in the preface to this book, by making her appear to be a liar. They wanted to eliminate her because she was a truth teller.

This has occurred in El Salvador in many ways. The paradigm case is Archbishop Romero. Why did they eliminate him? To be sure, it was for having told the truth, exhaustively and straight out, about the deaths, the disappearances, the torture, about thousands of people receiving unjust salaries, and about those—especially the poor and simple—who had to flee the country. Archbishop Romero got in their way because he was, as he put it, "the voice of the voiceless." What most bothered them about his voice was that it was heard—and that it told the truth.

Archbishop Romero kept the eighth commandment perfectly: "Thou shalt not kill." On the thirtieth anniversary of his martyrdom, in an Anglican church liturgy, Dr. Rowan Williams, then archbishop of Canterbury, told of a remark made by an airport official when Archbishop Romero returned to El Salvador after the meeting of the Latin American bishops in Puebla. As Romero walked by, he heard the official say, "There goes the truth." In his first homily after the Puebla meeting, Romero said that phrase made him happy, "because in my suitcase I wasn't bringing contraband or lies; I was bringing the truth."

That was Archbishop Romero's way. Of course he wanted to keep the eighth commandment, but his relationship with the truth went much deeper than that. It was something that shaped him: loving the truth, being possessed by it and open to it, and being determined to bring it to bear. After that came telling the truth concretely, speaking about whether the commandments were being kept in El Salvador, especially the fifth—thou shalt not kill—and the seventh—thou shalt not steal. Telling the truth meant denouncing, and doing it in a way we've never seen again.

As for violations of the fifth commandment, he spoke of "violence, murder, torture, slashing people with machetes, dumping bodies, hurling the dead into the ocean; this is the reign of hell" (July 1, 1979). Shortly before he was killed, he said, "They keep massacring those who have organized, simply because they take to the street to ask for justice and freedom" (January 27, 1980).

As for violations of the seventh commandment, he said, "Don't steal! What you have, you've stolen from the people, who are perishing in misery" (March 18, 1979).

Speaking again of the eighth commandment, in the context of our country, he said, "What's missing here is the truth" (April 12, 1979). "There are too many people whose pens are for hire, whose words are for sale" (February 18, 1979). "They distort the truth" (January 21, 1979).

He denounced the way lies were used to make evil possible at all levels of society. With pain and bitterness, he complained, "We're living in a world of lies, where nobody believes anything anymore" (March 18, 1979).

At crucial moments he would invoke God's name, but without taking it in vain, uttering it in relation to his suffering people. In the well-known words of his final Sunday homily, "In the name of God, in the name of this suffering people whose cries rise to heaven more loudly each day, I implore you, I beg you, I order you in the name of God: stop the repression" (March 23, 1980).

❧

Archbishop Romero was shaped by the truth. To show this, I'll cite the words of a *campesino* whose wisdom is beyond doubt. He said Archbishop Romero was the most important person he had ever known, and he said these immortal words: "Archbishop Romero told the truth. He defended us, the poor. And that's why they killed him."

I don't recall him saying anything more than that. But it was enough. It said what has to be said about Archbishop Romero.

Surely that *campesino* took great joy in the fact that Archbishop Romero defended them. And surely, when Romero was killed, he cried bitterly, as one does when losing a father. But perhaps what had taken him by surprise, most of all, was the simple fact that Archbishop Romero had told the whole truth.

He could well have said, "We have been oppressed, killed, disappeared, left homeless." But he would have added: "And we have been silenced. Nobody ever said a word for us. But now Archbishop Romero has told the truth."

Archbishop Romero's defense of the *campesinos*, and his being killed for doing so, were intimately related to his being a person who *told the truth*. To tell the truth was, in itself, to defend the poor, who often had no other defense than the truth. And to tell the truth was, in itself, to risk death.

❧

Scripture has important words about the ultimate things for believers and all those of good will. Certainly love is central, but truth is, too.

Scripture places it in dialectical opposition to *the lie*. In the Gospel of John, 8:44, the evil one is described as a murderer and also as a liar.

John 8:32 speaks of the truth with great simplicity: "The truth will make you free."

Archbishop Romero and Lucía Cerna weren't identical. Both of them experienced difficult moments. On February 25, 1980, Romero wrote in his diary that he feared a violent death. While she was being interrogated, Lucía felt fear, too, and a moment came when she weakened and fell.

Archbishop Romero told the truth vigorously, insistently, repeatedly; he did it in public, in cathedrals, before microphones. Lucía told the truth while she was being threatened, guarded in official places, and submitted to lie-detector tests.

I want to end with a text from the last part of Jesus' life. In Bethany a woman came up to him and poured an expensive perfume on his head. Some were indignant, saying this was wasteful; the perfume, they said, could have been sold, and the money given to the poor. But Jesus defended the woman, saying, "When she poured this perfume on my body, she did it to prepare me for burial." And he added, "Truly I tell you, wherever this gospel is preached throughout the world, what she has done will also be told, in memory of her."

I hope that this book will proclaim to its readers, wherever they are, the fidelity and goodness of Lucía. She held firm in the truth till the end.

Acknowledgments

We are grateful. *Somos agradecido.*

Over the years Santa Clara University and its interwoven communities have been a source of nourishment to each of us at different times and often for very different reasons. Today, together, we are particularly grateful to SCU's president, Michael Engh, SJ, for sponsoring and co-publishing this work. He embraced the idea from the beginning, and Michael McCarthy, SJ, facilitated SCU's association with Orbis Books. Our editor, James Keane, has been an attentive and discerning advocate to bring the witness of the UCA martyrs to new audiences.

We are honored that Jon Sobrino, SJ, and José M. Tojeira, SJ, offered words of inspiration and challenge, along with their memories for this work. These essays echo the respect and love that Lucía experienced all those years ago at the UCA.

We appreciate the time and effort of those who read and commented on portions of this manuscript, including Sister Mary Annel, MM, Geraldina Cerna, Rev. Penelope Duckworth, Karen Filice, Sister Lilla Hull, MM, Sonny Manuel, SJ, Michael McCarthy, SJ, Susan Raffo, Francis Smith, SJ, Mark Torres, SJ, Sister Cecilia Vandal, MM. A special note of gratitude is due to both James Torrens, SJ, and to Gary Kass for important conversations at critical stages in this process.

Thank you to Gene Palumbo of the UCA for translating both the Preface and the Epilogue, and to Jesús Ramos of Sacred Heart Schools Atherton for translating the poems of Alfredo Espino.

Santa Clara University Archives provided some of the images here. We are grateful for the help of Sheila Conway and her assistants in locating information and photos. Other photos were taken by Lisa Ignoffo when she traveled to El Salvador in 2011, and by Edward Fassett, SJ, when was there in 2013.

Sometimes encouraging words and insightful comments usher a work along inevitably rocky paths. On several occasions throughout the interviewing and writing of this book Francis Smith, SJ, offered those words and insights. His support is deeply appreciated.

Each of us has a heart full of gratitude to God for our families, who accept our love and offer theirs in return.

Esperamos que este libro habla de verdad y el respeto de todos los mártires del Salvador—It is our hope that this book speaks of truth and respect for all the martyrs of El Salvador.

Bibliographic Essay

Mary Jo Ignoffo

Nothing about this book is easily classified. Is it primarily a memoir or a history? Is it a book about civil war or a testimony of witness to a crime? Are there strands of theology, or is it spirituality? Ultimately, this book is a fusion, a blending of cultures and languages, traditions and histories. Sources that were consulted also drift across the spectrum from history to religion, from the voices of the UCA to official government documents. And finally, there are reflections of those who reported or mourned after the fact.

Lucía

The most important source for this book is Lucía Cerna. Her willingness to open her heart and recount events of her life has brought both pain and joy. The audio recordings of our interviews and transcriptions will be placed in Santa Clara University's Archives and Special Collections.

Lucía's first official testimony was given before a Salvadoran judge in the Spanish and French embassies in San Salvador five days after the massacre on November 21 and 22, 1989. Next, she and her family were sequestered in Miami by the FBI. The Cernas' testimony there is not available, and in fact, access to the official recordings of those interviews was denied even to the congressional committee investigating the Jesuit murders in 1990.

Upon release from the FBI, Lucía was interviewed by two human rights lawyers on December 3, 1989, in Miami, and on December 9 and 10 at an undisclosed location, which Lucía now believes was Spring Hill College in Alabama. The authors of this report, R. Scott Greathead, assistant attorney general of the State of New York, and Martha Doggett, author of reports on human rights in El Salvador, had been to El Salvador on numerous occasions. They issued "The Jesuit Murders: A Report on the Testimony of a Witness," for the

Lawyers Committee for Human Rights on December 15, 1989. Doggett and Greathead write: "It is our firm conclusion that Lucía Cerna's testimony of what she observed on the night of the murders is credible and trustworthy. . . . The declaration she gave to the investigating judge in El Salvador and the statements she made to us are consistent" (32).

Martha Doggett went on to write *Death Foretold: The Jesuit Murders in El Salvador* (Washington DC: Georgetown University Press/ Lawyers Committee for Human Rights, 1993), a highly detailed account of the crime, of what led up to it, and of American officials' various viewpoints. The case against the criminals is laid out, with a commentary on the workings of the Salvadoran judicial system.

Jim Torrens among the first of the California Jesuits to meet Lucía, interviewed her in the summer of 1990, in the first months of her relocation. Torrens's resulting article, "UCA—The Witnesses Talk," appeared in *America*, a national Jesuit publication, on November 24, 1990, one year after the massacre. Torrens's article was the first published interview with Lucía Cerna.

Voices of the UCA

Serious analysis of the scholarly work of the Jesuit martyrs is a task that will be undertaken by others. Both Lucía and I looked to some words from the UCA to inform our conversations. Important commentary came out of the UCA before the massacre and since. The best concise retelling of the events of the night of November 16, 1989, is Dean Brackley's "Remembering the UCA Martyrs: Ten Years Later," *Conversations on Jesuit Higher Education* 16/3 (1999), which is also available online. Brackley gives a precise chronology of that night, and his article adds details that were not available in the initial investigations.

Teresa Whitfield's *Paying the Price: Ignacio Ellacuría and the Murdered Jesuits of El Salvador* (Philadelphia: Temple University Press, 1995) illuminates reasons that Ellacuría and the others were targeted. She looks at the background, education, and particular talents of some of the martyrs, including their publications. In the minds of some military officers the Jesuits were Marxists who supported opposition to the government. In this line of thinking, the priests were enemies of the state. While the focus of this book is Ignacio Ellacuría, his philosophy and life path, in many ways he embodied the institution, and he ultimately "paid the price."

Ellacuría received invitations to speak from around the world. When he was killed, he had just returned from Spain, where he had addressed a number of groups. Several years earlier, in 1982, he had been invited as the commencement speaker at Santa Clara University and was awarded an honorary degree. His message to the graduates that year is available on the scu.edu website.

The most comprehensive history of the UCA is Charles J. Beirne's *Jesuit Education and Social Change in El Salvador* (New York: Garland Publications, 1996). It clarifies how the institution came to the vanguard of social change in El Salvador. Beirne highlights many remarkable aspects of the short—twenty-four years from founding to massacre—evolution of the university. He also outlines weaknesses in its development and administration.

Lucía and I rewatched, after twenty years, the 1990 episode of *60 Minutes* on which she had been interviewed. Most startling was to see a brief clip of Ignacio Martín-Baró, Padre Nacho, in a video that had been filmed months before he died. Lucía let out an audible gasp upon hearing his voice again and in hearing the urgency of his perspective on the situation in El Salvador. He believed that the country's problems were primarily solvable economic challenges, not ideological ones.

Ignacio Martín-Baró's *Writings for a Liberation Psychology* was edited by Adrianne Aron and Shawn Corne in 1994 and brought out by Harvard University Press. A biographical article published in 2012 entitled "The Life of Ignacio Martín-Baró: A Narrative Account of a Personal Biographical Journey," by Nelson Portillo, was published in *Peace and Conflict: Journal of Peace Psychology*, American Psychological Association 18/1 (2012). Portillo is a visiting professor of sociology and political science at the UCA; he had met Martín-Baró there and follows in his path in psychology.

Segundo Montes Mozo and Juan José García Vasquez undertook the first major investigation of its kind in El Salvador, the statistical data and analysis of migration flows from El Salvador to the United States. *Salvadoran Migration to the United States: An Exploratory Study* (Washington DC: Georgetown University, Center for Immigration Policy and Refugee Assistance, Hemispheric Migration Project, 1988) offers a glimpse into social, economic, and political patterns. One surprising result of studies like this one was and remains the fact that El Salvador's poor are a crucial element to the country's economy. The poor have introduced remittances from the United States as an economic factor that the country is now dependent upon.

Jon Sobrino, world-renowned theologian, has written extensively. His remarks at Mission Santa Clara for the twentieth anniversary of the massacre, "The UCA Martyrs: Challenge and Grace," November 5, 2009, are quoted here. Sobrino's *Where Is God? Earthquake, Terrorism, Barbarity, and Hope,* translated by Margaret Wilde (Maryknoll, NY: Orbis Books, 2004), offers insights into suffering and the importance of acknowledging the suffering of so many in the world. Likewise, Dean Brackley's *The Call to Discernment in Troubled Times: New Perspectives on the Transformative Wisdom of Ignatius of Loyola* (New York: Crossroad, 2004) examines an Ignatian perspective in the face of suffering and evil.

Official Documents

Without a doubt, Congressman Joe Moakley (D-MA) was the highest-ranking and most forceful American to put his credibility on the line while investigating the UCA murders. The John Joseph Moakley Archive and Institute at Suffolk University, Boston, has preserved the congressman's papers and oral history interviews. One invaluable resource is "Congressman Joe Moakley and El Salvador: A Research Guide," available on the suffolk.edu website.

In addition, Robert Allison and Joseph McEttrick, both of Suffolk University, interviewed Joe Moakley in 2001. Transcriptions of the interview, "John Joseph Moakley, Oral History Project," are available on the suffolk.edu website.

Moakley's firsthand impressions, including those from leading a congressional task force to El Salvador, add a crucial dimension to Lucía Cerna's experiences. The congressman reiterates what happened to her and outlines his very disturbing insight that "we were fighting our own country on this one."

The congressional task force, known as the Moakley Commission, issued an interim report on its finding on April 30, 1990. The "Interim Report of the Speaker's Task Force on El Salvador," available on the Center for Justice and Accountability website, cja.org, and other sites, is an alarming indictment of the U.S. policy in El Salvador and of the culprits involved in the UCA murders. The "Final Report," issued on November 18, 1991, is a short verification of the "Interim Report."

The Lawyers Committee for Human Rights, New York (today's Human Rights First) published "The Jesuit Case: The Jury Trial" *(La Vista Pública)* in September 1991. It documents the trial held in

El Salvador in the case of the UCA murders. It also can be found on the cja.org website.

The Peace Agreement reached between El Salvador's warring parties was signed at Chapultepec, Mexico, on January 16, 1992. The full text of the agreement can be found in several places online. A preliminary agreement had been reached the previous year, calling for the United Nations to establish a Commission on Truth for El Salvador. The commission issued *From Madness to Hope: The Twelve-Year War in El Salvador* in 1993. The text of this document has been posted by the United States Institute of Peace on the usip.org website.

As a result of the Truth Commission, the United States released formerly classified documents—approximately twelve thousand memos, cables, and telexes—relating to U.S. involvement in El Salvador during the 1980s. In a special supplement the *National Catholic Reporter* reproduced dozens of them. Arthur Jones's "El Salvador Revisited: A Look at Declassified State Department Documents—Some of What the U.S. Knew—and When It Knew It" (September 23, 1994) remains an amazing piece of reporting and news gathering, particularly since many of the documents have been "reclassified" in recent years. Some of the memos outlined in Jones's article were used for this work.

Historical Background

A few histories of El Salvador published beginning in the 1970s provide some to understand the experiences that Lucía relayed. I purposely looked at Alistair White's *El Salvador* (New York: Praeger Publishers, 1973). Although outdated in many ways, it offers a perspective of El Salvador in the 1950s and 1960s, when Lucía was growing up. Likewise, David Browning's *El Salvador: Landscape and Society* (Oxford: Clarendon Press, 1971) accounted for how the Cerna family managed to maintain land ownership and therefore avoid the fate of the landless.

Jeffery M. Paige, *Coffee and Power: Revolution and the Rise of Democracy in Central America* (Cambridge, MA: Harvard University Press, 1997) gives an overview of the coffee commodities markets of Central America, explains El Salvador's role in the region, and provides a sturdy framework to understand the country's elites and dominance over the economy throughout the twentieth century. It gives an insightful description of *La Matanza* of 1932, linking it with the civil war of the 1980s.

Lucía's descriptions of Walter Thilo Deininger particularly captured my attention, and I was able to understand his story through Max Paul Friedman's *Nazis and Good Neighbors: The United States Campaign Against the Germans of Latin America in World War II* (Cambridge: Cambridge University Press, 2003). This book describes the under-reported U.S. World War II policies in Latin America.

There are dozens of publications on El Salvador's civil war of the 1980s. A few, chosen from the beginning of the conflict, include Robert Armstrong's and Janet Shenk's *El Salvador: The Face of Revolution* (Boston: South End Press, 1982). Others that were published toward the end of the war, like *El Salvador at War: An Oral History of Conflict from the 1979 Insurrection to the Present*, edited by Max G. Manwaring and Court Prisk, and published by the National Defense University Press in 1988, give voice to U.S. military officials, Salvadoran military officers, leaders of the FMLN, and foreign diplomats.

The Church

Archbishop Óscar Romero is a pivotal figure in El Salvador's history and the history of Catholicism in Latin America. Some of his homilies were compiled and translated by James R. Brockman, SJ, in *The Violence of Love* (Maryknoll, NY: Orbis Books, 1988 and 2010). Romero's open letter to President Jimmy Carter, February 17, 1980, can be found on the villanova.edu website.

Romero's close friend, Rutilio Grande, SJ, is recalled by Joseph E. Mulligan, SJ, in "Remembering a Salvadoran Martyr," also available online, for example, on the thewitness.org website. A small publication on Rutilio Grande was published by the UCA in 1978, the year after Grande's assassination. Specific authors are not identified except to say they were Jesuits of the UCA. *Rutilio Grande, Mártir de la evangelización rural en El Salvador* (UCA, 1978) is one of only a handful of publications about this important figure whose life and death prophesied the fates of his colleagues and his country. I hope this gets translated into English, as the authors personally knew this important martyr of El Salvador.

The Second Vatican Council, held in Rome beginning in 1962, and the Second General Conference of Latin American Bishops, held in Columbia in 1968, were watershed events in the history of the Catholic Church. Both conferences had social and political implications far beyond the confines of church walls. Hundreds of publications detail the proceedings. A radio address of Pope John XXIII just before the opening of the conference on September 11, 1962, is quoted herein. The full address and the other documents of Vatican II are available on the vatican.va website. Documents from the Second General Conference of Latin American Bishops are published in *The Church in the Present-Day Transformation of Latin America in the Light of the Council* (Washington DC: USCC Division for Latin America, 1968) and also online.

Official church comments about liberation theology were articulated by Joseph Cardinal Ratzinger, approved by Pope John Paul II, in the Sacred Congregation for the Doctrine of the Faith's "Instruction on Certain Aspects of the 'Theology of liberation,'" August 6, 1984. A different, more nuanced understanding of liberation theology is found in the German Bishops' Conference document *The Church's Confession of Faith: A Catholic Catechism for Adults*, translated by Stephen Wentworth Arndt, edited by Mark D. Jordan and Walter Cardinal Kasper (San Francisco: Communio Books Ignatius Press, 1987).

Human Rights

America's Watch, which currently operates as Human Rights Watch, offers details about its work on its website, hrw.org. Its account of human rights abuses in El Salvador during its civil war was published as America's Watch, *El Salvador's Decade of Terror: Human Rights Since the Assassination of Archbishop Romero* (New Haven, CT: Yale University Press, 1991). The foreword was authored by the late María Julia Hernández, at the time the executive director of the San Salvadoran Archdiocesan Tutela Legal, a Catholic human rights advocacy organization. She interviewed and questioned Lucía and ultimately counseled her to flee the country.

The Center for Justice and Accountability is an international human rights organization that attempts to deter torture and other abuses; it helps victims to recover and seek justice. It litigates against abusers in international court and currently has taken the Jesuit massacre case to trial in Spain. Its website is cja.org.

The horror that occurred in a small Morazán village in 1981 is detailed by Mark Danner in *The Massacre at El Mozote* (New York: Vintage Books, 1994). The U.S. State Department denied many massacres by the Salvadoran military during the 1980s, and when it acknowledged some, it pointed out that the violence may have been caused by the opposition.

Disturbing the Peace by James Hodge and Linda Cooper (Maryknoll, NY: Orbis Books, 2005) focuses on civil disobedience by Maryknoll priest Roy Bourgeois and two colleagues who took issue with the School of the Americas' training of Salvadoran soldiers at Fort Benning, Georgia.

Margaret O'Brien Steinfels wrote "Death and Lies in El Salvador: The Ambassador's Tale" for *Commonweal Magazine* 133/18 (October 26, 2001). It is a lengthy interview with former U.S. Ambassador to El Salvador Robert White. It was during his tenure that Archbishop Romero was assassinated and the American churchwomen were slain in 1980.

Reflections

Immediately after the massacre at the UCA, memorials were held around the world. Some reflections by Jesuits have been quoted, including Stephen Privett's untitled homily for a mass of resurrection on November 17, 1989, at Mission Santa Clara. A copy of Privett's talk is in the Archives and Special Collections at Santa Clara University. Joseph O'Hare's talk on November 22, 1989, at St. Ignatius Church in New York City, "In Solidarity with the Slain Jesuits of El Salvador," can be found on the onlineministries.creighton.edu website. Dan Germann spoke at Mission Santa Clara on the one-year anniversary of the massacre and again at a California Province meeting in 1991. He gave me copies of his remarks, and they are quoted herein.

Index

Alas, José, 65, 161
Amaya, Rufina, 62–63
Amaya Grimaldi, Óscar Mariano, 92
America, 154
America's Watch (Human Rights Watch), 60, 177
Antiguo Cuscatlán (El Salvador), 1, 10, 15–16
APDHE (Spanish Association for Human Rights), 149
ARENA (Nationalist Republican Alliance; Alianza Republicana Nacionalista), xviii, 60–61, 72–73, 98
Arrupe, Pedro, 52, 94, 147
Arrupe Partnerships for Community-Based Learning, 154
Ascencio, Sierra, 92
Atlacatl, 13–14
Atlacatl Battalion, xviii–xix, 14, 63, 76–77, 80, 81, 92, 94, 112
Avalos Vargas, Antonio Ramiro, 92
Avilés, Carlos, 115

Beirne, Charles J., 91, 153–54, 173
Benavides Moreno, Guillermo Alfredo, xviii–xix, 77, 93, 112, 114, 115, 134, 148, 149
Benedict XVI. *See* Ratzinger, Joseph
Berlin Wall, fall of, 80
Berra, Joseph, 47, 121–22, 127, 130–31
Bettelheim, Bruno, 58
boat people, Vietnamese, 147
Bourgeois, Roy, 76, 178
Brackley, Dean, xxiv, xxv, 144–45, 150, 151–53, 172, 174
Bradley, Ed, 116
Buckland, Eric Warren, 115
Bush, George H. W., xiii, 63, 79–80
Bustillo, Juan Rafael, 93

Cádiz Deleito, Francisco, xii
Calero, Luís, 128
Call to Discernment in Troubled Times, The (Brackley), 151–52, 174
Calmus, Ellen, 152
Cañas, José Simeón, 31, 161
Cardenal, Ernesto, 63–64
Cardenal, Rodolfo, 66, 70
Carter administration, 59, 60, 62
Casa Cinquenta, 51, 70
Catholic Charities, 138
Catholic theology, 32, 34
Center for Justice and Accountability, 149, 150, 160, 177
Central America
  Germans in, during World War II, 15
  social justice in, 34
  U.S. involvement in, 74–76
Central Intelligence Agency (US), 75
Cerna, Cecilia, 24, 25, 26, 36
Cerna, Geraldina, 104, 123, 125, 146, 159
Cerna, Jorge, xiii, xxii–xxiii, 37, 41, 42, 122
  in Alabama, 123–24
  as baker, 47–51
  family of, 25–26, 36–37
  interrogation of, 103–9
  leaving Soyapango, 72, 81
  not talking about the massacre, 96, 97
  parents of, 49–50
  polygraph testing of, xiii, 113
  protection of, 88–90. *See also* Cerna family, protection of

recanting his story, 108–9
testimony of, xiii, xx, xxii, 88, 111, 144, 150
in Washington, DC, 124–26
as witness to the murders, xix, xxii
working in California, 138–39
Cerna, Lucía, xxvi, 3, 4, 5, 7, 43–46, 68, 163–64
brother of (Fernando), 3, 6–7, 9
brother of (Óscar), 2, 3, 4, 8, 9, 12–13, 19, 86, 111, 126, 132, 137, 147
buying a house in Soyapango, 41–42
childhood of, 1–10, 16, 17
children of, from first marriage, 22, 23, 24, 26, 30, 142–43
church of, during childhood, 17
credibility of, xxiv, 19
daughter of, 41, 42, 48, 69, 70. *See also* Cerna, Geraldina
dizziness of, in childhood, 8
effects on, of the massacre and its aftermath, 128, 138, 146, 158
escape to the U.S., 101–2
family of, 1–7, 8, 9–10, 25–26, 105–6. *See also individual family members*
father of, 2, 3
first U.S. job of, 138
grandfather of, 5, 6, 10, 12–13
grandmother of, 5–6, 9–10, 13
healing process for, 120, 131, 154, 158
home of, 3–4
husband of (first), 19–24, 24–26, 27, 29–30, 42
interrogation of, by the U.S., xx, 23, 30, 102, 103–9
learning by watching others, 4–5, 6
leaving home to go to work, 10, 19, 26
leaving Soyapango, 69–70, 72, 81
loyalty of, to the Jesuits, xxiv
mother of, 2–3, 8, 9–10, 13, 19, 26
moving to the U.S., 50
Nacho appearing to, after the murders, 84, 96
not talking about the massacre, 96, 97
polygraph testing of, xiii, 108, 113
prayers of, 24, 142, 146
protection of, 87, 88–90, 98. *See also* Cerna family, protection of
raised in poverty, 3, 7, 8
reacting to the murders, 86–88, 93–94, 96, 97–98
recanting her testimony, xx, 108–9, 113, 121, 122, 132
rescued from the FBI, 121–22
on returning to El Salvador, 37
schooling of, 7–10, 17–18, 19, 52
talking to God, 9. *See also* Cerna, Lucía, prayers of
testimony of, xii, xiii, xx–xxiii, 88, 95, 110, 111–12, 144–45, 150, 171–72
in Washington, DC, 124–26
witness to the murders, xi, xii, xv, xix–xx, 83–85. *See also* Cerna, Lucía, testimony of
working as a child, 7
working at the Loyola Center, 39–40, 51
working in the provincial's office, 41
working at the rectory, 51, 67–68
working at the UCA, xvii, xxiv, 41, 42–47, 52, 53
working in the U.S. as a CNA, 139–44, 155, 158
Cerna family
achieving middle-class status, 51
adjusting to US life, 139, 154–55
admiration for, xiii–xiv
attempts to discredit, xii, xiii
dealing with the war in Soyapango, 68–69
in FBI custody, xii–xiii, xx, 102–17, 131, 148
flown to Miami, 110
leaving Soyapango, 71–72
moved to Alabama, 122–23, 131
moved to California, 127, 132, 137, 147
moved to Texas, 126–27, 132
protection of, xi–xiii, xx, 99, 101–2, 126
retracting their story, xiii
returning to El Salvador, 146
selling home in Soyapango, 146
staying at UCA, 69–71

testifying before the Moakley Commission, 131
US immigration status of, 154–55
Chapultepec Peace Accords, 118–19, 134, 135, 149, 175
Chávez, Luis, 32, 34
Chema. *See* Tojeira, José María
Chidester, Richard, xii, 90, 101–3, 106–11, 113, 115–19, 125
China, 79
CIHD (Commission for the Investigation of Criminal Acts), 95, 117
CJA. *See* Center for Justice and Accountability
Clarke, Maura, 62, 64, 161
Clinton, Bill, 73
Clinton administration, 135
Cold War, 73, 79–80
Commission for the Investigation of Criminal Acts, 112
communal farms, 36
communism, fear of, 73
Conference of German Bishops, 56
Contras (Nicaragua), 75
Cortina, Jon, 54
Cristiani, Alfredo, xviii, xix, 75, 80, 86, 95, 101, 104, 109, 113–14, 119, 128, 134, 145, 147, 164
cuchubal, 142

Darwinism, spiritual, 31
D'Aubuisson, Roberto, 60–61, 66–67, 72–73, 74, 161
Death Foretold: The Jesuit Murders in El Salvador (Doggett), 172
Deininger, Walter T. (Don Baltita), 1, 2, 6, 12, 13, 14–16, 20, 27
Delgado, José Matías, 161
Development of Peoples, The (Paul VI), 34
Dia de la Cruz, 9, 16
Diem, Ngo Dinh, 73
Doggett, Martha, 171–72
Don Baltita. *See* Deininger, Walter T.
Donovan, Jean, 62, 64, 161
Duarte, José Napoleón, 67, 74–75
Dueñas family, 26

Eastside Project, 154
ECA (*Estudios Centroamericanos*), 63
el Despertar, 51
Ellacuría, Ignacio (Padre Ellacu), ix, xx, xxv, 52, 68, 66, 67, 75, 138, 172–73
accused of Marxism, 53–54, 67
death threats against, xviii, 53, 80
fleeing to Spain, 61
getting more work hours for L. Cerna, 41–42
as leading voice of the UCA, 53
murder of, 81, 85, 92, 93
personality of, 42, 44, 45
political involvement of, 43
publications of, 56–57
Santa Clara University and, 153
speaking for the oppressed, xvii, xviii
steeped in philosophical thought, 53–54
trying to broker peace in El Salvador, 80
on US aid to El Salvador, 78–79
El Libro de San Cypriano, 22, 24, 29
El Mozote, massacre at, 57, 62, 177
el Puerto del Diablo (the devil's gate), 20, 29
El Salvador
acknowledging crimes at El Mozote, 63
Amnesty Law in, 144, 149, 150–51
Atlacatl in history of, 13–14
Catholic priests murdered in, 63
children in, 2, 11
civil war in, xvii, xxv, 14, 28, 54, 68, 72, 77, 78, 80, 134, 155–56
coffee families' control of, 27–28
convictions in, for UCA massacre, 149
coup in (1931), 28
current conditions in, 156–57
democratic hopes in, 12
denying extradition requests from National Court of Spain, 151
denying large-scale massacres, 57
Dia de la Cruz in, 9, 16
education in, 17–18
Fourteen Families' rule of, 13
history of, 175–76
human rights crimes in, 97, 98
independence of, 12, 31

insecticide use in, 25
insurgency in, 29
Jesuit households in, 51
La Matanza's importance in, 28. See also *La Matanza*
law in, 128
memorial in, to civil war deaths, xxv
midwives in, 25, 37
migration from, to the U.S., 21, 58, 173
military in, xi, xii, xiv, xviii–xix, 13, 28, 78
name of, hope in, 159
oligarchy in, 14–15, 27, 28, 31–32, 78
peace negotiations in, xviii
plantation life in, 12
political refugees from, 147
poor in, 13, 26, 58
ranking of, in Human Development Index, 11
reaction in, to Reagan's election, 61
reform movement in, 62
remittances to, 156–57, 173
unstable government of, 74
U.S. aid to, 73, 77, 78–79, 128–29, 133
U.S. limiting military involvement in, 76
violence increasing in, after Reagan's election, 61, 62
violence institutionalized in, 35
wealth gap in, 27
El Salvador's Decade of Terror (America's Watch), 98, 177
Espino, Alfredo, 14, 16–17
Estrada, Miguel Francisco, xiii, 85, 86, 120
Estudios Centroamericanos (ECA), 31, 78–79
Externado San José, 51

Farah, Douglas, 94
FBI (U.S. Federal Bureau of Investigation), xii–xiii, xx
contacting Cernas about trial in Spain, 145
interrogation of the Cernas, xx, 23, 30, 102, 103–9, 148
Federal Republic of Central America, 12
FMLN (Farabundo Martí National Liberation Front; Frente Farabundo Martí), xi, xiii, xviii, 54, 68, 72, 80, 134, 164
Foley, Thomas, 116, 129–30
Ford, Ita, 62, 64, 161
Fort Benning (GA), 76, 77. *See also* School of the Americas
Fourteen Families, 13, 20
France, involvement of, in protecting the Cernas, xii, 88–89, 99, 101–2, 110
From Madness to Hope: The Twelve-Year War in El Salvador (UN Commission on Truth for El Salvador), 175
Funes, Mauricio, 156, 157, 161

Galvin, John R., 77
Garcia Alvarado, Roberto, xviii
García Vasquez, Juan José, 173
Gaudium et spes (*The Church in the Modern World*), 33
Germann, Daniel, xxi, 99, 100, 127, 128, 133–34, 137–42, 153–55, 158–61
Gondra, José María, 40, 51
Gorbachev, Mikhail, 79
Grande, Rutilio, 35–36, 61, 65, 158–59, 161, 176
Greathead, R. Scott, 114, 171–72
Guatemala, genocide in, 150
Gutiérrez, Gustavo, 55

Haig, Alexander, 62, 75
Hernández, María Julia, xiii, 87, 97–99, 161, 163–64, 177
Hernández Ayala, José Vicente, 93
Hernández Barahona, Carlos Camilo, 93
Hinton, Deane, 54, 75
Hockstader, Lee, 94
hope, 159–61
Howard, Richard, 47, 94, 137, 144, 147
Hull, Lilla, 64
Human Development Index, 11
hunger, 11–12, 34

Ibisate, Francisco Javier (Ibis), 66, 70, 86
Idoate, Florentino, 31
Ignatius, xxiv–xxv
Ignoffo, Lisa, 152–53
international obligation laws, 150
Iran-Contra affair, 75
IUDOP (University Institute of Public Opinion), 58
Izalco, 29

Jardín Botánico La Laguna, 15
Jesuit Conference (Washington, DC), 120
Jesuit Education and Social Change in El Salvador (Beirne), 153–54, 173
Jesuit Refugee Service, 94, 147
Jesuits (Society of Jesus), 18, 39–40, 159–60
  community of, 90–91
  controversy surrounding, 91
  deaths of, effects of, 81
  differing opinions of, 40
  households of, in El Salvador, 51
  listening for God's will, xxiv–xxv
  in Miami, 119–20
  suppression of, 91
  role of, in Cernas' narrative, xxiv
Jesus, crucifixion of, 160
Jicaras Tristes (Sad vessels; Espino), 17
Jiménez, Laura, 154
John XXIII, 33, 176–77
John Paul II, 56, 63–64, 177
Johnson, Lyndon, 73, 74
JRS. *See* Jesuit Refugee Service

Karl, Terry, 150
Kazel, Dorothy, 62, 64, 161
Kennedy, John, 73–74
Kolvenbach, Peter-Hans, 94, 159
Kouchner, Bernard, xii, 99

la chusma, 13, 32, 34
La Matanza (the slaughter), xvii, 28, 57, 72
Latin America. *See* Central America
Lawyers Committee for Human Rights (Human Rights First), 100, 118, 174–75
Lenin, Vladimir, 73
Leonard Neale House, 131
liberation psychology, 57
liberation theology, 32, 52, 55, 177
  criticism of, 55–56
  sin and, 56
  UCA and, 56–57
Locatelli, Paul Leo, ix, 97, 153
López, Arnando, xxv, 92
López y López, Joaquín, xxv, 18, 40, 52, 65, 85, 92
Loyola Center, 39–41, 51

Mackin, Theodore, 99–100
Magaña, Álvaro, 63
malnutrition, 11
Mandela, Nelson, 79
Manuel, Sonny, 154
Martí, Agustín Farabundo, 28, 72
Martín-Baró, Ignacio (Padre Nacho), xv, xvii, xix, xxv, 33, 35, 42, 43, 52, 66–71, 78, 81, 83, 138, 158–59, 173
  appearing to L. Cerna after the murders, 84, 96
  insisting on national historical memory, 98
  known as a subversive, 57
  murder of, 85, 92
  personality of, 43–44, 45, 46
  political involvement of, 43
  studying human behavior, 58
  threats against, awareness of, 95–96
Martínez, Maximiliano Hernández, 12, 28
Martita, Niña, 19
Marxism
  Ellacuría accused of, 53–54, 67
  liberation theology and, 55–56
Mathies family, 26
McGovern, James, 129
Medellín, bishops' conference at (1968), 34, 55
memorials, for UCA massacre victims, 96–97
Mendoza Vallecillos, Yusshy René, 149
midwives, 25, 37
Moakley, John Joseph "Joe," 116, 124, 129–33, 135, 161, 174

Moakley Commission, 115, 116, 130, 131, 133, 148, 149, 174
Moakley-DeConcini Bill of 1983, 129
Moakley Report, 100
Monan, J. Donald, 115
Monseñor Romero Pastoral Center, 81
Montes Mozo, Segundo, xxv, 33, 46, 67, 58, 66, 92, 157, 173
Monumento a la Memoria y la Verdad, xxv
Moreno, Juan Ramón, xxv, 40, 92

Nacho. *See* Martin-Baró, Ignacio
National Civilian Police, 118–19
Navas, Milagro, 10
Nicaragua, 75
North, Oliver, 63
Nutting, Wallace H., 77

Obama, Barack, 156, 157–58
O'Hare, Joseph, 96, 100, 159
On Essence (Zubiri), 53
Order of José Matías Delgado, 161

Padre Chema. *See* Tojeira, José María
Padre Nacho. *See* Martin-Baró, Ignacio
Parque Nacional Walter T. Deininger, 16
Paul VI, 33, 34
Paying the Price: Ignacio Ellacuría and the Murdered Jesuits of El Salvador (Whitfield), 172
Pedraz, Rogelio, 65–66, 87
Pérez Vásquez, Angel, 92
philosophy house (for El Salvadoran Jesuits), 47, 51, 71
Pinochet, Augusto, 150
Pipil, 13
PNC (National Civilian Police), 118–19
Poland, 79
political action, measure of, 54–55
Ponce, René Emilio, xviii, 77, 80, 93, 115, 134, 135, 145
populist movements, worldwide, 79
Portillo, Nelson, 173
poverty, 11–12, 34. *See also* El Salvador, poor in
preferential option for the poor, 32
pride, 39
Privett, Stephen, 97, 100, 145, 150, 154, 159–60

Rahner, Karl, 53, 163
Ramos, Celina, xi, 92
Ramos, Elba, xi, 71, 85, 92, 158
Ramos, Obdulio, xi, 71, 85
Ratzinger, Joseph, 56, 177
Reagan, Ronald, 61, 62, 73, 75, 78
Reagan administration, 54, 63, 75, 77, 81
rectory, 51
  L. Cerna's work at, 47
  rules at, 46
Regalado, Concepción (Concha), 20, 22, 29
Regalado, Tomás, 20–21, 27
Regalado Dueñas, Ernesto, 20, 21, 22, 26, 28–29
Regalado-Dueñas, Helen de, 21, 29
Regalado family, 20–22, 26–27, 29, 30, 158
Regalado González, Tomás, 30
remittances, 58, 156–57, 173
respect, as human need, xxiv
Revista Latino-americano de Teología, 57
Revolutionary Democratic Front (FDR), 61
Rhee, Syngman, 73
Rivas Mejía, Manuel Antonio, xiii, 30, 77, 93, 95, 105–6, 111, 112, 113, 115–19, 132, 134, 148
Rivera y Damas, Arturo, xiii, 94, 96, 114, 134, 163
Rivero, Fred, 101, 102, 107, 110
Rodríguez-Porth, José Antonio, xviii
Roman Catholic Conference of Latin American Bishops, 34
Romero, Óscar Arnulfo, 34, 35–36, 54–55, 72–73, 76, 97, 157, 161, 164–67, 176
  calling for change in U.S. approach to El Salvador, 59–60
  murder of, 60–61, 64, 65
Roncalli, Angelo Giuseppe. *See* John XXIII
Rutilio Grande, Mártir de la evangelización rural en El Salvador, 176